Explore Pennsylvania's Northcentral Highlands
Volume 2: The Susquehannock State Forest

Short Hikes in God's Country

by Chuck Dillon

Pine Creek Press
R.R. 4 Box 130B
Wellsboro, PA 16901
(717) 724-3003

Cover: A view of "God's Country" from the Cherry Springs Vista on Route 44. Photo by Curt Weinhold.

Although this guide accurately reflects conditions along these trails at the time of writing, it is impossible to detail every possible hazard that you might encounter. Conditions in the natural world are constantly changing, and changes may be made by the Bureau of Forestry, particularly in conjunction with logging activities. All persons hiking these trails do so at their own risk, and this guide is no substitute for the use of common sense and good hiking practices. The author and publisher disclaim any and all liability for conditions along the trail, occurrences along it, and the accuracy of data, hazards, and material contained in this book.

Library of Congress Catalog Card Number: 95-92730

ISBN 0-9639328-3-7

Printed in the United States of America
Reed Hann Litho Company
Williamsport, PA 17701

ACKNOWLEDGMENTS

Many people provided information and suggestions that were helpful in making this book possible.

I would like to thank Dave Shiller, District Forester, Susquehannock State Forest, and Malcolm "Mac" Waskiewicz of his staff for maps and information on trails and management activities in the Susquehannock State Forest. Chip Harrison, Park Superintendent, and Jeff Hahn and Lois Morey of his staff provided information for the trails in Lyman Run State Park.

Ed and Carol Szymanik of the Susquehannock Lodge were involved throughout this effort, and their patient prodding was sometimes the catalyst that helped keep this work going. Ed and Roger Buck accompanied me on a couple of exploratory hikes, and I am sure that they will be glad to learn that some of the trails they experienced did not make it into this book (for the record, I did not purposely choose those trails to discourage them, and I can suggest a few others that were worse experiences, but not by much).

Darlene Madarish provided an encyclopedia of information on plant identification for the Guide to the Susquehannock Trail System. The information she compiled was used for several of the hikes in this book.

In the course of hiking these trails I met Leo Fontanella, whose farm you must cross to ascend Johnson Brook - his directions and commentary were both helpful and entertaining. Tim Morey and Larry Nordheimmer both suggested Bristol Swamp as a possible hike, but that was after this hike had already been suggested by Curt Weinhold. Henry Lush suggested the Beech Flats area for possible hikes.

Willis Conable provided some of the historical and trail information used in this book.

Curt Weinhold, whose photos graced *Pennsylvania's Grand Canyon - A Natural and Human History*, provided the cover photo for this book.

My wife, Susan, provided encouragement, technical support, editing and suggestions which made this book possible. She can attest to the many hours of sacrifice that went into this project - hiking, researching, and writing (hey, it's a dirty job, and somebody had to do it). She went on a few of these hikes, too, and can tell you why Etienne Brulé's "silver mine" is called the "lost" silver mine, as can my son, Jon, and my daughter, Alison.

This is my Father's world,
And to my listn'ing ears,
All nature sings and round me rings
The music of the spheres.

This is my Father's world:
I rest me in the thought
Of rocks and trees, of skies and seas;
His hand the wonders wrought.

This is my Father's world,
The birds their carols raise,
The morning light, the lily white,
Declare their Maker's praise.

This is my Father's world:
He shines in all that's fair;
In the rustling grass I hear him pass,
He speaks to me everywhere.

- Maltbie D. Babcock, 1901

The natural world supplies much more than mere physical needs, for it was given that we might be reminded that there is an eternal God, by Whose mighty power this world was created, and that man, by nature, is a spiritual, as well as physical, being, created to enjoy a personal relationship with Him. It is my prayer that the reader, in discovering and exploring a natural world of great beauty and by recognizing the wisdom in which all of its parts work together, might also seek and come to know the God Who created it.

CONTENTS

Finding Your Trail & Cautionary Notes 9

State Forest Regional Map 10

Introduction 12

Safety 22

Regional Geology 25

Regional Forest History 30

The Forested Environments 33

The Wet Environments 35

Edge Environments 38

Forest Management 40

STS WEEKEND TRIP CONNECTOR TRAILS

Connector Trails Map 46
WEST BRANCH TRAIL 48
CHERRY SPRINGS TO WILD BOY RUN 51
YOCHUM RUN TO BLACK MARK HOLLOW 55
DRY HOLLOW RIDGE TRAIL 59

DAY HIKES

DAY HIKES - NORTH 65

1 BRISTOL SWAMP: PHOENIX TRAIL 66
2 BRISTOL SWAMP: JOHNSON BROOK TRAIL 69
3 BRISTOL SWAMP: GAME BREAK/
DRY BOTTOM TRAILS 72
4 HEMLOCK TRAIL 76
5 BUCKSELLER TRAIL 78
6 CROWELL HOLLOW TRAIL 81
7 DENTON HILL NORTH 84
8 DENTON HILL 88
9 SPLASHDAM/BINKY HOLLOWS 92
10 ROCK RUN ROAD VISTA/LOSEY RUN 97
11 LYMAN RUN NORTH 102
12 LYMAN RUN STATE PARK 105
13 LYMAN RUN STATE PARK: BEEHIVE/
WILDCAT TRAILS 108
14 LYMAN RUN SOUTH (EWING TRAIL) 111
15 WETMORE RUN 115
16 BEECH FLATS: TOM CABIN HOLLOW 119
17 SPLASHDAM HOLLOW 124

DAY HIKES - CENTRAL 127

18 CAPTAIN SHELTON TRAIL 129
19 FORD HOLLOW/PATTERSON PARK 134
20 EAST FORK - SINNEMAHONING/FORD HOLLOW 138
21 WATER TANK HOLLOW 141
22 B & S GRADES 144
23 MT. BRODHEAD 148
24 HOGBACK HOLLOW 152
25 WILD BOY NORTH - STONY LICK RUN 157
26 WILD BOY SOUTH - STONY RUN 161
27 PINE HILL (JAMISON RUN TRAIL) 165

DAY HIKES - SOUTH 171
28 ROBIN HOLLOW 172
29 WINDFALL RIDGE 176
30 YOCHUM RUN 179
31 OLE BULL STATE PARK 183
32 BERGSTRESSER HOLLOW 186
33 HOPPER HOLLOW 190
34 SPOOK HOLLOW 194
35 SPRING BROOK 198
36 WELCH RIDGE 202
37 LEFT BRANCH - YOUNG WOMAN'S CREEK 205
38 LIEB RUN - SCOVILLE BRANCH 209

DAY HIKES - HAMMERSLEY WILD AREA 213
39 BLACK MARK HOLLOW 215
40 BUNNELL RUN 218
41 BLACKSMITH HOLLOW & LOST SILVER MINE 220
42 TWIN SISTERS 224
43 ELK LICK RUN/GRAVEL LICK RUN 228
44 MURDOCKS (ROAD HOLLOW) 232
45 ELKHORN RUN 237
46 COUNTY LINE - DUMP HOLLOW 240
47 BEECH BOTTOM HEMLOCKS 244
48 TROUT RUN 247
49 BELL BRANCH 251

FINDING YOUR TRAIL & A FEW CAUTIONARY NOTES

Most of these hikes require some map reading skills or some easy bushwhacking. Your first test is finding the starting point - if you cannot do that then you may have real problems out in the woods on some of these routes.

Minimal verbal descriptions are included in this book to help the reader locate the starting point for each hike. A regional map, showing each area of the Susquehannock State Forest, can be found on pages 10 and 11. In addition, at the beginning of each section, an area map can be found with a number that corresponds to the starting point of each hike. A topographic map for each hike is also included (and has been updated to show known changes as of this writing). The starting point for each route is indicated on these maps by the appropriate hike number. Additional details, if needed, can be found on county maps, an atlas, U.S.G.S. topographic maps, or the Bureau of Forestry Public Use Map for the Susquehannock State Forest.

Parking can usually be found at the start point of each hike. Unless the hike starts at a public facility parking is usually limited to a space or two where you can pull off the road. Please do not block access to driveways or to gated Forestry logging roads and trails.

Most of the trails covered in this book are not blazed. Although most are easily followed, they are not maintained - some can be very rough and can be hazardous if proper care is not exercised by the hiker. A good map and compass, and the ability to use them, are highly recommended.

Hiking times are approximate - your time will vary by physical ability and number of times you stop.

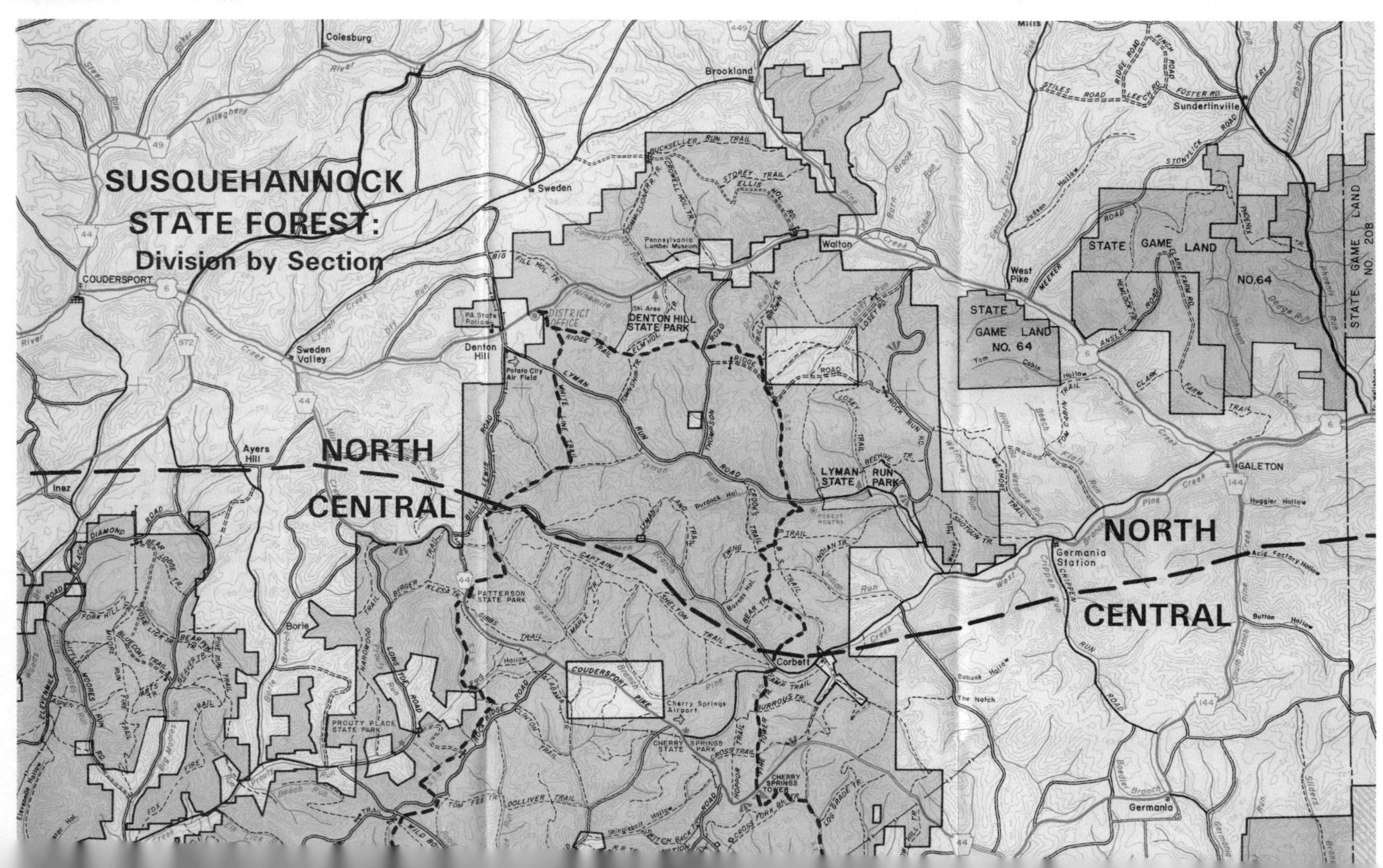
SUSQUEHANNOCK
STATE FOREST:
Division by Section
NORTH
CENTRAL
NORTH
CENTRAL
Coudersport
Sweden
Sweden Valley
Coalesburg
Brookland
Walton
West Pike
Denton Hill
Ayers Hill
Inez
Borie
Corbett
Germania Station
Galeton
Germania
Sunderlinville
DENTON HILL STATE PARK
LYMAN RUN STATE PARK
PATTERSON STATE PARK
PROUTY PLACE STATE PARK
CHERRY SPRINGS STATE PARK
Pennsylvania Lumber Museum
DISTRICT OFFICE
PA State Police
Potato City Air Field
Cherry Springs Airport
Ski Area
CHERRY SPRINGS TOWER
STATE GAME LAND NO. 64
STATE GAME LAND NO.64
STATE GAME LAND NO. 208
COUDERSPORT PIKE
LYMAN RUN ROAD
THOMPSON ROAD
LEWIS ROAD
LONG TOE ROAD
CRIPPEN RUN ROAD
ROCK RUN RD.
LOSEY RD.
WHITE LINE TRAIL
RIDGE TRAIL
SHELTON TRAIL
CAPTAIN TRAIL
CROOK'S TRAIL
HARDWOOD TRAIL
BEAR LODGE TR.
FORK HILL TR.
BLUECOAT TRAIL
PINE RUN TRAIL
MOORE RUN FIRE TRAIL
LITTLE MOORES RUN RD.
BUCKSELLER RUN TRAIL
STOREY TRAIL
COMMISSIONER TR.
CROWELL HOL TR.
BIG FILL HOL TR.
TOWNSHIP TR.
BILLY BROWN TR.
HEMLOCK TR.
CLARK FARM RD.
ANSLEY ROAD
TOM CABIN TRAIL
WETMORE TRAIL
SHOTGUN TR.
INDIAN TR.
BEEHIVE TR.
FIRE TOWER TR.
BURROUS TR.
HOPPOR TRAIL
CROSS TRAIL
LOG GRADE TR.
DOLLIVER TRAIL
CLINTON TRAIL
ALABAMA TR.
GIBBS TRAIL
BERGER KLESA TR.
MAPLE TR.
EWING TRAIL
BEAR TR.
CROSS FORK BK TR.
SWITCH BACK TR.
TOM FEE TR.
WILD BOY
DIAMOND ROAD
BLACK ROAD
ELEVENMILE
STONYLICK ROAD
STILES ROAD
RIDGE ROAD
FINCH ROAD
LEECH RD.
FOSTER RD.
MEEKER
PHOENIX TR.
Pine Creek
Allegheny River
Genesee Forks
Huggler Hollow
Acid Factory Hollow
Button Hollow
Bohunk Hollow
The Notch
Judson Hollow

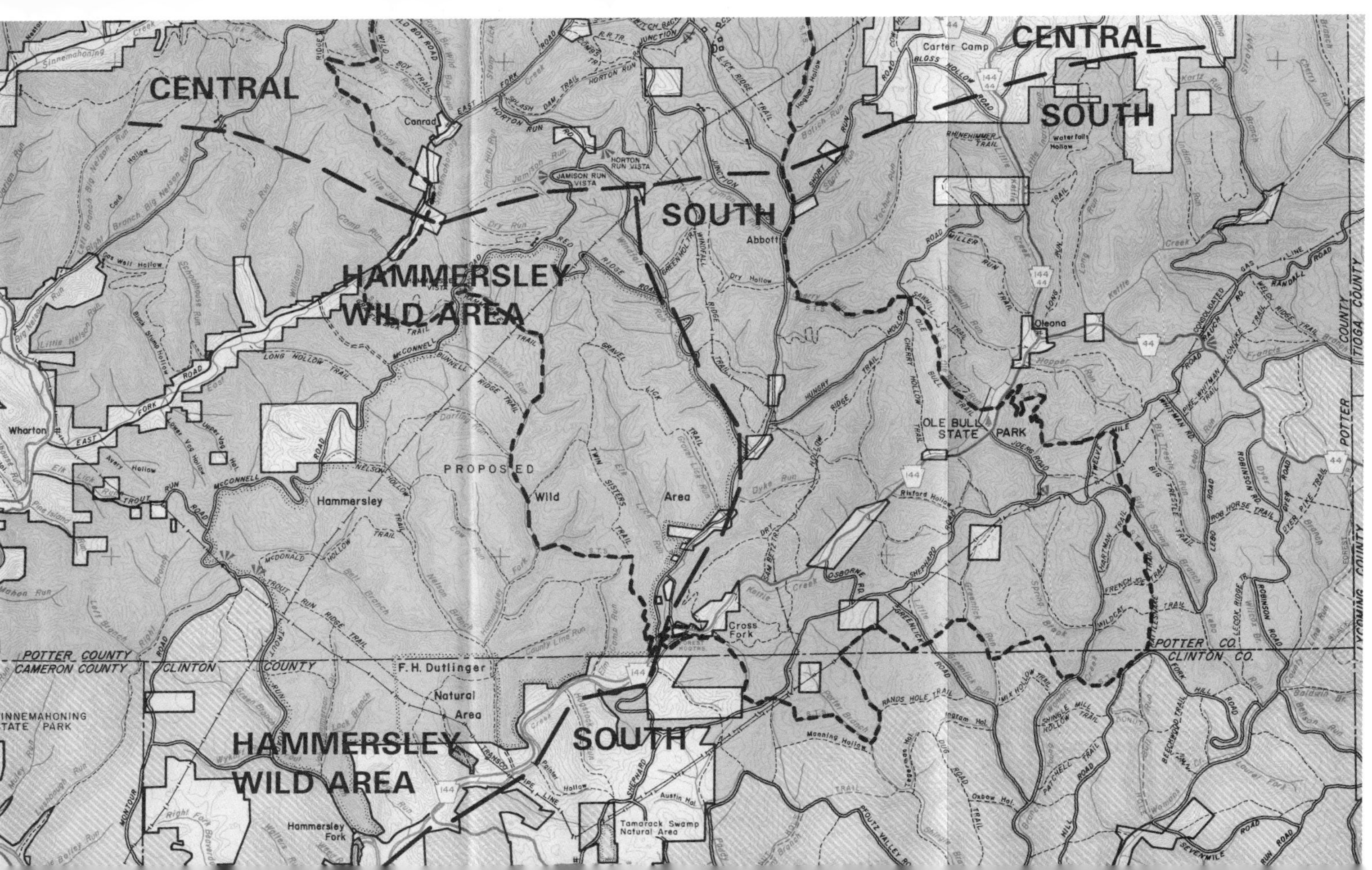

CENTRAL
SOUTH
CENTRAL
SOUTH
SOUTH
SOUTH
HAMMERSLEY WILD AREA
HAMMERSLEY WILD AREA
PROPOSED Wild Area
OLE BULL STATE PARK
SINNEMAHONING STATE PARK
F.H. Dutlinger Natural Area
Tamarack Swamp Natural Area
POTTER COUNTY
CAMERON COUNTY
CLINTON COUNTY
POTTER CO.
CLINTON CO.
POTTER COUNTY
TIOGA COUNTY
LYCOMING COUNTY
Carter Camp
Conrad
Abbott
Oleona
Wharton
Hammersley
Cross Fork
Hammersley Fork
HORTON RUN VISTA
JAMISON RUN VISTA

INTRODUCTION

Potter County is known as "God's Country", a name that certainly speaks volumes as you look out over endless green waves of mountains extending to the horizon in summer or the brilliant orange, red, and yellow fall foliage against the deep blue sky. The hardwoods of its forests grow straight, tall, and wide with a magnificence that you can scarcely imagine until you walk below the forest canopy. With a population of only 17,000 people, the land is owned as much by the whitetail deer, the black bear, the coyote, and the wild turkey as it is by humans. It isn't heaven, but it comes close to the tranquility and beauty of the garden where God placed Adam and Eve.

Potter County's "forest primeval", however, is rich in human history. In the late nineteenth/early twentieth centuries the original forest was razed to provide timber for a growing nation. After stripping the land bare, the lumber companies of Pennsylvania's Lumbering Era moved on, giving the land back to God to see what He would do the second time around - the barren landscape provided ideal conditions for the sun-loving hardwoods to regenerate, providing the majestic cherry, ash, beech, and maple that dominate the landscape today.

Along its trails, many of which were constructed to skid the original timber out or haul it out over a logging railroad, you will find metal relics of this former age - bits of woodstove, rail, railroad engine, chain, nails, saws, barrels, and horseshoes, and a variety of objects of unknown origin. It is difficult to imagine that the forest today was once bustling with activity - the workplace and home of tens of thousands of people whose brief presence would produce profound changes in the forest, a few scattered settlements, names for hollows and streams, and little else.

Today much of this territory, now the 262,000 acre Susquehannock State Forest, is managed for timber products, watershed protection, wildlife needs, natural forest regeneration, biological diversity, protection of specialized environments, visual aesthetics, and low-density recreational opportunities.

The 85-mile Susquehannock Trail System, initiated in 1966 by Potter County Recreation, Inc., links a series of old railroad grades, skid trails, and foot trails that traverse the heart of the state forest and is its focal point for hiking and backpacking. Since its inception, the Susquehannock Trail System has served as the route of choice for thousands of hikers and backpackers - about 750 of which (as of this writing) have been certified by the Susquehannock Trail Club as official "circuit hikers", who have hiked and documented their experiences over the entire route.

Over the years the demographics of our society have changed, and an 85-mile circuit backpacking trip has been difficult for some to do, whether by virtue of time, family, or physical limitation. At the same time, there is increasing interest in family hikes, day hikes, and weekend-length backpacking trips, hence the need for a book like this one, documenting possible cross-routes to make weekend trips a reality, and providing shorter, circular routes for the day hiker.

My intent, however, is more than just practical. This book is part of a series to encourage the pioneering spirit inside many of you - to get you off the beaten track and "explore" a very special region of Pennsylvania. Pennsylvania's Northcentral Highlands, or "Keystone Mountain Country", is a region that relatively few Pennsylvanians know much about and one which its inhabitants sometimes take for granted. A region of few people and little economic and political capital remains at the mercy of outside political forces unless it has a political constituency that extends beyond its borders. By discovering this region and seeing it for yourself, you will want to keep coming back and to see its beauty and environmental quality protected for future generations.

If you seek solitude there are many trails included in this book that will provide this easily, particularly on weekdays (I encountered only a handful of people over the five years and almost 2,000 miles hiking trails for this book). The number of possible routes included here will help preserve this experience for you.

Finally, but most important, experiencing these trails provides a different and refreshing alternative to the spiritual impoverishment of our modern, manmade environment. The beauty, diversity, and purpose of each part of the natural environment speak of God's character - His intelligence, power, and creativity - and encourage an awareness and a perspective that will enrich your life far more than the materialistic world view of our age.

THE ROUTES: The routes these hikes follow can be traversed in less than a day by the average person. Unless otherwise noted, no special equipment is required for these trails - the hiker with a copy of this book should be able to follow the suggested route easily. Whenever possible, private land is avoided, and use of gravel Forestry roads minimized.

Included in each hike is a summary of the trail: features, distance (measured by pedometer, except for measurements along the STS, which were made with a Rolotape wheel), elevations (low and high), type of terrain crossed, approximate hiking time, whether the trail is blazed, and where to park. A brief commentary for the hike, a short description of the trail route, and a more detailed trail guide commentary are included.

Each hike includes a black & white reproduction of the U.S.G.S. topographic map(s) indicating the route of the trail. The hiker should refer to the appropriate U.S.G.S. 7.5' topo maps, or to the STS maps for details, if necessary. The reader should be aware, however, that most maps of the area are not updated frequently: they may lack valuable reference points (such as the Susquehannock Trail System itself, new logging roads, and trail changes) and may show trails that can no longer be found. I have made the relevant changes (of which I am aware) on the reproduced maps.

Your comments and suggestions regarding these hikes, as well as suggestions for other routes, may be directed to: Chuck Dillon, c/o Pine Creek Press, R.R. 4 Box 130B, Wellsboro, PA 16901.

WHAT TO WEAR: Dress for the conditions. Under most circumstances, wear long pants to save your legs from insect bites and from minor scratches. A T-shirt, wool shirt, or a light jacket or sweatshirt is usually appropriate, depending on conditions. In winter or in cold weather, layer clothing, beginning with polypropylene or other non-cotton long underwear.

Footwear deserves special attention for any hike. Although many of these routes can be made wearing sneakers, a better choice would be a light hiking shoe or hiking boot (Gore-Tex, nylon, or leather) with a pair of wool socks and polypropylene sock liners. Each type has its own advantages and disadvantages over which hiking enthusiasts can debate endlessly - the most critical aspect is fit. If they don't fit correctly, your feet will blister equally well in any of these boots! If you do a lot of hiking, think of hiking boots as an investment that will last a number of years.

FOOD & LODGING: A number of commercial establishments provide quality, reasonably-priced food and lodging in the Potter County region. Contact Potter County Recreation, PO Box 215, Coudersport, PA 16915 or phone (814) 435-2290 for more information and a complete listing. A partial listing follows by location:

Galeton Area:

Nob Hill Motel 814-435-6738
Doc's Motel 814-435-6787
Ox Yoke Inn 814-435-6522
West Pike Motor Lodge 814-435-6552

Denton Area:

Susquehannock Lodge 814-435-2163
Susque Homestead 814-435-2966
Pine Log Motel 814-435-6400
Ninemile Motel 814-435-2394
Potato City Motor Inn 814-274-7133

Coudersport Area:

Paul's Motel 814-274-8700
Lindy Motel 814-274-0327
Laurelwood Motel 814-274-9220
Crittendon Hotel 814-274-8320
Sweden Valley Motel 814-274-8770
Frosty Hollow Bed & Breakfast 814-274-7983
The Lush Victorian Bed & Breakfast 814-274-7557

Oleona/Cross Fork Area:

Carter Camp Lodge 814-435-1192
Kettle Creek Lodge, Ltd. 814-435-1019
Germania Hotel 814-435-8851
Susquehannock Forest Cabins 814-435-6577
Cross Fork Motel 717-923-0602
Cross Fork Inn 717-923-1258
Tom & Kathy's Bed & Breakfast 814-435-8582

SHUTTLES & TRAIL INFORMATION: The hikes described in this book should not require a shuttle. Shuttles along the Susquehannock Trail System are available through Susquehannock Lodge, RR1 Box 120, Ulysses, PA 16948, phone (814) 435-2318.

ATVs: ATVs are allowed ONLY on the ATV Trail, which is open to ATVs from Memorial Day Weekend through September 24. The ATV Trail is also available for use by hikers throughout the year.

BICYCLES: Bicycles are not permitted on the Susquehannock Trail System, nor are they permitted in the Forrest H. Dutlinger Natural Area. Other trails are open, but not all are suitable - there is no maintenance on them, so most are too clogged with blowdowns or too rough for pleasurable bicycling. Mountain bikers are encouraged to use the ATV Trail.

HORSES: Horses are not permitted on the Susquehannock Trail System. Other trails are open, but not all are suitable.

SKIING: Some of these trails are suitable for x-country skiing, assuming there is enough snow. The difficulty will be access. The Bureau of Forestry has marked a number of cross-country ski routes in the Denton Hill area, and a map can be obtained at the District Forest Office.

PARKING: Parking is noted for each hike, but is usually limited at most locations to only one or two cars (usually just pulled off the road). PLEASE DO NOT BLOCK THE GATED FORESTRY ROADS AND DO NOT PARK ON PRIVATE PROPERTY WITHOUT THE OWNER'S PERMISSION. Parking is more abundant at the Northern Gateway (District Forest Office, which is also open most every day of the week 8 A.M. - 4 P.M. and has toilet facilities), Lyman Run State Park, Patterson Park, Ole Bull State Park (toilets, water), and Forest Foreman's Office in Cross Fork.

WHAT TO BRING:

Pack: If you think you need a pack for these hikes, use a large fanny pack. You won't feel any weight on your shoulders, as it is carried on the hips. You can hike all day with hardly noticing that you are carrying anything, and you will have unrestricted freedom of movement. If you are backpacking, a suitable external or internal frame pack or rucksack is recommended.

First Aid Kit: A small one containing a few bandages, moleskin, aspirin, and ointment.

Water: A quart-sized nalgene bottle will suffice for most of these hikes. You can carry it in the fanny pack or in its own belt-mounted carrybag. This size should last a half-day per person.

Food: A mixture of raisins, peanuts, and M&M's/Reese's Pieces will give you a quick boost of energy and keep you going for a long time. Mix your own. If you are concerned about fat content, mix dried fruit, pretzels, and cereal (square shapes resist crumbing). Sandwiches tend to get crushed or overheated. Bring more than you think you need, just in case you're out longer than expected.

Extra clothes: Possibly a raincoat or poncho if it looks threatening (check the forecast before you leave, but expect it to be wrong on occasion). If you're unsure about being chilled wear a wool shirt - wrap it around your waist if you get too hot.

Other gear: Map, compass, guidebook(s), Swiss Army knife, walking stick, toilet paper, whistle. It is a good idea to carry a lighter or matches and a small flashlight just in case darkness overtakes you or you spend an unexpected night in the woods.

BACKPACKING: The Susquehannock Trail System provides excellent backpacking opportunities, and the cross-trails in this book will allow you to split this 85-mile trail into several weekend loops. The trail guide and maps for the Susquehannock Trail System, *Guide to the Susquehannock Trail System,* are available through the Susquehannock Trail Club, Pine Creek Press, or your local backpacking supply store. If you are backpacking, please note the following:

Fires: The use of a lightweight backpacking stove is recommended to minimize environmental impact. Such stoves are also more efficient for cooking and reduce the danger of fire. No fire permits are required, however. Small campfires for cooking and warming are permitted except during periods of high fire danger. Contact the Susquehannock State Forest District Office at (814) 274-8474 for information. Fires should be constructed in such a manner as to prevent their spread: a water source should be nearby, the site should be well away from mountain laurel, you should not leave your fire unattended, and you should extinguish your fire completely before leaving. PLEASE BE CAREFUL WITH FIRE!!

Camping & Permits: Camping in the Forrest Dutlinger Natural Area is not permitted. Camping elsewhere is permitted, and a camping permit (currently) is not required elsewhere if you arrive by a primitive means and stay at any one site for just one night. There is NO CAMPING permitted on: State Game Lands, State Parks, Picnic Areas (except at designated sites with a permit), or within 100 yds. of buildings. Contact the Susquehannock State Forest District Office for changes in these regulations.

Bathing & Cleaning: Please do not wash either yourself or your equipment in or near streams.

PORCUPINES: You may laugh, but porcupines are a much greater danger than bears or rattlesnakes if you leave your vehicle parked next to the State Forest, particularly overnight. They are attracted to salt and will destroy cooling hoses, brake lines, electrical wires, and fuel lines. Protect your parked car by spreading mothballs around it. When sleeping, don't leave your shoes or favorite fly rod where porcupines can reach them!

FLIES: Deer flies may be present at times in summer, particularly in open areas and near water.

TRAIL ETIQUETTE:

1. Bring out EVERYTHING you bring in. Don't trash our environment. Pick up any litter others may have left behind.
2. When nature calls, don't use any area near a stream, spring, seep, or wetland. Go off the trail and dig a small hole in which to bury feces (burn toilet paper or carry it out in a ziplock bag) - DON'T just let them lay on the forest floor! An astounding number of people just don't know what to do if it can't be flushed away!
3. Avoid private property whenever possible. Be courteous to property owners. The few trails in this book that do cross private property are either not posted, the owners have stated that they do not mind hikers passing through, or have given their permission when these hikes were mentioned for inclusion in this book.
4. Be courteous to other trail users.
5. Keep your dog leashed, if it accompanies you. This is

required in State Parks. Wildlife suffers stress in the presence of dogs.

6. On designated trails, please stay on the trail. Deviating from the trail will create additional areas of potential erosion.

TRAIL CLUBS:

Susquehannock Trail Club: The Susquehannock Trail Club, formed in 1967, maintains the Susquehannock Trail and meets regularly for business and social activities. The purpose of the club is to build and maintain trails, to aid in the conservation of wildlands and wildlife, and to promote fellowship through hiking and nature study. The trail club publishes a quarterly newsletter. New members are welcome. You are encouraged to join as a hiker who benefits directly from the trail club's activities - your dues (currently $6/year) and voluntary participation help maintain the trail system. In addition, the trail club's activities are always educational and fun. For membership, contact the Susquehannock Trail Club at P.O. Box 643, Coudersport, PA 16915.

Keystone Trails Association: The Keystone Trails Association is a statewide organization of individuals and organized groups dedicated to promoting the interests and serving the needs of hikers in and around Pennsylvania. Its quarterly newsletter keeps you informed of issues affecting hikers and trails in the state. The organization also publishes a number of maps and guides and encourages trail maintenance programs. For membership, contact the Keystone Trails Association at P.O. Box 251, Cogan Station, PA 17728.

STS CIRCUIT HIKER AWARD: Circuit hiker awards are given to those who hike the entire Susquehannock Trail System. To qualify:

1. Each applicant must hike the entire STS in one or many trips, in either direction. All sections hiked need not be in the same direction, nor geographically consecutive. There is no time limit.

2. Each individual hiker should sign every trail book encountered along the STS.

3. Each applicant must maintain a log of the trip in considerable detail, preferably with accompanying photographs.

a. Groups hiking together may keep a combined log, but

each member of the group must sign the log.

b. If the group covers only a part of the circuit, each member of the group must sign the log. Each copy must bear the names of all members of the group. The individual applicant must then submit a copy of the group log, together with other logs for other parts of the trip, when applying for the award.

4. Each applicant must submit his (her) logs of the circuit hike to the STS Circuit Hiker Award Committee. A group who has hiked the entire distance together may submit a combined log to the committee, but each member of the group must sign it.

5. The Circuit Hiker Award Committee will review the log(s). If the committee is satisfied that the applicant has hiked the entire STS, the committee will certify the applicant as "Susquehannock Trail System Circuit Hiker No. ___."

6. Each certified STS Circuit Hiker is eligible to purchase and wear the STS Circuit Hiker brassard. Additional brassards may be purchased by certified circuit hikers.

7. Certified STS Circuit Hikers will be given identification numbers by the STS Circuit Hiker Award Committee in the order in which they are certified by the committee.

8. Relocation of any part of the STS after an applicant has hiked through that portion shall not disqualify the applicant.

9. The STS Circuit Hiker Award Committee may require applicants to appear before it to testify about the hike.

Requests should be sent to: Susquehannock Trail Club, P.O. Box 643, Coudersport, PA 16915 Attn.: Circuit Hiker Award Committee.

CLIMATE: To help you plan, average temperatures and precipitation follow. Please note that averages may occur within a wide range:

Month	Temperature (F) average range min/max	Precipitation average (in.)
January	15/36	2.5
February	13/37	2.4
March	23/43	3.6
April	32/59	3.8
May	41/71	4.5
June	50/79	4.5
July	53/82	3.7
August	52/81	3.4
September	45/74	3.5
October	35/63	3.3
November	27/47	2.9
December	17/36	3.5

SAFETY

A trip in the woods exposes you to hazards that are different, but not necessarily more dangerous, than you experience each day. Common sense, familiarization, and preparedness will minimize these risks. If you are not willing to accept these risks and assume responsibility for your actions and personal safety, then it is best that you stay at home. It is recommended that you not hike alone. Tell others where you plan to hike and when you expect to return - give them a time to initiate a search if you do not contact them.

EMERGENCIES: Dial "911" for Emergency Services
District Forestry Office: 814-274-8474
Cole Memorial Hospital (Coudersport): 814-274-9300
Soldiers & Sailors Memorial Hospital (Wellsboro): 717-724-1631

WATER SOURCES: While water is available from springs along many of these hikes, fill your canteen with potable water before the start of your hike. Trailside water sources should not be used unless treated chemically, appropriately filtered, or boiled to avoid giardia.

INSECTS: You may have an encounter with hornets, wasps, bees or yellow jackets along any of these trails. Your most dangerous encounter would be to step on an underground nest, and there isn't much you can do in that situation except to run and swat. Such situations can be life threatening if you are allergic to bee stings. Tell others in your party beforehand if you are allergic to bee stings.

TICKS & LYME DISEASE: You can eliminate most ticks by wearing long pants and checking for ticks at the end of the day. Ticks can be removed by placing the end of a recently burned match to the body of the tick or by placing Vaseline or gasoline on the tick. Do not yank the tick out with tweezers, as the head may remain imbedded in your skin. Cameron County, adjoining Potter County to the southwest, is the closest area where ticks are known to carry Lyme Disease. The highest risk period is early summer, when nymphal ticks are small enough to be unnoticed.

RABIES: Avoid animals that act in strange ways or allow you to approach them. The more common carriers of rabies are foxes and raccoons.

POISON IVY: Leaves three, let it be! (Poison ivy is not that widespread in the area covered by the hikes in this book.)

SNAKES: The Eastern Timber Rattlesnake inhabits the region. Encounters, though uncommon, could take place where snakes might warm themselves - sunny rock piles. Given notice of your presence, snakes avoid humans and strike only when surprised. Bites will make you sick, but are rarely fatal. Accounts of rattlesnake encounters by others have been mostly in the Hammersley Wild Area. I have never had an encounter with a rattlesnake on these trails, so, statistically, neither should you. To put things in perspective, I have witnessed dozens of trees and sizeable tree limbs fall while hiking (yes, they did make a sound, but I was there to hear them).

BEARS: Black bears live throughout the region, but they generally avoid humans whenever possible and are not frequently sighted. If you should see one, do not approach it. If cubs are nearby, do not place yourself between the cubs and the mother. Do not leave food around your camp, and do not camp where traveling bears have no choice but to go through your campsite.

GETTING LOST: Before your start out, tell someone where you are going and when you expect to get back. Have them call "911" if you do not return or contact them by a prearranged time. Study your map closely and try to visualize the surrounding terrain along your route. As you walk, compare the terrain to the contours on your map.

Although it shouldn't happen, occasionally people do get lost. Don't panic - retrace your steps if you can. If you can't, use your map and compass to figure out where you are by sighting any available landmarks or characteristics of the terrain. If you still can't figure out where you are, sit tight, don't panic, and wait for help to arrive. If for some reason you did not tell anyone where you were going or for how long and do not expect a search to be initiated, follow water downstream - or if you know there is a road in a certain direction, travel to the road and wait for the first passing motorist. The key advice here is "don't panic": evaluate your situation and the probability of a search being initiated, and decide on an appropriate course of action. On these hikes, a road, a camp, a familiar stream, and assistance should not be too far away.

LIGHTNING: Lightning is a hazard on top of the ridges, in open areas, and near large trees. Head down the slope to trees of medium, uniform height.

HUNTING SEASON: You are most apt to find hunters along the trail from mid-October to mid-December. Spring Gobbler Season is late April to mid-May. Most hunters will be out the last Saturday of October for turkey, the first day of Buck Season, and Doe Season - avoid these days. Wear blaze orange when you expect to be sharing the woods with hunters. There is no hunting on Sundays.

HYPOTHERMIA: This is your most common, but most understated, hazard you will face in the outdoors: your body cools down quicker than its heat can be replaced, particularly if you are wet. You shiver, and if you do not begin to warm up, you become incoherent in your thinking, lose coordination, and eventually just give up doing anything and slip into unconsciousness. Prevention is the best approach - polypropylene under wool, but if it is too late for that, wet clothes should be removed and replaced with dry ones, the body warmed by others, by starting a fire, or by giving the victim warm (not hot or cold) non-alcoholic fluids. Medical attention may be required in the more extreme cases.

REGIONAL GEOLOGY

The Susquehannock State Forest and Potter County are part of the Allegheny Plateau region of Pennsylvania. The plateau is composed of parallel sedimentary rock layers, predominantly sandstone, which are only gently folded and is characterized by flat-topped mountains and deep valleys formed by drainage and erosion.

Sedimentary rocks - sandstone, shale, and conglomerate - are composed of silt, sand and stone particles of various sizes that were brought into the region by water and deposited. Over the years they accumulated to great depths, and the heat and pressure of successive layers of sediments covered, compressed and hardened the earlier accumulations into rock.

Each type of stone tells us about the early environment of the region when the various sediments were deposited. Shale is composed of very small particles of silt, so its presence indicates times when the water was moving rather slowly. Sandstone, which makes up the vast majority of the sedimentary rock layers of Potter County, is composed of larger particles of grit and sand large enough to see with your eye, so the water was moving somewhat faster when these sediments were brought in. You can differentiate between these two rock types on the trail by observing the size of the particles that comprise the rock or by the way in which they decompose, or weather: shale splits along its bedding planes into thin layers and disintegrates into sharp pieces of rock, whereas sandstone will remain somewhat rounded and may leave piles of sand below certain formations. Both eventually separate into the particles which have been "cemented" together as rock.

Sometimes sandstone does not undergo sufficient heat and pressure to form a hard rock - this is known as "unconsolidated sandstone". It erodes much more quickly than does the harder sandstones.

Since most of the rock in Potter County is sandstone, with only little shale, the water that brought these sediments into the area was moving, not still or slow.

Conglomerate is composed of a mixture of pebbles and sand which has been cemented together over time. Often these pebbles will be quartz, a metamorphic rock which is not indigenous to the area. Very fast-moving water brought these pebbles great distances before slowing sufficiently to allow them to "drop out" and be deposited. The highest portions of the plateau contain a conglomerate of quartz and sandstone, so a more recent portion of its history was under swift-flowing water.

Within the sandstones may be other evidence of the early environment - ripple marks believed formed by the action of gentle waves or relatively quiet water, linear marks caused by the action of currents, stream beds, and larger waves, such as in a river or at the seashore. Flagstones, sandstones which split along their horizontal bedding planes in a uniform manner, usually display "current lineations" on their flat surfaces where they split. These ribbonlike ridges that parallel one another are depositional characteristics that indicate the direction of flow. Beach deposits are usually more uniform in particle size than are river deposits. Beach deposits usually extend a much longer distance perpendicular to the direction of flow (a broad area with a short, strong current) than stream deposits (a narrow area with long, strong current). Parting surfaces of rocks in Potter County show few, if any, ripple marks characteristic of slow-moving water, and the linear current lineations which are found appear to have been made by flowing water. The size and dimensions of the flagstone deposits suggest waves along a beach.

Rocks may also contain various fossils that provide additional clues about the early environment of the area: fossilized seashells tell us when the water was warm, salty, and shallow; plants tell us of periods when portions of the region were above water. Although some fossilized shells are found along the trails in this book, these shells are relatively small, so conditions for marine life (warm, shallow, relatively still water) were less than optimum when sedimentation occurred. Plant fossils, particularly tree branches and roots, are abundant, so the area in the vicinity of the trail spent regular and significant periods above water.

The most common fossils you may observe in the area are:

Brachiopods: Locally, most types of fossilized seashells are "brachiopods" - marine animals with a hinged shell. They attached themselves to rocks or the sea bottom and filtered water for their food. Unlike clams, they were sedentary and their lack of mobility meant that they were quickly smothered by incoming silt and sand, providing ideal conditions for fossilization to occur. One of the relatively few brachiopods that has survived until today is the barnacle.

Mollusks: Unlike brachiopods whose shells are symmetrical when viewed face-on, mollusks do not have symmetrical shells when viewed from this angle. When viewed edge-on, however, also unlike the brachiopods, the two shells joined by a hinge are symmetrical. Clams and mollusks moved about more readily than the brachiopods.

Crinoids: An echinoderm (a relative of the starfish), these creatures attached themselves to the sea bottom with a root system, to which a "backbone" stalk of hollow disks was attached. At the top of the stalk was a more delicate frond of material that filtered the water for food. Usually the only portion that was fossilized was the root-like structure that anchored it to a rock or sea floor and the "backbone", which usually scattered over the bottom of the sea as individual hollow disks.

Plants: Usually found in the form of fossilized branches, the plants most commonly found as fossils along these trails are sphenophytes (relatives of the horsetail rush) and lycopods (relatives of the clubmoss). The sphenophytes are generally preserved as pieces of tree trunk, and the most common of these, known as calamites, contained vertical ribs stretching between regular nodes where leaves or branches grew. Their trunks were hollow and looked somewhat like bamboo. The lycopod most likely to be found is sigillaria, the "seal tree". Its leaves left scars in vertical rows along ridges also aligned vertically along the trunk. It branched only once or twice at the top of its trunk.

To the east and adjacent to the Susquehannock State Forest there are several geological differences that give clues to the regional environment: there is more shale there (indicating slower-moving water to the east); there are significantly more marine fossils (indicating slower-moving, warm, salt water there); there is coal (black rock of compressed layers of organic plant material that has hardened, indicating the presence of swamps and land); and there are fossilized corals and wormholes.

There is one more clue that is a key to understanding the geological history of the Potter County area - the presence of gas wells and gas lines, particularly in the southern half of the trail. The presence of natural gas is believed to have originated where organic debris mixed with mud (components of dark shale) was covered by sediments of sand, the weight of which created pressure and heat sufficient to squeeze organic compounds (oil and gas) out of the rocks. The oil and gas migrated out of the source shales and filled pores and cracks in adjacent sandstones (reservoir rocks), which were then covered and trapped by less porous rock or blocked by the faulting of less porous rock, sealing them until drilled.

In fact, the southern portion of the Susquehannock Trail System lies over the Leidy Gas Field, a long gas reservoir stretching to the northeast in a thin band. The field is composed of two pools: the Leidy Pool on the northwest side of an anticline near the crest, south of Kettle Creek, and the Tamarack Pool, a faulted section at the crest of the same anticline but separated by the fault. Gas was discovered in this area in 1934 in the Oriskany sandstone formation, almost 7,500 feet below the surface.

The Leidy Pool is believed to have been a series of ancient sandbars and beaches at the edge of a shallow sea about 350 million years ago. Many miles long, but only a few miles wide and running NE to SW, this sand mound separated the open sea to the west from a lagoon which served as a catch basin for organic materials which became the dark shale source rocks. After the area was covered by additional sediments, the sandbar served as a convenient, porous reservoir for the migrating natural gas. The natural gas was trapped in this porous sandstone formation by later layers of less-porous shale and by faulting, which sealed the gas in two separate pools adjacent to each other, approximately 200 - 250 million years ago, when the North American and African continental plates collided to form the Appalachian Mountains to the south and raised the area north and west of Williamsport as a gently-folded tableland.

Regionally, the area was once a shallow sea during the Devonian Period (405-350 million years ago). It was during this time period that the gas-holding Oriskany Sandstone was deposited and then covered by the finer shales deposited by slower-moving water. This was followed by alternating periods of slow and fast-moving water, resulting in the shales and sandstones of the period. More recent portions of the Devonian Age are marked by a gray sandstone sequence (Oswayo Formation) found on the lower elevations of the Susquehannock Trail System.

The Mississippian Period (350-310 million years ago) was marked by faster-moving water which deposited great quantities of sand in the region. The coarse gray and light gray sandstones

(Burgoon Sandstone) and conglomerates (coarse sandstones and quartz pebbles) of the Pocono Group comprise the upper elevations and high plateaus of Potter County. Later depositions of shale have been removed by erosion and are not found here.

The Pennsylvania Period (310-280 million years ago) was the age of coal swamps, a period in which the land was alternately above, then below sea level. The conglomerates and sandstones of this era have also been removed by erosion except in the southeast corner of Potter County.

Upon the close of the Pennsylvania Period, the North American and African continental plates collided, creating severe folding south and east of Williamsport, producing the Appalachian Mountains. North and west of Williamsport, however, the sediments rose as a gently-folded tableland, the Allegheny Plateau. The tops of these gentle folds, known as "anticlines" remain as the high plateau. The bottom troughs, ("synclines") provided the drainage channels for the ancient sea and the creeks and rivers of the region.

Geological activity remained relatively static, limited primarily to erosion. The Pleistocene Epoch (1.8 million to 11,000 years ago) saw the advance of massive glaciers southward, but only a small portion of Potter County (north and east of the Genesee Fork and Main Branch of Pine Creek) provides evidence of being covered by the advancing glaciers. The cold local climate and its freeze-thaw cycles, however, accelerated the fracturing of bedrock and the erosional process.

REGIONAL FOREST HISTORY

The Potter County forest we see today is a second-growth natural forest, nearing maturity in many areas. While it substantially represents the tree species that had become established at the time European settlers arrived on this continent, the relative composition of the forest has changed quickly and dramatically in response to man's activities in the region.

White pine and hemlock were subclimax tree species and were more predominant than they are today - the white pines along the slopes of the stream valleys, and the hemlock (with its beech association and a mixture of various oaks and red maple) were found throughout the plateau, comprising up to 85% of the forest. Hardwoods were also common, but not as predominant as they are today, making up the balance of the forest, but dominating some areas. Logging and fire produced sudden, extensive, and catastrophic changes in the forest environment, resulting in a forest today where the hardwoods dominate and the pine and hemlock are secondary, localized species.

White pine, a wood of many uses, was the first to undergo extensive cutting. Pine was scattered, and pine loggers did not clear-cut large areas of Potter County. Usually located near streams, the pine was cut and floated out. Splashdams, erected along many of these streams, usually solved the problem of insufficient water.

The invention of the low-geared Shay and Climax engines enabled narrow-gauge railroads to negotiate steep terrain. Beginning in 1885 narrow-gauge logging railroads were being constructed throughout the forest, making previously inaccessible timber now easily accessible. Many of these logging railroad grades and associated skid roads are now hiking trails.

Although white pine was needed for certain uses, the less-expensive hemlock could substitute for some of them. In addition, its bark was rich in tannin and could be used for tanning leather. Local tanneries were established throughout the region, and as the price of hemlock rose, so too did the potential to make substantial profits, particularly if the hemlock logging operation was large.

Thinking big was easy for Frank and Charles Goodyear. After starting what would become the largest hemlock logging operation in Potter County, the Goodyear Lumber Company, the

Goodyears then formed the Buffalo & Susquehanna Railroad in 1893 to transport their hemlock to mills and then to market. Their activities would have a profound effect on the forest and the region. The Goodyears cut more than 25% of the Potter County forest, followed by the Lackawanna Lumber Co., which cut almost 20%.

When the Goodyears started logging, the surrounding forest was about 85% hemlock and 15% hardwoods. They constructed logging railroads to access their timber, large lumber camps for use over a year or two period, and employed several hundred men to cut their timber quickly and then move on. This practice, based purely on a value system rooted in short-term economics, was known as "cut and leave". Their timber was transported to nearby sawmills in Galeton or Austin, mills that worked round-the-clock to convert it to lumber and ship it out. Little was done on a small scale, and towns grew up overnight, then disappeared almost as quickly after logging was complete. The Goodyears finished cutting in early 1911 and disposed of their Pennsylvania operations to concentrate efforts in Bogalusa, Louisiana. Their holdings are now part of the Crown Zellerbach Corp.

After the Goodyears had cut the hemlock, they sold the hardwoods and associated rail lines to others, notably the Emporium Lumber Co. Emporium cut the large hardwoods for flooring and lumber. Upon completion, Emporium then sold the remaining smaller hardwoods to the National Chemical Company, which converted them into carbon, wood alcohol and acetate of lime, an ingredient of gunpowder. By 1915, even this was complete, stripping a large portion of the Potter County forest. The Lumbering Era in Potter County was over.

The intent of the Commonwealth of Pennsylvania when it began to acquire land for the Susquehannock State Forest in 1901 was to replant the forest with pines and other evergreens. The forest we have today, however, is primarily a natural second growth forest, one that resulted from widespread, unplanned regrowth.

The forest, stripped of its canopy, was flooded with light. This stimulated the growth of sun-loving hardwoods, such as cherry and ash, sprouting from the stumps of hardwoods that had been logged, germinating from seeds that lay dormant in the former dark, shaded forest, or left because they were too small to be of economic value.

With such large amounts of land stripped bare, erosion and fires carried much of the soil away. Natural second growth produced the forest we see today, but the increased sunlight favored the sun loving cherry and ash, thereby changing the composition of the hardwood forest. The Susquehannock State Forest today is about 70% northern hardwoods and red maple, 11% mixed oak forest, and 3% aspen - gray birch. White pine and hemlock, as a forest type, predominate over only 1% of the Potter County forest, though they are scattered throughout the other forest types as well.

The forest of today is not a static system. It is always undergoing stress and change. Just as logging and fire changed the forest in the early 20th century, so too other influences have produced significant changes and continue to do so today. The chestnut blight virtually has eliminated that species, except as saplings. Over-browsing of new sprouts by deer limits the natural reproduction of the forest. Insects, such as cankerworm, oak leaf rollers, larch sawfly, elm spanworm, and gypsy moth defoliate and prey on certain species. Beech scale disease, the combined work of an insect and a fungus, is removing many beech from the forest. Increased sugar maple mortality, believed to be associated with insect defoliations of the 1970's, has been occurring on the mountaintops. Acid precipitation is another factor, the long-term effects of which are now being studied. The steady advance of the hemlock wooly adelgid, a native of Asia with few known natural enemies, now threatens the hemlock in north central Penn's Woods.

Man can slow down some processes, speed up others, and introduce new influences that change the forest. No matter what actions he may take, there are some influences over which he has little or no control which will continue to change the forest environment.

THE FORESTED ENVIRONMENTS

There is more to a forest than just trees - there is a complex, interrelated system of animal and plant communities that are intimately related to the physical environment. In addition to trees are a greater number of shrubs, herbs, ferns, fungi, mosses and lichens. The physical environment includes water, soil, rock, temperature, sunlight, air and space. Together these help create a variety of localized environments on which animals, from large mammals to insects, depend. Each element performs an essential function to the existence, maintenance, and future development of the forest.

The hiker on a typical walk passes through a variety of different types of habitats or environments - associations of different plants that create conditions preferred by certain types of animals and birds and not preferred by others. This may be due to availability of certain types of food (including other species of animals dependent on certain plant types), variations in sunlight, temperature and water, housing needs.

The 262,000 acre Susquehannock State Forest, primarily a maturing northern hardwood forest, is a transition forest that contains several different forest types, including evergreen, mixed deciduous, and oak-hickory forest types. Combine these with differing stages of development, streams, wetlands, flood plains, meadows, and cut areas, and a mixture of many different environments is produced. Although there are a number of ways to categorize these environments, the following may assist the reader in identifying most of the forest types found along the hikes found in this book:

Northern Hardwood: The northern hardwood forest is noted for its spectacular autumn colors and for its spring wildflowers. Sugar maple, beech and yellow birch compose over half of the wood present in a stand. Associated with the northern hardwoods are red maple, hemlock, red oak, ash, black cherry, pine, basswood, black and white birch. The world finest furniture-grade black cherry, of which Pennsylvania is the leading producer, can be seen along these trails. The understory frequently contains striped maple ("moosewood") or ferns. Deer, turkey, ruffed grouse, black bear, squirrels and chipmunks find beechnuts, other nuts, and seeds for food, and browse is found by deer and porcupines. Because the forest canopy is usually more closed than the mixed oak forest type, the floor is generally more shaded, cooler and moist - habitat for salamanders who must keep their skin moist to breathe. Gray fox, bobcat, coyotes, owls, and hawks find ample food by preying on rodents and small mammals found on the forest floor.

Aspen - Gray Birch: This is the pioneer forest of aspen, gray birch, and red maple, typically found in areas of poorer soil, cleared areas, and burned areas. The understory may be grassy, fern-covered, or of mountain laurel. Wildlife might include ruffed grouse, who find cover, food, nesting and breeding grounds here. In young stands particularly, beaver (near water), and deer like to browse here. Squirrels and chipmunks find food on the forest floor in the older stands, while porcupines will feed above in the canopy.

White Pine - Hemlock: These are generally found in cool, moist ravines. When the ravines are oriented east-west, the hemlocks prefer the north-facing side, while the white pine will be found on the south-facing side. This type of environment provides shelter for deer, roosting places for ruffed grouse and wild turkey, and food for squirrels.

Mixed Oak: Various mixtures of oak species - red, black, white, scarlet, and chestnut oaks. The chestnut oaks will generally be found in the dry, rocky areas. The understory is generally mountain laurel. Acorns provide food for deer, wild turkey, black bear and squirrels. Since the forest is more open and generally warmer and drier than other areas of the forest, eastern timber rattlesnakes might be found, if seen at all, in rock piles where they warm themselves and find shelter. Rodents and small mammals provide food for gray fox, owls, hawks, bobcat, and coyote.

Plantations: These are areas composed of single species, usually planted in rows. Species planted are usually red pine, white pine, scotch pine, various spruces (primarily Norway spruce, an introduced species), and larches. The density of these stands often eliminates the forest understory, and thick plantations provide shelter for black bear and deer. When cones are produced, squirrels will gather them into piles for food.

THE WET ENVIRONMENTS

Along most of the hikes suggested in this book you will find several types of wet environments, some seasonal and some existing throughout the year. In them the presence of water is the prime environmental factor that defines the types of plants and wildlife that may be found there. In addition, these "wetlands" have an important impact on other environments.

Flat areas on top of the plateau may serve to collect water and filter it into the ground. These areas are vital groundwater (or aquifer) recharge areas. Without them, springs and seeps would run dry, rivers and streams would cease to flow during dry periods. Pollution in these areas is easily transmitted into the aquifer, affecting wells, springs, seeps, and streams dependent upon the aquifer as a source. By collecting and releasing water over a long period, the recharge area moderates water levels, easing the potential for flooding and providing water when no rainfall is present.

When water collects at the top of the plateau and remains long enough to affect the types of vegetation growing nearby, it is called a depressional wetland. These provide specialized habitats for frogs, salamanders, and similar creatures who depend on them for seasonal needs, such as breeding.

Springs and seeps differ in the amount of water they release. They can become contaminated by pollution sources located above them or at recharge points along the aquifer. Often the types of plants that grow near them differ from other areas along the trail - bee balm, jewelweed (or touch-me-not), cardinal flower, and smartweed.

The outflow of springs combines to produce streams, or riverine wetlands. Fast-moving and cold, these streams produce healthy populations of native trout that feed on a variety of aquatic insects. Along the banks are a wide variety of trees, shrubs and flowers. Periodically, streams overflow their banks, spilling into flood plains that slow the floodwaters, depositing sediments on which sycamores and willows grow.

The more typical "wetland" environment is the habitat covered by shallow water or where the water table is near the surface, forming a transitional zone between an aquatic environment and a terrestrial environment. These we usually associate with marshes, wet meadows and shrub swamps. They play an important role in controlling floodwaters, holding great amounts of water, releasing it slowly, recharging groundwater, filtering pollutants, and providing habitat for a wide variety of wildlife with unique requirements not satisfied by drier or wetter environments.

The beaver pond is a classic example of the "typical" wetland, yet it is composed of several specialized wetland environments: a flowing stream (suddenly impounded and slowed, releasing sediment), an emergent wetland of cattails and soft-stemmed plants along the edge (many of these plants grow with their stems "emerging" from the water, partly in and partly out), and the pond itself. As the beavers clear the area, the amount of light increases, encouraging the growth of willows and shrubs.

The beaver pond is part of a dynamic wetland progression, for the beavers move on to more favorable feeding grounds, their dams fall into disrepair, and the ponds begin to drain. The loss of standing water makes life difficult for the emergents (cattails), but the rough sedges find the less aquatic environment more favorable and become more dominant, changing the marsh into a wet meadow, or sedge meadow. As more vegetation is added, incomplete composting of the dead vegetation adds material to the black muck of the area. As it dries, shrubs and trees (red maple, alder, and willow) take root in the enriched soil, creating a shrub swamp. The amount of light is diminished and the light-demanding plants give way to more shade-tolerant species. Each change of plants brings changes in animal types and populations.

Knowledge of the plants found in these wetland environments and of their specialized habitat requirements tells you what is happening in these local wet ecosystems:

Streams: Vegetation in the stream itself is generally limited to algae. Falling leaves, sticks, grass, and assorted organic materials make up the detritus that enriches the stream and provides food for some fish and shelter for aquatic insects. Near the stream is either the floodplain forest, various hardwoods, or the pine-hemlock forest. The stream provides an edge-type environment, or change from forest to an open area, providing water and food for a variety of species. Belted kingfishers nest in cavities excavated in sandy banks that may be found along the larger streams. Mink, raccoon, and river otter find crayfish and fish here, while an assortment of waterfowl swim and feed here, and great blue herons stalk the shallows. Mayflies, stoneflies, caddisflies, and hellgrammites make up the bulk of the aquatic insects, depending upon the quality of the stream. Small native brook trout inhabit the cold pools and mountain streams of the county.

Flood plains: These flat areas are found adjacent to rivers and streams and are inundated by flooding waters. Typical vegetation includes sycamore, elm, hornbeam, elderberry, red maple, black willow, ferns, ragweed, jack-in-the-pulpit, jewelweed, mayapple, stinging nettle, sedges, and turtlehead. The area provides nesting for mink, river otter, wood ducks and mergansers. Deer often find ample cover in which to hide here. Opossum, raccoon, and a host of rodents can be found here too.

Marshes: The marsh supports a variety of plant life. Emergents include cattails, arrowleaf, bulrushes, reeds, sedges, and rushes. Bladderworts may be found submerged in the water, while duckweed floats on the surface. The marsh provides nesting for red-winged blackbirds, wood ducks, mallards, teals, and other waterfowl, and provides food for muskrats, mink, raccoons, great blue herons, and green herons, among others. A variety of frogs, including bullfrogs and spring peepers breed in this environment. Several species of turtles (snapping, painted, box, spotted, and wood) are apt to be living and feeding here, in addition to various salamanders and newts. Beavers are often the creators of this type of wetland, as they dam running water to provide cover from predators, access to feeding grounds, and their homes.

Sedge Meadows: These normally do not have persistent standing water, as marshes do. Vegetation includes sedges, tussock sedge, bedstraw, cattail, horsetail, goldenrod, aster, rushes, sensitive fern, spotted joe-pye-weed, milkweed, and willows. Mallards and teals, and red-winged blackbirds may nest here or nearby. King rails, Virginia rails, and common snipes may be found here. Voles and mice provide food for marsh hawks.

Shrub Swamp: Richer and drier soils encourage the growth of various shrubby plants, such as alder, blueberry, pussy willow, and red-osier dogwood, found with viburnums, arrowleaf, tearthumb, bulrushes, crested wood fern, goldenrod, asters, bedstraw, sedges, sensitive fern, spotted joe-pye-weed, turtlehead, and virgin's bower. These areas provide cover for a variety of moles, mice and shrews, and nesting and cover for songbirds. Hawks will use these areas to perch, watching adjacent marshes and fields for rodents.

EDGE ENVIRONMENTS

The edge, or ecotone, is a specialized transition zone where the forest meets an opening, such as a field, wetland, stream, or logged clearing. It is a place rich in wildlife variety. A number of species either live along an edge or use it to pass from one type of environment to the other. The forest provides cover - the opening provides food. Young, thick growth along the edge provides both.

This transition zone usually contains several times the number of species normally present elsewhere, as predator species have learned.

Within the Susquehannock State Forest, we can consider the meadow or field as an environment related to the ecotone or edge - unless adjacent to a farm, the meadows and fields are relatively small. Usually they contain a variety of grasses, wildflowers (most commonly asters, black-eyed Susan, daisy, buttercup, and vervain) and "weeds", such as milkweed, goldenrod, common mullein, and ragweed. Here in spring, snow cover is lost first and "green-up" begins, providing deer with a richer diet than the woody browse of winter.

We think of deer as a woodland animal, but it is an edge-dweller, using fields for food and thickets for cover. When most of the land is forested and maturing, food and shelter decline, bringing a decline in the number of deer that the land can support unless new openings and new edges are created. The decline in the number of deer in certain areas of the forest is related to this change: thickets of the 1950s, which favored large deer populations, are now maturing. The changing habitat now supports fewer deer or forces them to relocate their territories to include new edge areas.

Fields are needed for a variety of songbirds, such as bluebirds, who nest along their edges and feed within them. Various snakes, mice, shrews, woodchucks, and other rodents provide food for owls, red-tailed hawks, and red foxes. Insects are drawn to the flowering plants, and birds prey upon them.

The other type of typical edge environment is the clear-cut or thinning. These areas typically have been logged and are in various stages of growth. New clear-cuts quickly offer a tremendous amount of new growth that has been stimulated by sunlight and increased warming of the ground.

At first, the clear-cut will be used for feeding by deer (new clear-cuts are fenced because deer have been hindering regrowth). The slash left behind and the thicket that quickly emerges provides ideal cover, particularly during hunting season. Rodents proliferate, providing food for owls and hawks. As the forest begins to grow back, songbirds use the area for nesting and cover until the environment changes back to a forested one.

FOREST MANAGEMENT

Today's forest is a "managed" forest, a term that has changed over time: from a focus on reforestation, land acquisition, and fire control, to recreational development and timber management, to multiple use, to what is now "ecosystem management". The change in focus has been to meet scientific, social, and economic demands and changes that have developed over time. The Bureau of Forestry solicits input from the public for its management plans through regularly scheduled "roundtables", special meetings, and public hearings. These discussions help shape future management plans, so it is important for the public (you) to become knowledgeable about how forests develop and function, about their role in our world, and about how they are managed, then to evaluate the effectiveness of present management approaches through field observation.

The concept of forest management was derived from past failure to manage an important, limited resource that is capable of renewing itself naturally. Not to manage is as much a management decision as to manage, as can be seen by the great changes in the forest that resulted from the "cut and leave" philosophy of the Lumber Era. The difference is that by deciding to purposely manage the forest we try to control the outcome, enhancing the aspects we consider desirable and trying to eliminate the consequences we are trying to avoid. The concept is sound, but the ends we manage toward will sometimes conflict, and our finite knowledge and available resources guarantee something less than perfect success in implementing any forest management plan.

If today's forest was allowed to continue without interference by man, the trees would mature, hollow out, drop dead limbs, and dominate the forest canopy as old growth. Natural regeneration would be inhibited by limited sunlight on the forest floor. This would promote the dominance of the forest by a few tree species, reducing the diversity of forest environments and the number and variety of animal and plant species that could be sustained as their habitats disappeared.

The extent to which the forest would emulate this model is limited by other factors, however. Stress from gypsy moths, insects, disease, fungus, temperature and drought would kill some of the trees, opening the forest canopy to some degree. Dead branches in the under story would provide ideal fuel for forest fire (from lightning) to open the forest further. While the general trend can be predicted, the actual course of development in any area is less certain than the theoretical model. We cannot know with 100% certainty all the details.

At the same time, man is part of the forest equation - he is a user of its physical products (and has been since the beginning of time). The region's managed forest provides a variety of high-quality hardwoods. A managed forest enhances the quality of these woods. Man is also a consumer of the intangible properties of the forest - recreation, solitude, and beauty - and of many secondary forest benefits, such as clean water, clean air, and protection from flooding. Therefore, it is not a question of whether man *should* manage the forest, but one of *values* - which (or whose) values govern how the forest is to be managed.

The present forest management approach is shifting toward "ecosystem management": the forest is viewed as a dynamic system of many parts (humans, plants, animals, nutrients, water, energy), functions, and processes with complex interrelationships and needs. The goals are to maintain a variety and abundance of species ("biodiversity") and to maintain the health and proper functioning of the forest subsystems so that it renews itself, accommodates short-term stresses, and adapts to long-term changes. The wisdom of this approach is undeniable, but our finite understanding, knowledge, and abilities will always limit our success in managing a forest with the complex ordering that God put into creating it.

The forest today is divided into zones according to forest type, unique features and value, site characteristics, and use. Certain areas have been set aside to protect their ecologies or natural beauty ("Natural Areas") and are allowed to function without human intervention. The 1,551 acre Forrest H. Dutlinger Natural Area enjoys this protection in the Susquehannock State Forest. Some extensive, undeveloped areas (3,000+ acres), such as the proposed Hammersley Wild Area (30,253 acres), have been designated as "Wild Areas", set aside for non-intensive, primitive recreational uses, and forest management limited to salvage and wildlife habitat improvement. Other areas are wetlands, ponds, streams and meadows that are managed solely for wildlife, water quality, and recreational use. The remaining forest is zoned either noncommercial, where site and topography inhibit timber development and primary uses are for wildlife, water quality and recreation, or as commercial forest.

Almost 80% of the Susquehannock State Forest is classified commercial forest, but this does not necessarily mean that 80% of the forest will be timbered. Steep slopes and the proximity of trails place additional constraints on logging, and aesthetics in some areas also limit timbering activities. Commercial forest is broken down further into zones that will be managed by even-age forest management (a euphemism for "clear cutting"), and uneven-age management ("selective cutting"). Uneven-age management is limited to sites where regeneration is inhibited and where aesthetics and recreational needs (e.g., hiking trails, roads, etc.) may suffer.

"Even-age" forest management is the "modus operandi" that has covered almost three-quarters of the Susquehannock State Forest since 1965. The reasons given for this approach are several: many hardwood species can only be regenerated in this way; it provides a forest that regenerates itself naturally in cycles of about 100 years; it enhances biodiversity and wildlife management; and it stimulates the greatest amount of vegetative growth in the shortest period of time.

Clear cutting is limited annually to 1% of the forest that is zoned for "even-age management". This is presently a maximum of 1,907 acres per year, and each clear-cut is limited to a maximum of 70 acres. Each area must be regenerating naturally, and the slash that is left is intended to protect the young plants that will form the next generation of forest in the area. Areas adjacent to one another cannot be clear-cut any less than five years apart. The decision to clear-cut a given area is dependent on a number of factors as well, including tree species, vigor and age, habitat, special species needs, availability of den trees, presence of spring seeps, streams, trails, and biodiversity needs.

Trail protection is limited to a 100 ft. buffer on either side of a "State Forest Hiking Trail". In the Susquehannock State Forest this includes only the Susquehannock Trail System, North Link Trail, and South Link Trail. Trails within the Forest H. Dutlinger Natural Area are protected fully under its "no cut" policy. All other trails (most of the trails included in this book) enjoy no official status or special protection. That means that you will almost certainly encounter logging activities along these trails, particularly in the flatter areas, such as the ridges.

New clear-cuts look ugly, but the appearance is temporary.

A closer inspection from the trail will show that new growth is present even in the newest clear-cut, for regeneration must be present before clear cutting is undertaken. Areas that lack regenerating undergrowth are treated as "uneven age" management areas, and certain species (such as hemlock) are left to provide species diversity. If heavy browsing by deer were allowed to continue unchecked for five years, the deer would clear the area of new growth, and the forest would not regenerate, producing an area of grass, ferns and shrubs. Consequently, slash is left to provide some protection for young growth from deer, and clear-cuts are now fenced to discourage deer from entering until the new forest can survive browsing.

The opened forest stimulates sprouting and growth, creating a brushy habitat within five years. Within about 20 years, the brushy appearance is gone, and the area has taken the appearance of a young forest. Within 40 years, the area once more looks like a forest, with trees up to 10 inches diameter.

Like any management concept, things in the field do not always follow theory. For example, while the slash left in a clear-cut is supposed to decompose within five or 10 years, it is more likely to take 10 to 15 years for this to occur. Similarly, deer browsing in a clear-cut eliminates certain species, such as blue beech. Although these species may not have commercial value, they add to the forest's biodiversity, one of the prime management goals, so these species are sometimes provided special protection.

To the trail user, a clear-cut in the Susquehannock State Forest is a temporary tradeoff of aesthetics for increased wildlife habitat and diversity, very possibly a view that would otherwise be blocked by the forest, and a personal opportunity to evaluate the extent to which the theoretical methods used to manage our area's forests actually work in the field.

Comments and needs of trail users are considered by the Bureau of Forestry in updating its forest management plan, but only if you tell them. Send them to: District Forester, Susquehannock State Forest, P.O. Box 673, Coudersport, PA 16915.

STS WEEKEND TRIP CONNECTOR TRAILS

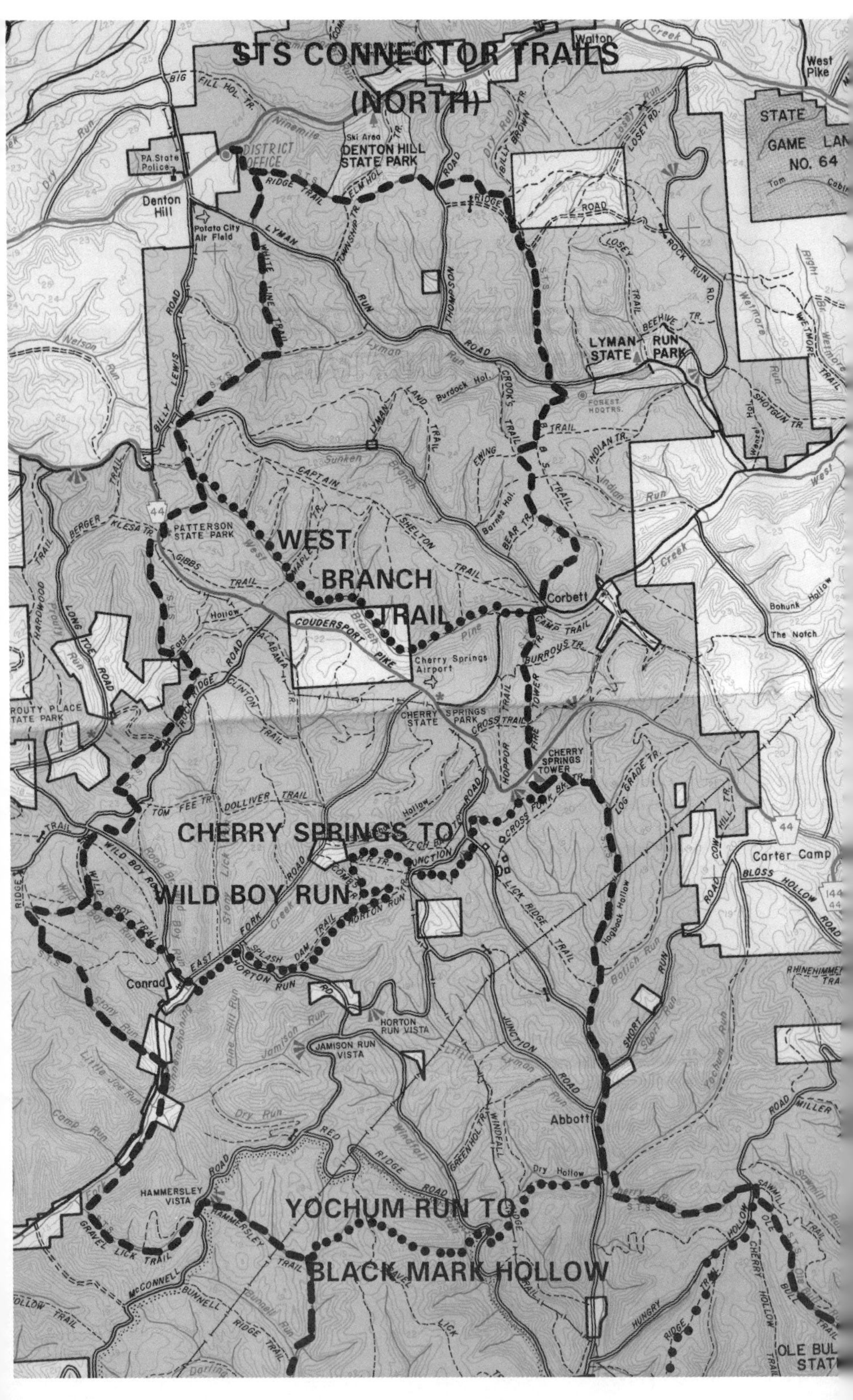

STS CONNECTOR TRAILS (NORTH)
WEST BRANCH TRAIL
CHERRY SPRINGS TO WILD BOY RUN
YOCHUM RUN TO BLACK MARK HOLLOW
DENTON HILL STATE PARK
DISTRICT OFFICE
PA State Police
Denton Hill
Potato City Air Field
LYMAN STATE RUN PARK
FOREST HDQTRS.
STATE GAME LANDS NO. 64
PATTERSON STATE PARK
PROUTY PLACE STATE PARK
Corbett
Cherry Springs Airport
CHERRY SPRINGS STATE PARK
CHERRY SPRINGS TOWER
Carter Camp
Conrad
HORTON RUN VISTA
JAMISON RUN VISTA
HAMMERSLEY VISTA
Abbott
Walton
West Pike
The Notch

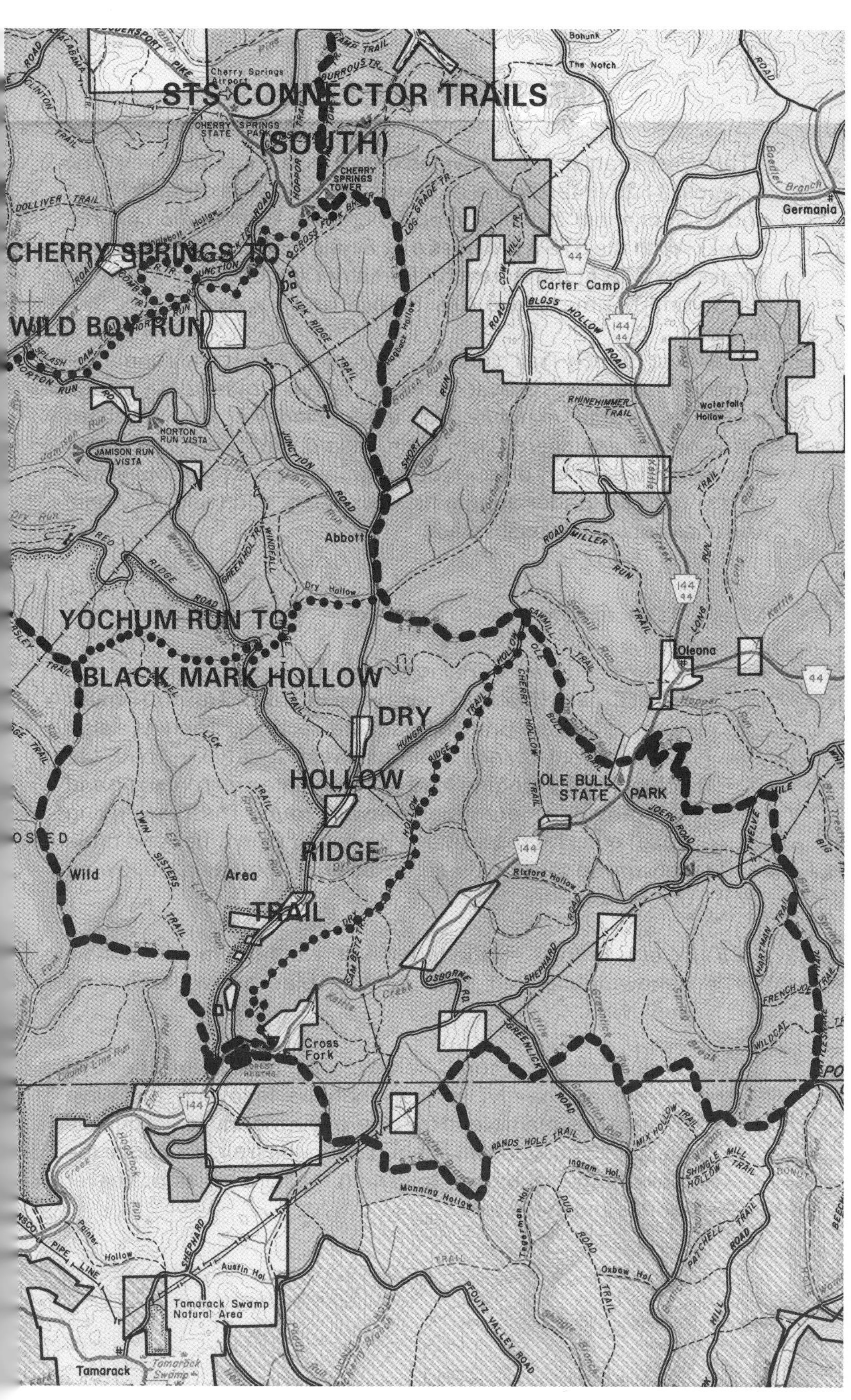

STS CONNECTOR TRAILS (SOUTH)
CHERRY SPRINGS TO WILD BOY RUN
YOCHUM RUN TO BLACK MARK HOLLOW
DRY HOLLOW RIDGE TRAIL
Cherry Springs Airport
CHERRY SPRINGS STATE PARK
CHERRY SPRINGS TOWER
Bohunk
The Notch
Germania
Carter Camp
HORTON RUN VISTA
JAMISON RUN VISTA
Abbott
Oleona
OLE BULL STATE PARK
Wild Area
Cross Fork
Tamarack Swamp Natural Area
Tamarack
DOLLIVER TRAIL
LOG GRADE TR.
LICK RIDGE TRAIL
JUNCTION ROAD
RED RIDGE ROAD
WINDFALL
SHORT RUN
RHINEHIMMER TRAIL
MILLER RUN TRAIL
SAWMILL TRAIL
CHERRY HOLLOW TRAIL
JOERG ROAD
TWELVE MILE
HARTMAN TRAIL
FRENCH JOE TRAIL
WILDCAT
OSBORNE RD.
SHEPHARD ROAD
GREENLICK ROAD
RANDS HOLE TRAIL
MIX HOLLOW TRAIL
SHINGLE MILL HOLLOW TRAIL
PATCHELL TRAIL
Manning Hollow
Rixford Hollow
PFOUTZ VALLEY ROAD
DUG ROAD TRAIL
PIPE LINE
TWIN SISTERS TRAIL
S.T.S.

WEST BRANCH TRAIL

The West Branch Trail provides a 6.75 mile route between STS milepost 11.25 (intersection of Tower Trail and West Branch Road) and STS milepost 79.06 (where STS crosses West Branch of Pine Creek). With the STS it provides a 22.8 mile loop (23.65 miles if you access the STS at the Bureau of Forestry District Office at Denton Hill Summit). Time to hike West Branch Trail is approximately 3 - 4 hours.

The West Branch Trail contains a variety of forest environments: hemlock swamps, beaver ponds, beaver meadows, sedge meadows, cattail marshes, streams, meadows, and northern hardwood forest (cherry, ash, birch, maple, and beech). The trail also includes a variety of trail types: logging road, snowmobile trail, former railroad grades, footpaths, deer paths, skid trails, ATV trail, and occasional easy bushwhack.

Miles	Description
0	Yellow and black Forestry gate at logging road near bend of West Branch Road, 0.5 miles west of Tower Trail (0.75 miles west of Sunken Branch Road intersection). There is a sign for the West Branch Trail just west at curve in road, but following the logging road will eliminate a wet crossing and will provide a more straightforward route. The trail (logging road) quickly crosses West Branch of Pine Creek and turns left on opposite side along base of mountain, following snowmobile trail.
0.25	West Branch Trail turns left at bottom of hollow (snowmobile trail exits right at blue arrow, ascending hollow).
0.75	Trail crosses second hollow. At this point the trail disappears briefly, so just continue following the West Branch upstream along the base of the mountain. Within the next 0.25 mi. you will again pick up the trail just above the base of the mountain, following it past a series of beaver ponds and meadows.

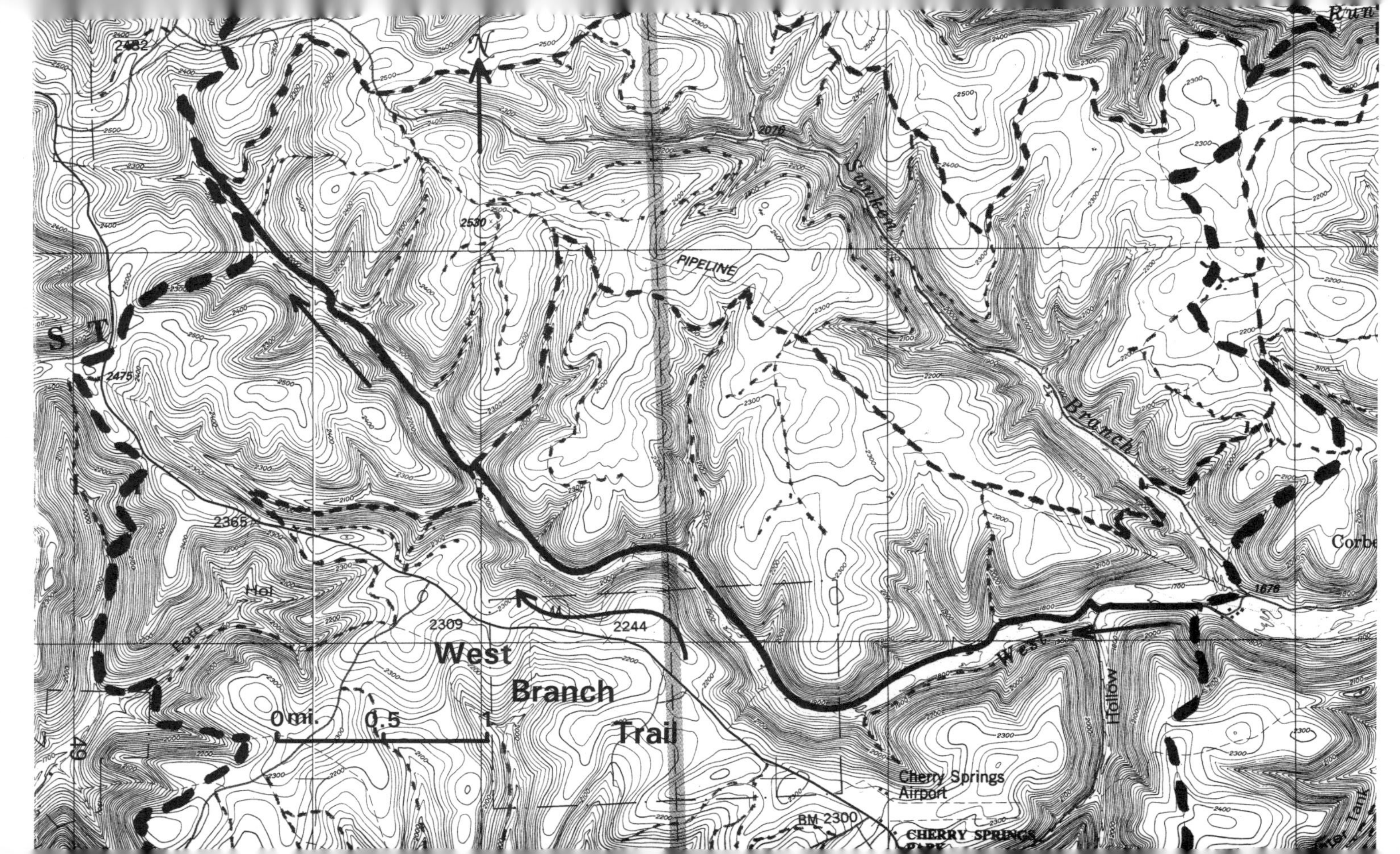

West Branch Trail
N
0 mi. 0.5 1
Sunken Branch
West
Hollow
PIPELINE
Cherry Springs Airport
CHERRY SPRINGS
BM 2300
2482
2530
2076
2475
2365
2309
2244
1676
Ford
Corbe
Run

1.25 After passing a small hollow, trail crosses onto private property (white blazes mark Forestry boundary) past additional beaver ponds and meadows. The trail becomes a footpath along the base of the mountain. NO CAMPING ON PRIVATE PROPERTY.

2.0 After passing old beaver pond, trail crosses small grassy hollow with running water. There is a grassy grade which descends left into the meadow at this point, but you follow a worn path, continuing along near the base of the mountain. The trail will become a rolling, somewhat uphill grade that is easy to follow.

2.6 West Branch Trail descends and crosses intersection of Old Cabin Trail at bottom of hollow. Nice camping here. After crossing this hollow the West Branch Trail becomes intermittent and more difficult to follow. If you lose the trail just continue along near the base of the mountain.

3.85 West Branch Trail crosses Maple Hollow. The ATV Trail ascends Maple Hollow. At this point you can continue following an intermittent series of footpaths, deer paths, and skid trails near the base of the mountain or you can turn left on the ATV Trail, crossing the West Branch of Pine Creek and following the ATV Trail along a well-defined route.

4.8 Beech Hollow enters from right. Nice camping with water.

5.05 Beech Hollow Trail (grassy logging grade) meets West Branch at small hollow. Cross this hollow and follow ATV Trail, paralleling West Branch of Pine Creek.

5.6 ATV Trail bends left where grassy trail enters on right. Continue along ATV Trail.

6.05 Where ATV Trail leaves West Branch, turning sharp right, continue straight. There is a grassy fork here - the left will join the STS on the other side of West Branch, the right (straight) fork will intersect the STS (m.p. 79.06) on this side of West Branch in 0.2 miles.

CHERRY SPRINGS TO WILD BOY RUN

This crossover route provides an 8.95 mile route between STS milepost 13.96 (just south of Cherry Springs Fire Tower) and STS milepost 68.86 (Wild Boy Hollow). The route utilizes the former B&S railroad grade from Cherry Springs to Shinglebolt Hollow, a footpath and short, easy bushwack over the hill and down into Horton Run, an old railroad grade and a logging road down Horton Run, the B&S grade again south along the East Branch of Sinnemahoning Creek, a road through Conrad and up Wild Boy Road, and an old woods road/railroad grade up Wild Boy Hollow to the STS. With the West Branch Trail as a return it provides a 29.05 mile loop that can be done in 2 - 3 days, or you can use it with the northern half of the STS to make a 48.75 mile loop that can be done in four days.

There are two options you may want to consider along this route. First, instead of exiting the STS after Cherry Springs Fire Tower you may want to continue along the STS south into Hogback Hollow, turning right in about 0.4 miles at the Cherry Springs Hunting Camp driveway (which is the B&S grade). This option adds a mile to the route, provides a vista of Hogback Hollow, and is easily followed.

Option #2 should be considered seriously if you are unsure of your bushwhacking skills: instead of exiting the B&S grade in Shinglebolt Hollow and following the bushwack over the hill and down into Horton Run, switchback along the B&S grade into Shinglebolt Hollow, following it down the hollow, then bending left, following the grade downstream along the East Branch of Sinnemahoning Creek. Although this route will add 0.65 miles to your trip, it is an easily followed, gradual downhill grade the whole way and will save you time (you avoid a climb and a bushwack). There is only one small detour along the grade, at the bottom of the Combs Trail where there is a grade washout.

Miles	Description
0	From STS milepost 13.96 at fork in trail (0.3 miles south of Cherry Springs Fire Tower), turn right, leaving STS along unblazed grade. Blowdowns and grapevines may necessitate minor detour along grade.

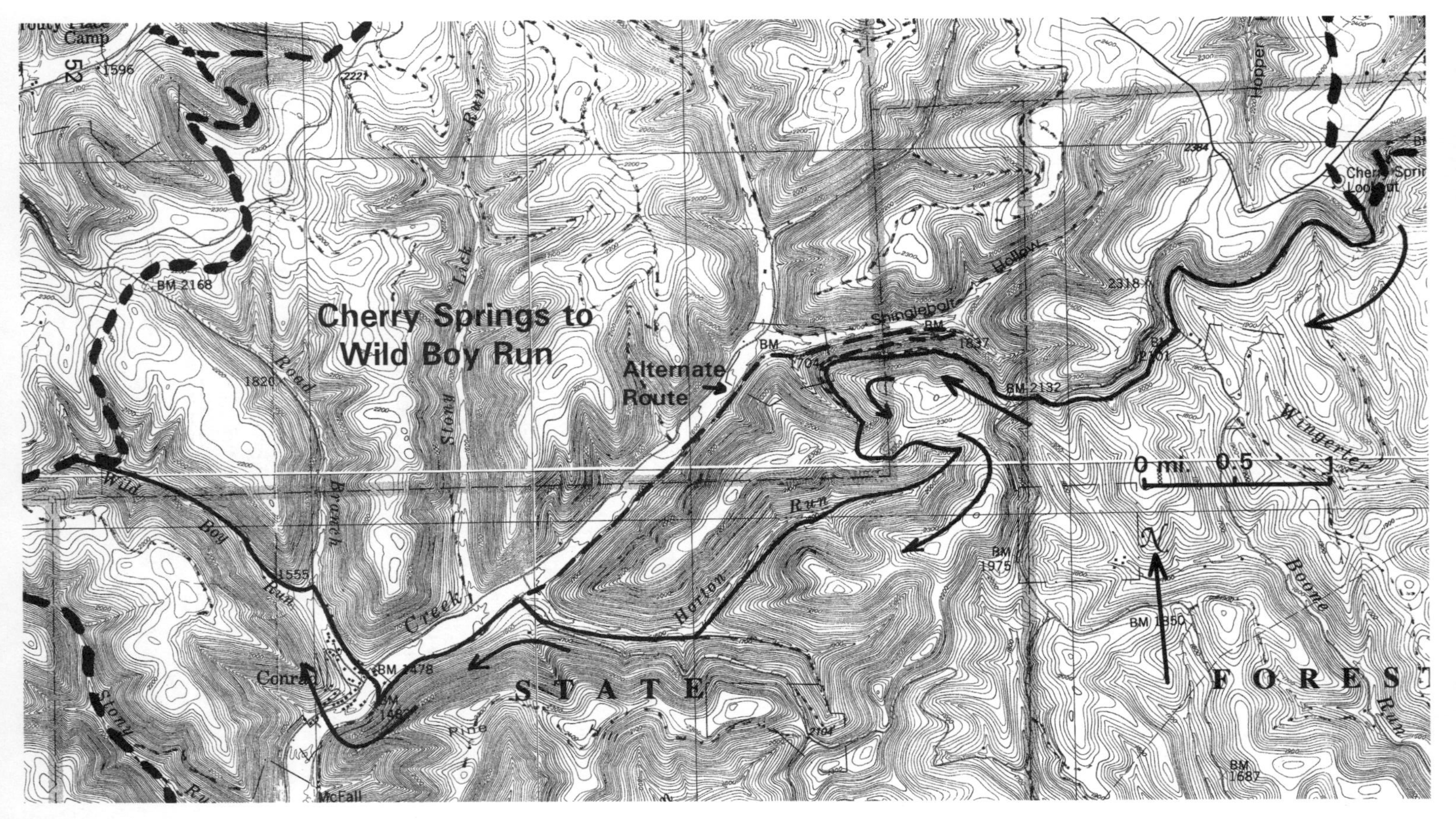
Cherry Springs to
Wild Boy Run
Alternate
Route
0 mi. 0.5 1
Camp
1596
2221
BM 2168
1820
Road
Branch
Stony
Lick
Run
Wild
Boy
Run
1555
Creek
Conrad
BM 1478
BM
1482
McFall
Pine
STATE
FOREST
Horton
Run
BM
1704
Shinglebolt
BM
1837
Hollow
BM 2132
2318
2384
Hopper
Cherry Springs
Lookout
Wingerter
Boone
Run
BM
1975
BM 1850
BM
1687
2104
Stony
N

0.1 Unblazed grade intersects former B&S grade, which has the appearance of a road. Follow the B&S west. There is one brief detour in another mile to traverse a grade washout.

1.45 B&S grade crosses Boone Road, continuing along well-defined grade.

2.35 After passing red hunting cabin, B&S grade crosses Junction Road. There are two grades on the other side of Junction Road - the left rises, the right descends through a railroad cut in the grade. Take the right grade, descending easily into Shinglebolt Hollow.

3.6 At this point the B&S switches back to the right, continuing descent into Shinglebolt Hollow, but you continue along the main grade another 0.2 miles, where the grade abruptly ends - here ascend the right-hand bank and ascend a steep, faint foot trail along the right side of Combs Hollow. [If you are following Option #2 above, then follow the B&S grade to the right and then turn sharply left in 0.7 miles at the next switchback, continuing either downhill or mostly level. Near the bottom of Shinglebolt Hollow you will bend left along the grade, following it along the base of the mountain along the East Fork of Sinnemahoning Creek. 3.25 miles after exercising this option you will end up where the grade crosses Horton Run Road.]

4.1 At top cross ridge (100 yds. wide) and turn left, following south side of ridge east and dropping down into Horton Run when slope allows. There is no trail to follow here. At the bottom of Horton Run is an old logging grade along the right side of the hollow. The grade sometimes follows the stream bed which may be wet.

5.2 Exit diagonally left where hollow enters on the left, rising along a moderate slope (no trail) to a logging road about 100 yds. above and on left of Horton Run. There follow it down along Horton Run. If you do not exit the bottom of Horton Run at this hollow then your route will become very wet and a trail will be found only intermittently. Good camping here.

5.95 Pass yellow and black forestry gate, continuing along former logging grade past four hunting camps to Horton Run Road.

6.2 Turn right on Horton Run Road, then left shortly onto B&S grade, following it downstream along East Branch Sinnemahoning Creek.

7.1 Turn right at driveway, following it down into the village of Conrad and East Fork Road.

7.25 Follow Wild Boy Road along north side of Wild Boy Run.

7.85 Turn left off Wild Boy Road following driveway across and up south side of Wild Boy Hollow past Davidsburg Hunting Club.

8.75 Cross to right side of Wild Boy Run and pick up old railroad grade. It will be necessary to make several crossings of Wild Boy Run in next half-mile.

9.25 Cross to left side of Wild Boy Run and follow old grade, bending left up branch of Wild Boy Run.

9.45 Intersection of STS at milepost 68.86. Camping in vicinity.

YOCHUM RUN TO BLACK MARK HOLLOW

This crossover route provides a 6.85 mile route between STS milepost 20.84 (Yochum Run and Cross Fork Creek) and STS milepost 58.17 (Hammersley Fork at Black Mark Hollow). The route utilizes a wire cable bridge to cross Cross Fork Creek, a driveway to Cross Fork Road, a logging road (Dry Hollow Trail), a short, easy bushwack and a logging road to the gas line on Windfall Ridge, a skid trail down Robin Hollow, Windfall Road, a logging road and old grades up Mud Lick Hollow, and a bushwack and old railroad grades down Black Mark Hollow to the STS. With the West Branch Trail as a return it provides a 33.9 mile loop that can be done in 3 days, or you can use it with the northern half of the STS to make a 53.4 mile loop that can be done in 4 - 5 days. With the Dry Hollow Ridge Trail to the south as a return it provides a 26.95 mile loop, or with the southern half of the STS a 44.2 mile loop trip.

Miles	Description
0	From STS milepost 20.84 just before Yochum Run, cross Cross Fork Creek on wire cable strand bridge. This tightrope cable bridge is not for the fainthearted (one cable across for your feet, one cable across for your hands). Once upon the opposite side follow the driveway to the road.
0.15	Upon crossing Cross Fork Road, follow the gated logging road with the sign for Dry Hollow.
1.3	Turn left where logging road makes a sharp right turn in Dry Hollow. Up to now the road has been clear and gently rising - now the grade will become an intermittent trail following the drainage along a moderately steep grade.
1.5	Main drainage continues, bending right. Trail disappears, so follow main drainage.
1.75	You will see the faint remains of an old skid trail to the right as your route begins to level out somewhat about 75 feet in elevation from the top of the hollow. Look closely for it,

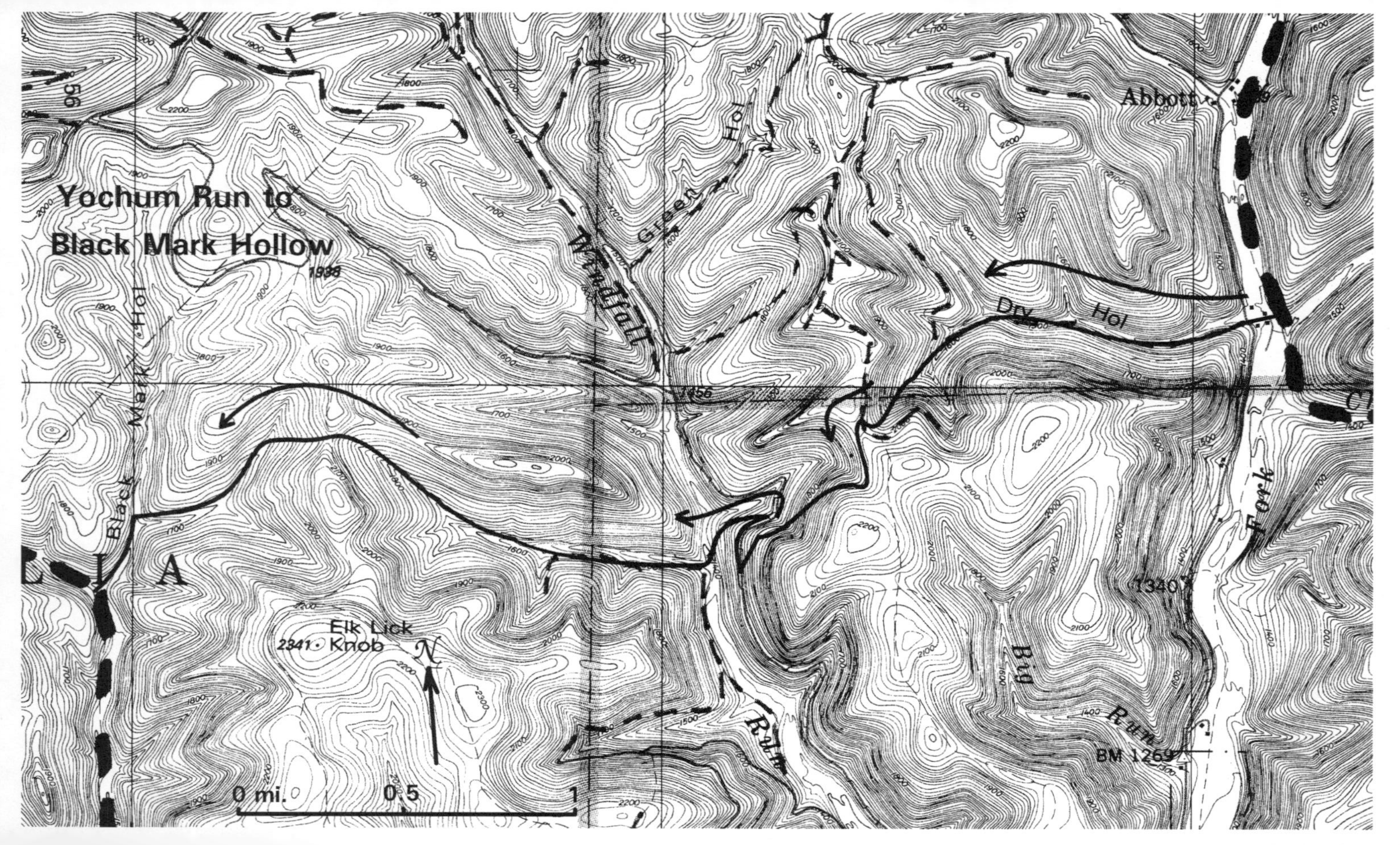
Yochum Run to
Black Mark Hollow
Abbott
Dry Hol
Green Hol
Windfall
Black Mark Hol
Big Run
Fork
Elk Lick
2341 · Knob
1340
BM 1269
1938
1456
0 mi.
0.5
1

then bushwack your way to it - it will descend briefly, then tend uphill, becoming more evident as you follow along.

1.95 Old woods grade enters onto a grassy logging road. As you follow the logging road you will have a few glimpses down into Dry Hollow. Logging road bends left around the hillside, becoming grassy and gently uphill.

2.25 Cross gas line on top of Windfall Ridge to a column of rocks on the opposite side. This rock column marks the top of Robin Hollow Trail: angle to the left behind a pile of slash to find the well-beaten woods trail. It will become an old grade just before the slope to the right becomes steep.

2.75 Robin Hollow Trail bends right in small hollow.

3.05 After a brief, steep descent, turn right on Windfall Hollow Road.

3.4 Just before Windfall Road bends sharp left a grassy logging grade enters from the acute left. Turn left and descend on grassy logging road, which is marked by a sign for the Mud Lick Hollow Trail.

3.75 After crossing Windfall Run (wet crossing, though a downed hemlock made this crossing easier), the logging road will split. Turn right, following along the left side of Mud Lick Hollow along an easy grade.

4.2 Where logging road makes a sharp left bend up a side hollow (it deadends in 0.15 mi.), leave the grade and descend to the bottom of Mud Lick Hollow, following it uphill as best you can (there is no trail, though there may be an occasional deer trail on either side of the hollow, and there may be several blowdowns along this route).

4.95 Mud Lick Hollow Trail levels and intersects Twin Sisters Trail, a well-worn trail with florescent orange blazes (near this intersection is a beech tree with "East Fork" carved into it.). Here continue straight across the flat ridge and drop down the hollow on the other side, bushwhacking your way along an easy to moderate descending slope through open woods.

5.75 To avoid most blowdowns, follow along the right side of the hollow after a hollow enters from the right. In about 0.3 miles you will find an old grade about 15 feet above the bottom of the hollow on its right side. A hollow just below enters on the left.

6.4 Turn left (S) into Black Mark Hollow and shortly follow an old grade down the center.

6.85 After crossing a small stream (Hammersley Fork) scramble up the bank to the STS, marked with orange blazes.

DRY HOLLOW RIDGE TRAIL

This crossover route provides an 8.7 mile route between STS milepost 25.92 (Hungry Hollow Road and the Ole Bull Trail) and STS milepost 49.57 (Cross Fork at Route 144). The route follows Hungry Hollow Road south from the STS to the Parker Hollow Trail (marked with a sign), where it turns left briefly, then bends right along the Dry Hollow Ridge Trail (a footpath, gas line, or old grade in portions) which follows the ridge, then descends to Route 144 just north of Cross Fork. With the Yochum Run to Black Mark Hollow route as a return it provides a 26.95 mile loop that can be done in 2.5 - 3 days, or you can use it with the southern half of the STS to make a 34.6 mile loop that can be done in 3.5 days.

Miles	Description
0	From STS milepost 23.65 (where STS leaves Hungry Hollow Road toward Ole Bull Trail), continue S along Hungry Hollow Road. You will pass a sign for the Dry Hollow Ridge Trail where the road bends right - ignore this sign as this section of the trail is overgrown with mountain laurel and is difficult to follow very far.
0.8	To the right of Hungry Hollow Road is a sign for Parker Hollow Trail. At this point turn left, following a trail through the mountain laurel for about 100 yds. The path will then make a sharp right turn at the Dry Hollow Ridge Trail (the portion of the trail to the left at this turn can only be followed a short distance before it disappears).
1.3	Dry Hollow Ridge Trail crosses top of Bergstresser Trail (marked with florescent orange surveyors' tape), then crosses logging road (white paint marks the Dry Hollow Ridge Trail on the other side of this logging road). As the trail rolls along the top of the ridge there is much mountain laurel and a small area of rhododendron which may make the trail difficult if you are carrying a backpack - an alternate route is to turn left at the logging road, following it south and west parallel to this trail.
2.15	A piece of surveyor's tape marks the trail crossing for

Cassidy Hollow and Tub Hollow, but these trails are difficult to discern. The trail approaches knob and goes off to the left side of the knob - surveyors' tape marks portions of the trail, halfway between the knob and the logging road to the left.

2.45 Dry Hollow Ridge Trail turns left, following gas line, which bends right and follows ridge.

5.0 At top of knoll gas line bends left and downhill. The Dry Hollow Ridge Trail continues straight crossing the ridge through hemlock, then more open oak woods. Vista of mountains and plateau across Kettle Creek.

5.15 Trail jogs diagonally to right, then becomes ill-defined: just continue paralleling the ridge.

5.65 View (when there are no leaves) of plateau to the east across Kettle Creek. The trail becomes more distinct and is also marked with surveyors' tape as it rises.

6.0 View of Gravel Lick/Elk Lick section of Hammersley Wild Area from top of knob.

6.3 Vista of Elk Lick Run and Hammersley Wild Area. Trail descends to the right of ridge.

6.9 A trail heads off to the right and descends, but you continue straight ahead here, descending along point of hill.

7.3 Nice view south from point down Kettle Creek toward Hammersley Fork, down Route 144. About 40 feet before this flat rock vista is a switchback skid trail cut into the mountainside. This trail descends from east side of point - follow this skid trail down.

7.6 In Dry Hollow trail crosses and turns right, following a skid trail along left (N) side of hollow.

7.95 Trail crosses Forestry boundary (white blazes), and does so again in 0.15 miles

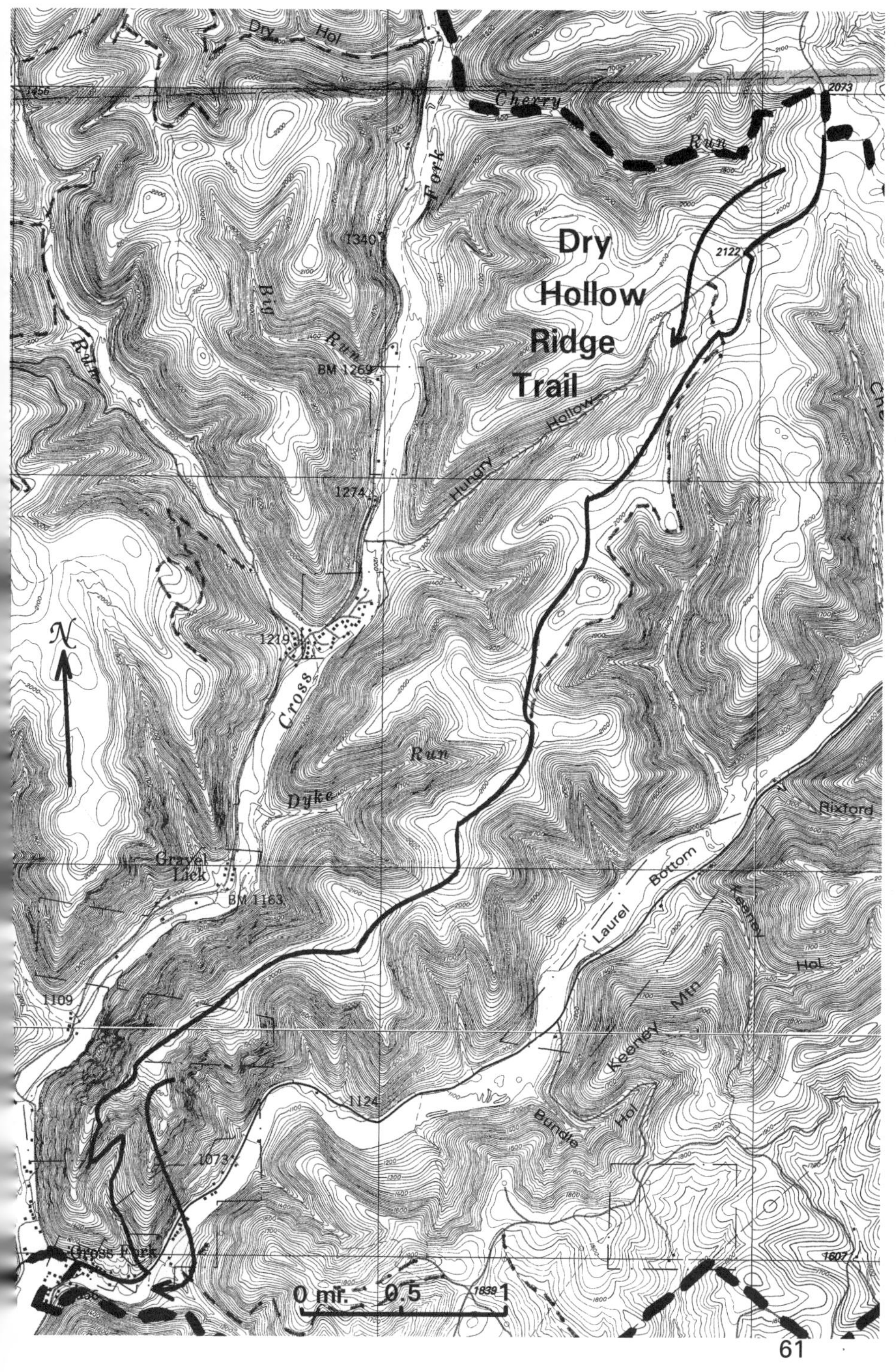

Dry
Hollow
Ridge
Trail
Dry Hol
Cherry
Run
Fork
Big
Run
BM 1269
1340
1274
Hungry
Hollow
2122
2073
1219
Cross
Dyke
Run
Gravel
Lick
BM 1163
1109
Laurel
Bottom
Bixford
Keeney
Hol
Keeney
Mtn
Bundle
Hol
1124
1073
Cross Fork
1607
1839
N
0 mi.
0.5
1

8.3 Trail bends left, just above mobile homes, then turns right and follows driveway to Route 144, where you turn right.

8.7 Intersection of STS milepost 49.57 in Cross Fork.

DAY HIKES

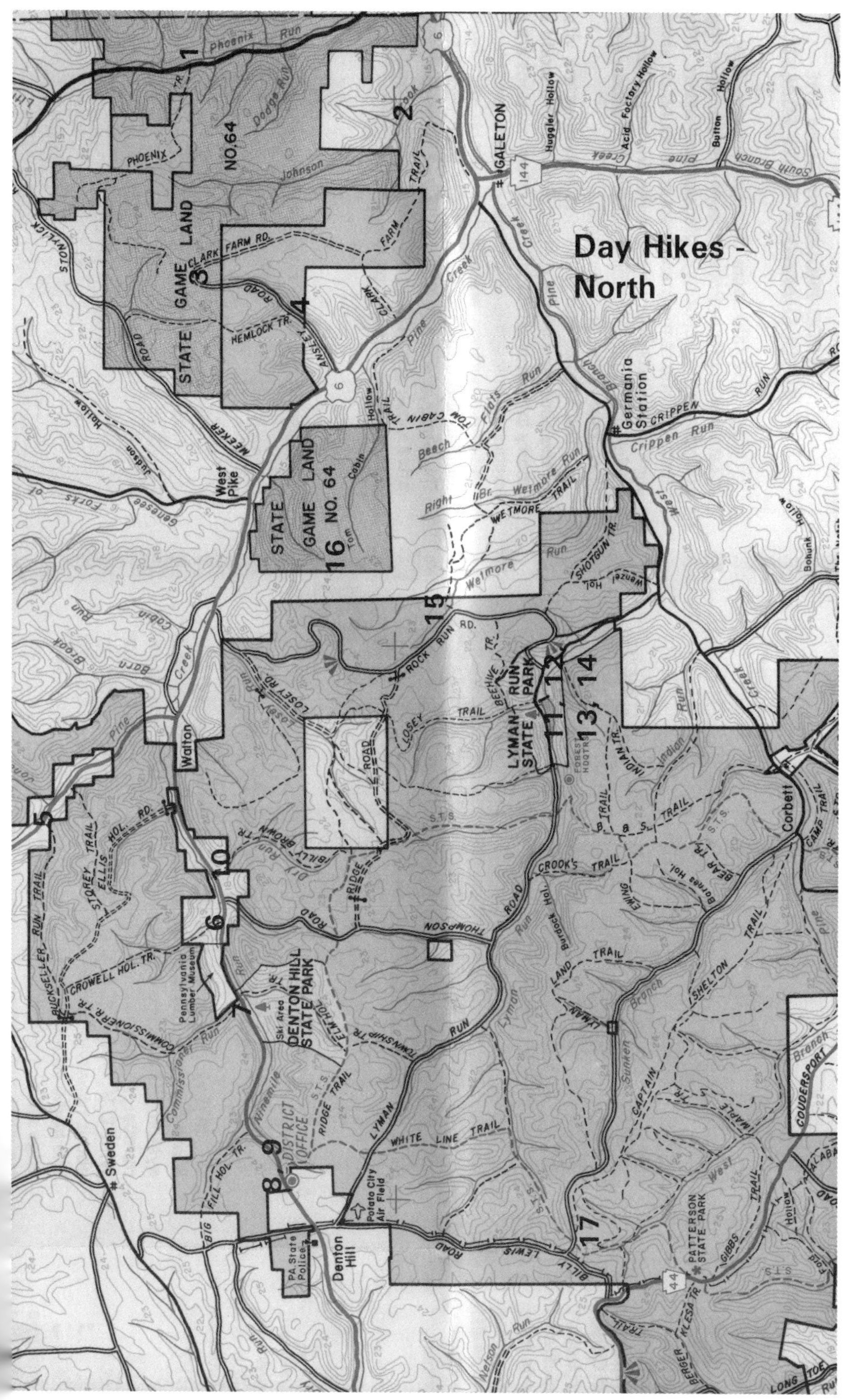

Day Hikes -
North
GALETON
Germania
Station
West
Pike
Walton
Corbett
Sweden
Denton
Hill
STATE GAME LAND
NO.64
STATE
GAME LAND
16 NO. 64
LYMAN RUN
STATE PARK
DENTON HILL
STATE PARK
PATTERSON
STATE PARK
Pennsylvania
Lumber Museum
Ski Area
DISTRICT
OFFICE
Potato City
Air Field
PA State
Police
FOREST
HDQTRS
Phoenix Run
Dodge Run
Johnson
PHOENIX TR.
CLARK FARM RD.
CLARK FARM TRAIL
HEMLOCK TR.
ANSLEY ROAD
STONY LICK ROAD
MEEKER
Judson Hollow
Genesee Forks of
Pine Creek
TOM CABIN TRAIL
Hollow
Beach
Flats Run
Right Br. Wetmore Run
WETMORE TRAIL
Wetmore Run
SHOTGUN TR.
Wenzel Hol.
CRIPPEN RUN
Crippen Run
Huggler Hollow
Acid Factory Hollow
Button Hollow
Pine Creek
South Branch
Bohunk Hollow
Cabin Run
Barn Brook
ROCK RUN RD.
LOSEY RD.
Losey Run
LOSEY TRAIL
BEEHIVE TR.
ROAD
S.T.S.
BILLY BROWN TR.
Dry Run
RIDGE ROAD
THOMPSON ROAD
CROOK'S TRAIL
B a S TRAIL
INDIAN TR.
Indian Run
EWING TRAIL
BEAR TR.
Barnes Hol.
Burdock Hol.
LAND TRAIL
LYMAN
Lyman Run
SHELTON TRAIL
Branch
Sunken Branch
CAPTAIN
MAPLE TR.
West
GIBBS TRAIL
ELLIS HOL. RD.
STOREY TRAIL
BUCKSELLER RUN TRAIL
CROWELL HOL. TR.
COMMISSIONER TR.
Commissioner Run
ELKHOL TR.
TOWNSHIP TR.
Ninemile Run
RIDGE TRAIL
LYMAN RUN
WHITE LINE TRAIL
BIG FILL HOL. TR.
BILLY LEWIS ROAD
Nelson Run
BERGER TRAIL
KLESA TR.
COUDERSPORT
LONG TOE
CAMP TRAIL
Hollow

1 BRISTOL SWAMP: PHOENIX TRAIL

FEATURES: forest types, manmade/natural wetlands
DISTANCE: 5.7 miles
TIME: 3 hours
ELEVATION: 1440 - 2265
TERRAIN: moderate grades
BLAZES: none
PARKING: Game Commission parking 3.0 mi. N of Rt. 6 on Loucks Mills Rd. along Phoenix Run. There is a red "#1" sign just S and another parking area with a bridge across Phoenix Run to the N.
COMMENTS: Fairly easy to follow - short, easy bushwhacking

Lakes and ponds primarily differ in water temperature - lakes are larger and deeper, producing layers of water temperatures (warmer on top, colder on the bottom), whereas pond temperatures are relatively uniform, but change quickly in response to air temperature. Lakes contain three zones of distinct environment: the littoral zone (close to shore, shallow water, marshes), the limnetic zone (open water, illuminated area, containing light and oxygen), and the profundal zone (lake bottom, little light and oxygen).

On this hike you will pass a natural pond, created by beavers, and a deeper, manmade pond. Both contain a littoral zone, but because the manmade pond is larger and deeper it also has a limnetic zone (seen close up near the dam). Both result in a progression of wet environments that enrich the diversity of the forest. The difference between them is that the manmade pond is a managed environment whose placement and construction were calculated for the sole purpose of creating a new environment that will attract certain types of wildlife (e.g., wood ducks and other waterfowl) that would not otherwise live here.

Altering the natural landscape with a pond creates new habitat, increasing biodiversity (varieties and numbers of species). The manmade pond mimics its natural counterpart in a purposeful way. On the other hand, the aesthetics of a beaver pond is something that is difficult for human engineers to match.

TRAIL DESCRIPTION:

This route follows the Phoenix Trail (an easily followed grade) over the mountain. The trail may be somewhat faint on top of the mountain before it drops down to a beaver pond and ends in an aspen meadow. An easy bushwack across the aspen meadow will get you to a Game Commission road along the edge of the manmade pond and the upper reaches of the wetland.

Miles	Description
0	Across from parking area on road to Loucks Mills (3.0 miles N of Route 6 - just S of parking area is a field with a red "#1" sign; just N of parking area is another parking area with a road that bridges Phoenix Run) there is an old grade that rises to the S, then quickly switches back N, ascending hill on W side of road.
0.7	Cross Forestry Boundary. Forest changes from northern hardwoods to mixed oak as you rise.
1.0	Older grade joins from acute left. Trail is easily followed, but is threatened by mountain laurel. After it levels and bends left trail will become an easily-followed grade.
1.35	Trail levels, bends right, then begins to descend.
1.8	At this point you can easily descend to observe lower swamp (beaver ponds) more closely.
2.2	Grade disappears in aspen meadow - follow deer trail to breast of dam, then follow road N along manmade pond.
2.85	Upper reaches of swamp. From this point the road will leave the swamp, descending north. Retrace steps to start.

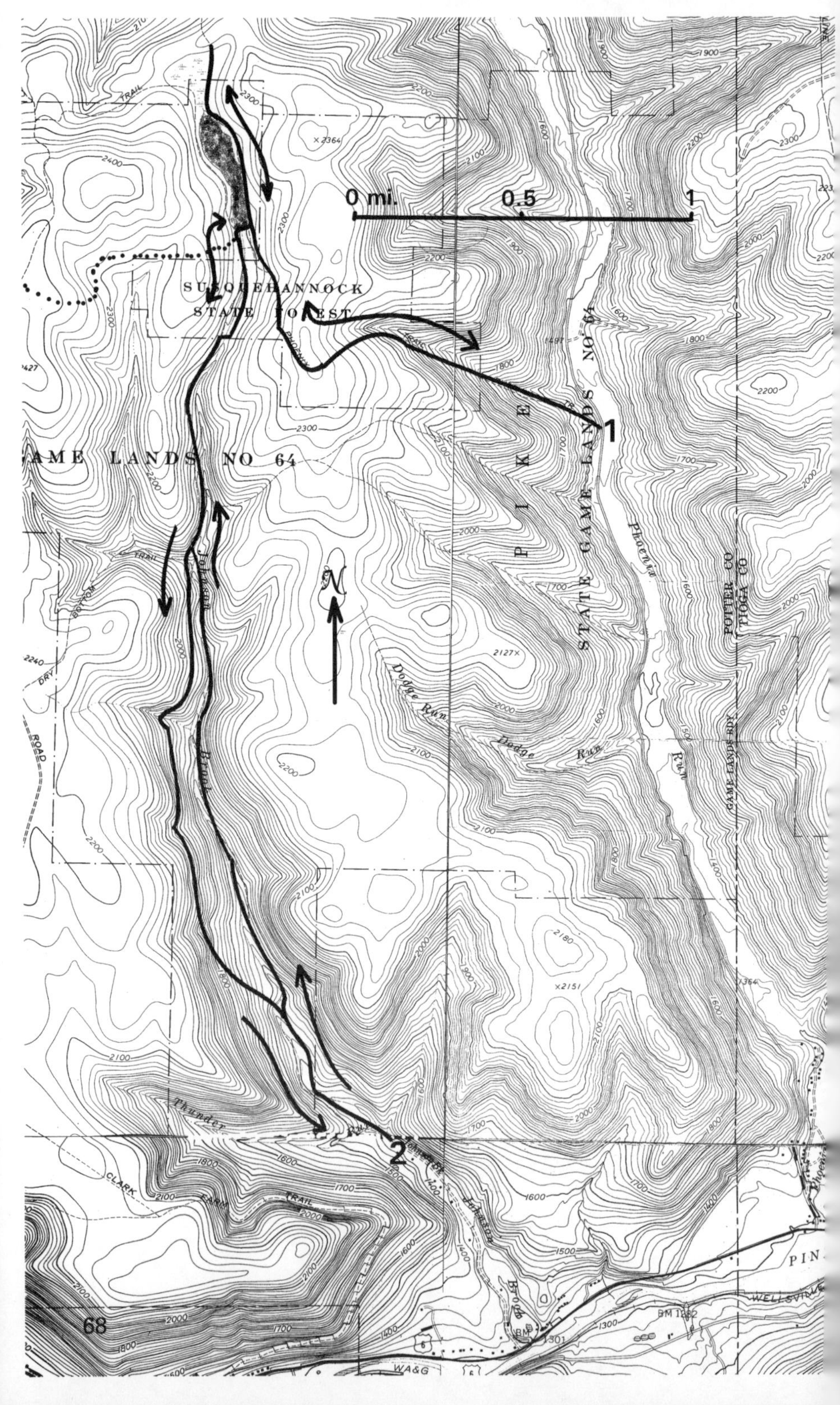

0 mi.
0.5
1
SUSQUEHANNOCK
STATE FOREST
GAME LANDS NO 64
STATE GAME LANDS NO 64
PIKE
POTTER CO
TIOGA CO
GAME LANDS BDY
Johnson
Brook
Dodge Run
Phoenix
Run
Thunder
CLARK
FARM
TRAIL
BOTTOM
DRY
ROAD
WELLSVILLE
WA&G
1
2

2 BRISTOL SWAMP: JOHNSON BROOK TRAIL

FEATURES: forest types, natural/manmade wetlands
DISTANCE: 8.9 miles
TIME: 5 hours
ELEVATION: 1430 - 2250
TERRAIN: moderate grade
BLAZES: none
PARKING: space for vehicle at end of Johnson Brook Road, 0.8 mi N of Rt. 6 (Permastone Inn). Let landowner know what you are doing.
COMMENTS: Fairly easy to follow, but bushwhacking skills required

Marshes are characterized by soft-stemmed herbaceous plants (cattails, sedges, arrowleaf), whereas swamps are characterized by the presence of trees, shrubs, and other woody plants. The soil is saturated with water for most of the growing season, and at certain times of year it may be covered with water. Marshes may follow a natural progression from marsh to swamp, but swamps are just as commonly found in poorly drained low areas.

In the swamp you will find red maple, willows, red osier dogwood, alders, and shrubby growth, or heaths. Heaths include mountain laurel, leatherleaf, blueberry, huckleberry, Labrador tea, buttonbush, and bog rosemary. Most heaths have leathery leaves covered with wax or dense hairs to reduce water loss. Although the heaths are found in wet environments, the acidic water of this type of environment is only slowly absorbed by the plant, so the heath vegetation is adapted to conserving its moisture, just as evergreens conserve theirs.

A thick heath characterizes the upper edges of both the natural and manmade ponds along this hike.

TRAIL DESCRIPTION:

This route follows a driveway through private land and an old grade and a dug path along Johnson Brook. The State Forest boundary is followed down to an old railroad grade, then a short bushwack gets you to a Game Commission road along the edge of the manmade pond and wetlands. You retrace your route back to the dug grade, which you follow all the way back down. After crossing Johnson Brook you follow the grade and driveway across private land back to your start.

Miles	Description
0	At end of township road at Leo/Rae Fontanella Farm (Private Road sign) (about 0.8 mi. from Route 6 at the Permastone). Park on right side near "no camping" sign and check in with owner to let them know who you are and what you are doing (if owner isn't there, leave a note on your windshield). There are signs directing you to walk in along the side trails. On this hike take the left side, passing along the rail fence and past the white barn, through a small opening in the rail fence at the far corner of the barn. Then turn right, following the road parallel to the split rail fence, past the back of the house, and across Johnson Brook. Be sure to close all gates that you have to open!!
0.22	Fork in road - bear right (straight) past the natural-sided barn, following along the edge of the pasture and base of the mountain to your left.
0.32	Cross barbed wire fence, leaving pasture and pick up old woods road along base of mountain. Cross onto State Gamelands shortly and to the right side of Johnson Brook.
0.45	Cross runoff from back channel on right and small open area. [This route ascends along the stream - the return descent will be via the Johnson Brook Trail, high above W side of stream and which intersects here in mountain laurel.]
0.6	Y - old grade goes up to right to more open area with birch, some maple. Continue through hemlock parallel to stream

along old woods road. [Last call to cross and use higher trail]

0.75 Grade disappears - follow path and you are on the grade again shortly. Although the grade is intermittent, generally you will find it along the right side of Johnson Brook.

2.75 Pass two piles of laid up stones on left side of grade, then a hollow on the left. Apple trees appear and stream bends left. Follow dug path located about 30 ft above left on the upstream side of the hollow.

3.6 White blazes of Forestry boundary. Here the trail deteriorates severely, so turn right and descend to the elevated grade along Johnson Brook below.

3.7 Turn left on top of elevated grade. Shortly you will cross the Forestry boundary enter an open area, and run out of grade. There angle left to woods edge to avoid wet areas.

4.05 Intersect snowmobile trail (road). Follow it across the crest of the dam and along the manmade pond.

4.75 Upper reaches of swamp. Retrace steps along road back to top of Johnson Brook Trail, to top of elevated grade, to Forestry boundary, and back to Johnson Brook Trail.

6.5 At the hollow where you left Johnson Brook to ascend to the dug grade (m.p. 2.75 above), continue along Johnson Brook Trail, which follows high route down W side of hollow paralleling Johnson Brook.

8.2 Johnson Brook Trail descends, somewhat steeply in places.

8.35 Trail crosses Johnson Brook to the left, or you can continue through the hemlock, crossing where you start to run out of room. There is red and white striped tape at the preferred crossing.

8.5 Exit State Game lands and return to start in 0.4 miles.

3 BRISTOL SWAMP: GAME BREAK/DRY BOTTOM TRAILS

FEATURES: forest types, natural/manmade wetlands
DISTANCE: 5.2 miles
TIME: 3 hours
ELEVATION: 1940 - 2425
TERRAIN: easy to moderate grades; short bushwack
BLAZES: none
PARKING: intersection of Ansley & Clark Farm Roads and at former fire tower site
COMMENTS: signs mark snowmobile trail; good bushwhacking skills required near top of Dry Bottom Hollow

Public lands are managed by a number of governmental agencies, among which is the Pennsylvania Game Commission. Using funds derived from hunting license fees, over the years the Commission has acquired land that provides habitats for important game species and which could be left open for public hunting purposes. These lands are managed to enhance habitats for these species.

While gameland management, being hunter-funded, had an original focus on hunting opportunities and game species habitat, the focus today is much more "systems" oriented. The interconnections between species and habitats are more complex than we imagine, so the emphasis in land management today is on maintaining viable biological systems by encouraging a variety and abundance of different species and the ecosystems in which they live. Biological diversity, or "biodiversity", preserves the web of life. Habitat degradation that adversely affects one species disturbs the environmental equilibrium, sometimes with disastrous effects on other species.

Biodiversity is diminished when habitat loss makes it impossible for a species to live in a certain place anymore or when a habitat is fragmented (a large habitat is changed into a patchwork of smaller habitats). Habitats are protected by the land acquisition and management programs of the Pennsylvania Game Commission and of the Bureau of Forestry, often with the assistance of other organizations, such as the Northcentral Pennsylvania Conservancy, the Western Pennsylvania Conservancy, and the Nature Conservancy, whose goals include wise land management and habitat protection. The acquisition and protection of certain habitats and the proper management of these lands are important to the environmental health of the region and to all species that live there.

TRAIL DESCRIPTION:

This route starts from the intersection of Ansley and Clark Farm Roads, following Ansley Road to the former fire tower site. There a wide grassy grade brings you to the snowmobile trail, where snowmobile directional signs will carry you down the rolling plateau to a Game Commission road along the edge of the manmade pond and upper wetlands. After retracing your steps back to the dam a short bushwack will bring you to an old railroad grade. The State Forest boundary will bring you up to a dug trail, which you follow to Dry Bottom Hollow. Old grades and a dug path are followed up the hollow to Clark Farm Road, which brings you back to start. Mountain laurel and a faint grade make good bushwhacking skills needed across the flat area at top of Dry Hollow.

Miles	Description
0	From intersection of Ansley Road/Clark Farm Road, head up Ansley Road (left Y) toward former fire tower site.
0.35	Former fire tower site. Turn right on Game Break Trail (grassy road with a "14A" sign and a gate).
0.8	Turn right onto snowmobile trail, marked with orange arrow and snowmobile trail signs, following blazed snowmobile trail as it winds across flat plateau.
1.05	Snowmobile trail bends left and descends along moderate slope, becoming more roadlike. The trail will parallel the Forestry boundary to your right, then descends.

1.7 Trail bends sharp left just before some white pine. Johnson Brook Trail (marked by "closed to snowmobiles" sign) enters from right at this turn. Follow snowmobile trail across the crest of the dam and along the manmade pond.

2.4 Upper reaches of swamp. Retrace steps back to intersection of Johnson Brook Trail and snowmobile trail.

3.1 Follow Johnson Brook Trail along edge of woods. When trail becomes difficult to follow, cut diagonally left toward raised grade next to Johnson Brook. After crossing the Forestry boundary (white blazes), turn right and cut back up toward Johnson Brook Trail (about 100 yds.) and resume travel along the trail.

4.3 Dry Bottom Hollow enters on the right - turn right and ascend the hollow along a skid trail on the N side of the hollow. [There may be surveyors tape in hemlock tree at the bottom of Dry Hollow. If you go too far, you come to apple trees and grade descends to the bottom of Johnson Brook.]

4.45 Hollow goes off to the right - you go off to the left at the small hemlock with the two white thumbtacks, following the right side of this left branch briefly before crossing and rising along the left side at a moderate slope through hemlock toward mountain laurel [crossing is marked with surveyors tape - the grade becomes less distinct if you miss this turn]. The trail bends right after steep portion.

4.6 Leave hemlock below and enter mountain laurel, rising moderately through mixed oaks.

4.8 Trail jogs left at semblance of Y, then levels, rising gently.

4.9 Trail bends up to the left, then bends right, winding its way though mountain laurel. [Looks like deer path here].

5.0 Cross Forestry boundary, following grassy path SW/WSW.

5.2 Turn right on Clark Farm Road at Dry Bottom Trail sign and return to intersection of Ansley Road in 1.0 mile.

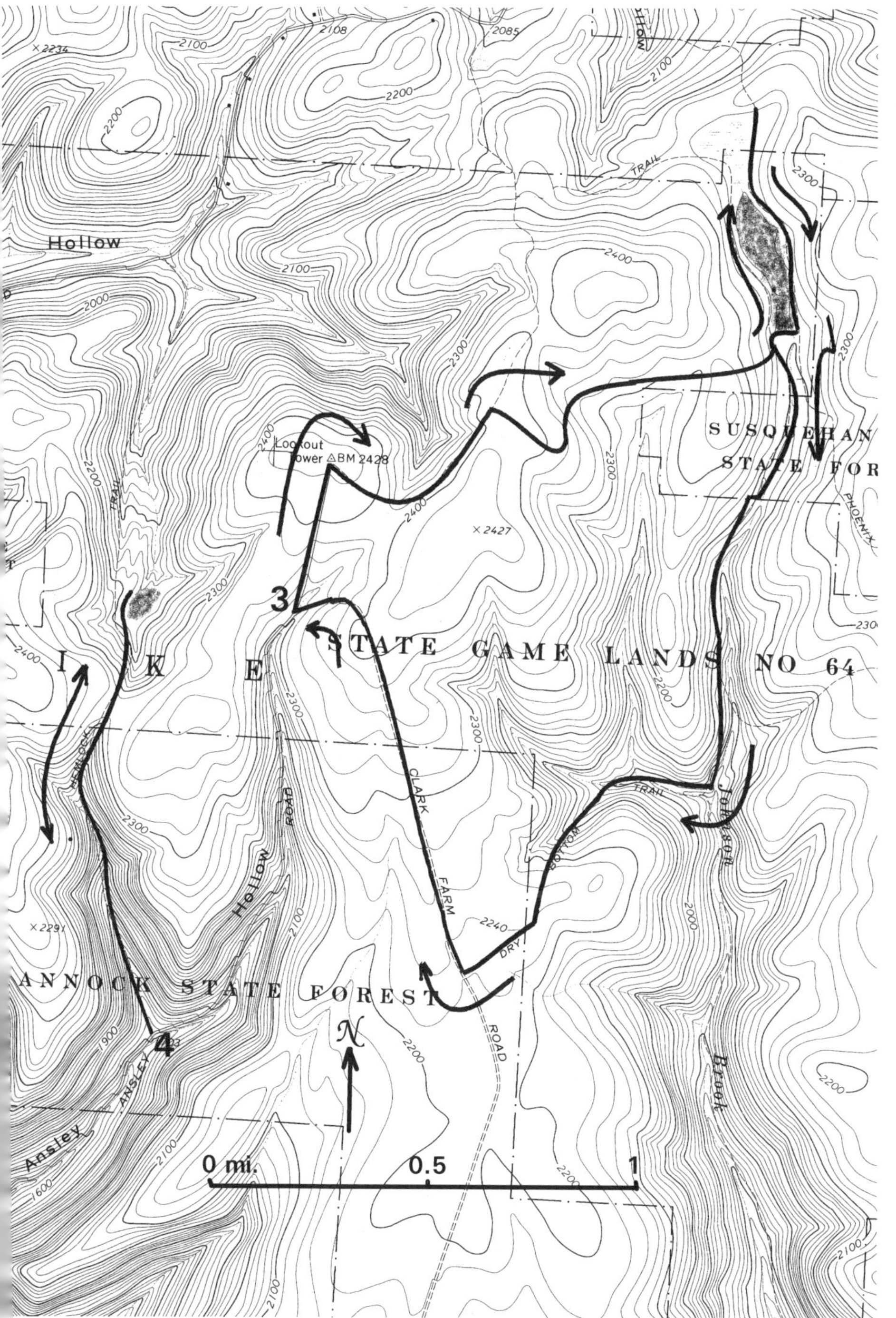
Hollow
Lookout
Tower △BM 2428
× 2427
3
STATE GAME LANDS NO 64
SUSQUEHANNA
STATE FOR
CLARK
FARM
ROAD
Hollow
HEMLOCK
DRY
BOTTOM
TRAIL
Johnson
Brook
ANNOCK STATE FOREST
4
ANSLEY
Ansley
× 2291
× 2234
PHOENIX
0 mi.
0.5
1

4 HEMLOCK TRAIL

FEATURES: forest types, wetland
DISTANCE: 2.75 miles
TIME: 1.5 hours
ELEVATION: 1700 - 2330
TERRAIN: moderate grade
BLAZES: none
PARKING: limited parking at trail head on Ansley Road
COMMENTS: Fairly easy to follow - short, easy bushwhacking

The wetland at the end of this hike is a relatively small one that shows a progression of wetland types. The area was originally ponded by a manmade log dam which has been partially destroyed and now lies in disrepair, covered by moss, much like an old beaver dam. Above the old dam is a ponded area, supporting algae, duckweed, submerged plants, and floating plants. As the water level becomes more shallow and variable, emergents such as cattails and arrowhead flourish, able to cope with the changing water level. The emergents give way to the tussock sedges and then to the bulrushes and horsetails as the environment becomes drier for longer periods. The grasses and ferns like somewhat drier ground, and finally the willows, alders, dogwoods, and red maples set their roots in the richer soils of the shrub swamp. If you trace the wetland to its source, you will find springs and seeps, each with their own specialized plant species.

The plants demonstrate a progression of wet environments, each with its distinctive plant types which thrive in certain ranges of environment defined by water level. Sometimes these ranges overlap in certain places, producing a mixture of wet-loving plant types known as interspersion.

TRAIL DESCRIPTION:

This route follows the Hemlock Trail over the mountain to a cattail marsh. The trail becomes faint as it tops the mountain.

Miles	Description
0	From Ansley Road follow grade on left side of hollow. Trail becomes rougher shortly, then, in 0.25 miles, switches over to the bottom right side of the hollow.
0.4	Trail bends right as two hollows enter on left and then shifts sides along bottom of hollow before becoming grade like.
0.7	Grade rises moderately steep along right side of right fork of hollow. Trail slope moderates and becomes pathlike as it passes from northern hardwoods to a mixed forest of white birch, oak with mountain laurel, beech-maple, and scattered pine and hemlock and old stumps.
0.9	Trail flattens approaching Forestry boundary, passing to right of large pine tree, then trail begins to descend easily. Trail may be difficult to discern here.
1.0	As you pass an old clear-cut above right, trail starts to descend more steeply. Descend along left side of drainage if trail becomes difficult to follow.
1.25	Trail bends left and crosses a small hollow along upper portion of swamp. The trail will become more difficult to find, so drop down to the swamp wherever convenient, following a deer tail at the bottom along the west edge of the swamp.
1.4	Overflow at bottom edge of the swamp. Retrace steps to return.

5 BUCKSELLER TRAIL

FEATURES: northern hardwoods
DISTANCE: 5.9 miles
TIME: 3 hours
ELEVATION: 1700 - 2460
TERRAIN: moderate path, steep and rocky in sections
BLAZES: none
PARKING: Rt. 449 on SW side of Buckseller Run, 2.8 mi. N of Rt. 6
COMMENTS: Fairly easy to follow, but some bushwhacking skills required

The earliest evidence of non-Native American activity in Potter County, it has been said, is a series of axe marks on a tree cut along Buckseller Run. These marks dated to about 1650. The Boon Road is believed to have been cut about 1757, and the Moravian missionary, David Zeisberger, camped along the Cowanesque River near Coudersport in 1767. William Ayers, about 1808, became the first permanent settler in Potter County.

Although the earliest evidence of European/Colonial activity is gone from Buckseller Run, this hike can still provide ample historical clues about the area: horseshoes and assorted metal from a blacksmith's shop and steel rails from the time this area was logged (about 1910 - 1913), the laid-up fieldstone placed by the Civilian Conservation Corps in the 1930s when the trail was built, and a clear-cut and road at the top from logging activities in 1994.

TRAIL DESCRIPTION:

The Buckseller Trail is a rolling CCC trail, sections of which may be difficult to discern. The upper portion is rougher - you may exit to a logging road to get to Ellis Hollow Road. Follow Ellis Hollow Road S from the Buckseller to the top of Root Hollow (a distinct left drainage along the road), where a short bushwack will get you to an old grade that descends Root Hollow back to the Buckseller Trail.

Miles	Description
0	From sign on Rt. 449, 2.8 mi N of Rt. 6, follow grassy grade on N side of Buckseller Run
0.45	The grade becomes a path after encountering washouts along hillside. Trail was built by CCC - stonework holds up trail along hillside (typical of CCC construction). The trail may become difficult to see in places - just continue along the right side of Buckseller Run when this happens.
1.2	Root Hollow enters Buckseller Run on left side. You will return to Buckseller Run via Root Hollow at this location. Continue along foot trail on N side of Buckseller Run.
1.7	Hollow with old grade enters on right side of Buckseller Hollow. Continue along Buckseller, picking up trail on other side. Note pieces of old rail across Buckseller Run. From here continue along main branch of Buckseller, eventually entering (1994) timbered area. Near the top if you have trouble following Buckseller, exit right along grassy skid trail and turn left on logging road above (moderate uphill) to Ellis Hollow Road.
2.75	Turn left at intersection of Ellis Hollow Road, Buckseller, Commissioner Hollow Trails, following Ellis Hollow Road.
3.65	Turn left off Ellis Hollow Road just before distinct drainage to the left, following top of flat to the left of the drainage along an easy bushwack. Eventually you want to follow an old skid road down the left side of Root Hollow (you could follow the bottom of the drainage, but the ferns hide holes, rocks, and blowdowns, creating a high potential for serious injury). After descending steeply you will come to the intersection of three hollows - continue downhill along an easy to moderate grade along the left side of the hollow.
4.7	Cross Buckseller Run and bear right on Buckseller Trail to return to Route 449 in 1.2 miles.

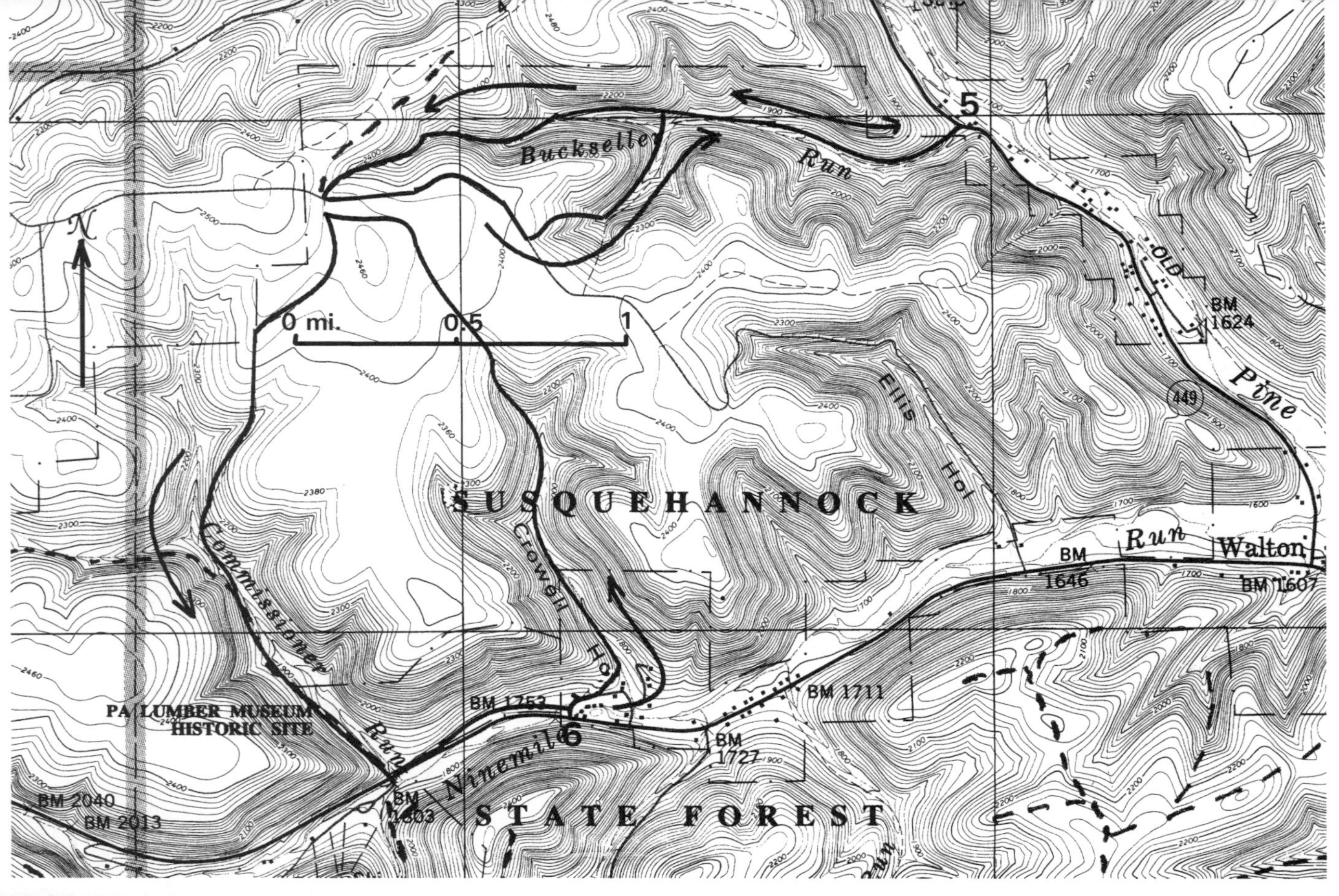
Bucksellev
Run
5
OLD
BM 1624
Pine
449
Ellis Hol
SUSQUEHANNOCK
Run
Walton
BM 1646
BM 1607
Crowell Hol
Commissioner
Run
PA LUMBER MUSEUM HISTORIC SITE
BM 1753
BM 1711
BM 1727
6
Ninemile
BM 1803
STATE FOREST
BM 2040
BM 2013
0 mi.
0.5
1
N

6 CROWELL HOLLOW TRAIL

FEATURES: northern hardwoods, stream, wetlands
DISTANCE: 6.3 miles
TIME: 3.5 hours
ELEVATION: 1760 - 2460
TERRAIN: steep and rocky areas
BLAZES: none
PARKING: Nine Mile Motel
COMMENTS: Not too difficult to follow

The Pennsylvania Lumber Museum was opened in 1972 and tells you the story of Pennsylvania's Lumber Era. You should stop at the visitor's center to see its comprehensive film that helps you to understand and appreciate the rich history of this era and the north central Pennsylvania region. There are also artifacts, tools, and photographs of the period, and you can take a self-guided tour of its reconstructed logging camp, its Shay logging engine and Barnhart log loader, and a fully-operational, steam-powered sawmill and log pond. The museum is open, except for state holidays, throughout the week from March to November and Monday through Friday from December through February. An annual "Barkpeeler's Convention", celebrating the region's lumbering history, is held over the July 4 weekend.

TRAIL DESCRIPTION:

This route follows a driveway from the Nine Mile Motel along the base of the mountain. A brief, easy bushwack avoids private cabins, and an old grade brings you up left branch of Crowell Hollow and winds across the top of the plateau. The Commissioner Hollow Trail winds across the top of the plateau and becomes a dug grade descending Commissioner Run (two short bushwhacks required). Near the bottom of Commissioner Run a logging road leads to Route 6 near the Lumber Museum. Rt. 6 (briefly) and an old railroad grade along the edge of the woods return you to the Nine Mile.

Miles	Description
0	From Nine Mile Motel follow driveway across Nine Mile Run and open area to base of mountain, where a road-like grade will bring you E. This grade ends shortly at hunting cabin, so bear left before you get to the cabin and bushwhack your way uphill through open woods.
0.25	Intersect jeep trail just below large sandstone outcrop marking a flagstone quarry. Large larch tree here also. Cut diagonally across the point to avoid the hunting cabins below, then drop down where convenient to pick up old, grassy, grade up Crowell Hollow.
0.7	Forest boundary.
1.0	Worn trail enters on left. Branch right at Y, descending to stream.
1.3	Turn left at bottom of 2nd hollow in Crowell Hollow (there is an arrow on a cherry tree on left here), ascending left side of hollow. Surrounding rocks may contain brachiopod, calamite, and plant fossils.
1.6	Trail becomes a running, rocky stream bed, then crosses fork at head of Crowell Hollow, becoming dry and following right side of Crowell Hollow.
1.65	Y intersection - take right branch here and just ahead, following shallow trench slightly uphill.
1.85	Well-defined trail here, winding its way generally NNW along top of plateau. Occasional orange blaze.
2.55	Turn left on Commissioner Run Trail 0.1 mi. W of Ellis Road. Commissioner Run Trail winds across flat plateau, paralleling large potato field off to right.
3.1	Trail crosses illegal "ATV trail" (orange arrow points left for ATVs) and becomes an easily followed woods trail. Turquoise camp to right. Trail begins to descend gently.

3.4 Trail bends left, descends easily, then levels somewhat.

3.7 After crossing ravine, trail disappears, so jog left, then right, crossing open area toward base of hemlock ahead and above left, picking up trail at base of hemlocks.

4.4 Trail washes out. Cross open grassy area. Pick up grade again shortly to right, parallel to and heading toward Commissioner Run.

4.7 Cross Commissioner Run and pick up grade along W side of Commissioner Run to Route 6.

5.5 Pass gate near Rt. 6 rest area and Lumber Museum. Turn left (E) on Rt. 6, passing Lumber Museum driveway.

5.7 At guard rail, ascend left to old RR grade, paralleling Rt. 6 through pines, ironwood, hardwoods and larch.

6.1 Pass through aspen grove. Wetland to right between grade and Rt. 6.

6.3 Turn right at Nine Mile Motel driveway to Rt. 6.

7 DENTON HILL NORTH

FEATURES: forest management, views
DISTANCE: 10.0 miles
TIME: 5 hours
ELEVATION: 1790 - 2480
TERRAIN: moderate grades
BLAZES: orange (STS), blue (access trail), and blue direction diamonds at some turns; none elsewhere
PARKING: Ski Denton or Lumber Museum parking lots or Rt. 6 rest area near Lumber Museum
COMMENTS: Fairly easy to follow

The Eastern Continental Divide follows Denton Hill Summit - to the northwest water flows down the Allegheny watershed into the Ohio, Mississippi, and Gulf of Mexico. To the southeast it flows down the Pine Creek watershed, the Susquehanna River, and into the Chesapeake Bay and Atlantic. If you were to go a few more miles northeast you would come to a triple divide, where the Allegheny and Pine Creek have their source and where a third river, the Genesee, flows north to the St. Lawrence and North Atlantic.

Technically rivers are traced upstream by following the fork with the most water. Based on flow rates, the Mississippi is actually a tributary of the Ohio, and the Monongahela is a tributary of the Allegheny, where they join to form the Ohio. The Mississippi River, therefore, is actually a tributary of the Allegheny, which flows from Potter County to the Gulf of Mexico. The rivers were named by Native Americans, however, without regard for flow rates.

The ecological health of Potter County is important to all three watersheds and to people who live along them. Poor environmental management, poor farming practices, or poor economic planning and development in Potter County have the potential for widespread detrimental effects in the eastern United States and southeastern Canada. History demonstrates that in the long-run it is much cheaper to prevent environmental damage than it is to clean it up later (if it is possible to clean it up).

TRAIL DESCRIPTION:

This route follows a logging road up Commissioner Run from Rt. 6, just west of the Lumber Museum. It becomes a winding jeep trail as it ascends to the top of the plateau at a moderate grade, then becomes a logging road again. An intersecting logging road along the edge of the plateau ends in a cul-de-sac, where a winding ski trail delivers you to Route 6 across from the District Forest Office. After crossing Route 6 blue blazes will lead you to the orange-blazed STS. The STS will follow a rolling level path across the top of Denton Hill to a clear-cut, where you leave the STS, following logging roads to Denton Hill State Park, past the top of the ski lifts, and winding down past the lodge and back to your start.

Miles	Description
0	From Route 6 rest area near Lumber Museum (across from Ski Denton), follow Commissioner Run Trail (grassy grade) north past gate.
0.7	At Y, bear left, leaving Commissioner Run Trail and following logging road easy/moderate uphill N.
1.05	Logging road bends sharp left to ascend hollow.
1.2	Cross wooden footbridge to right side of run. The logging road gets rougher and rocky on opposite side, following light blue diamonds and crossing several wet areas.
1.65	Cross to left side of stream over a series of culverts. After small hollow on left, trail will cross open area and become a dug logging road, rising at a moderate rate.
2.0	Grassy trail bends left then right, rising easily.
2.55	After crossing the flat, grassy road descends gently west, continuing to bend right, following hillside and crossing upper branches of Big Fill Hollow in about a mile.
4.1	Go straight at crossroads at top of Big Fill Hollow. Road bends left then ascends easily, skirting edge of clear-cut.

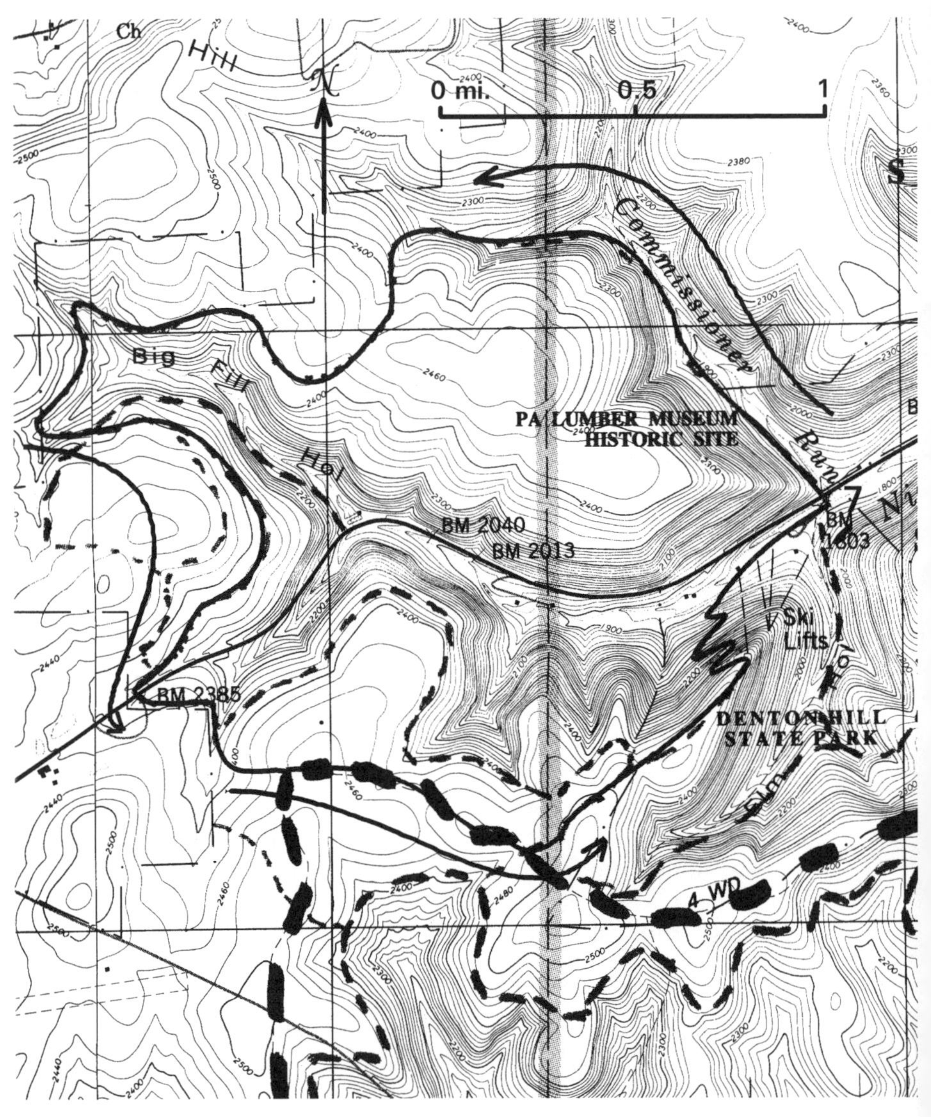

0 mi.
0.5
1
Hill
Big
Fill
Hol
Commissioner
Run
PA LUMBER MUSEUM
HISTORIC SITE
BM 2040
BM 2013
BM 2385
BM
1803
Ski
Lifts
DENTON HILL
STATE PARK
4 WD

4.45 Continue straight ahead at intersection of Big Fill Hollow Trail and Vista Trail (blue diamonds mark trails).

4.55 Bear left at Y intersection for Vista Trail. There are glimpses across Big Fill Hollow when the leaves are down, and in about 0.5 miles is the vista of Denton Hill, for which the trail is named (though it needs periodic cutting).

5.25 Cul-de-sac of logging road - look for blue diamond/skier sign and follow woods road SSW.

5.5 Trail turns left at blue diamond #19. Follow blue blazes as trail winds its way between new clear-cut and Route 6.

5.75 Trail joins connector grade to Rt. 6, then crosses Rt. 6, following driveway past Forestry Office, parking area, maintenance shed and yellow gate.

6.15 At left bend at bottom of hollow turn right, following blue-blazed connector trail (blue diamond #1) to STS.

6.45 Bear left at orange-blazed STS (grassy path). Trail register 50 ft ahead on left.

7.25 Trail passes through a small boulder field and through clear cuts (1984-85 cut to right; 1993-94 cut to left) along 100 ft. wide trail buffer zone.

7.4 Turn left where logging road crosses STS (blue diamond #3), following winding logging road across clear-cut.

8.15 Turn right at intersecting grassy grade (blue diamond #5), following grade along flat past chairlift.

8.7 Top of "Avalanche" by chairlift. Vista of N plateau and Ninemile Valley. Here turn left down ski area service road, which switches back several times to bottom of the hill.

9.55 Follow road past chairlift at bottom of "Avalanche" past brown pump building, maintenance building, and lodge to Route 6 and cross Route 6 to rest area.

8 DENTON HILL

FEATURES: views, ski area
DISTANCE: 9.4 miles
TIME: 5.5 - 6 hours
ELEVATION: 1850 - 2540
TERRAIN: easy to moderate grades
BLAZES: orange (STS) and blue (access trail); none elsewhere
PARKING: District Forest Office, Rt. 6 at Denton Hill Summit
COMMENTS: Fairly easy to follow

Denton Hill State Park consists of 700 acres which are leased to a ski area operator. One slope, "Avalanche", a 67% slope, is said to be the steepest in the east.

Annual snowfall at Denton Hill is about 100 inches, and is supplemented by manmade snow: water is taken from ponds, a nucleizing agent is added, and it is pumped through pipes and hoses and sprayed into the air in a fine mist, either by special electric or compressed air snowguns. The fine mist condenses around the nucleizing agent (or dust), and falls to the ground as snow or ice particles. The type of snow produced (ice, slush, powder, etc.) Is dependent upon temperature, humidity, and the air/water mixture, so a crew must check, adjust, and free the guns from ice each hour.

Having worked as a snowmaker here one winter (graveyard shift), I recall few sights more beautiful than sunrise at the top of Denton Hill on a clear, quiet, cold winter morning.

TRAIL DESCRIPTION:

This route follows a logging road from the District Forest Office to a clear-cut near the Denton Hill State Park border. There a grassy logging road leads into the park, passing the top of the ski lifts and winding down the hill past the ski lodge at the bottom. Logging roads then bring you up Elm Hollow and over the mountain to the orange-blazed Susquehannock Trail System. The STS brings you to a blue-blazed access trail and back to the District Forest Office.

Miles	Description
0	From District Forestry Office parking area, follow blue-blazed logging road past Forestry maintenance shed, past yellow gate. After crossing bottom of hollow the blue-blazed STS connector trail exits right (blue diamond #1). Here continue along the logging road, paralleling hollow on the left and catching glimpses of Route 6.
1.25	View E of Route 6 valley and surrounding plateau. Logging road continues to follow hollow, bending right, then left.
2.0	Enter new clear-cut (1993/94) bending right and ascending gently. At top the road is a view of the plateau to the north. Road then bends left and descends gently, then follows north and east edges of clear-cut.
2.45	Turn left at grassy road intersection (blue diamond #5). [If you continue straight ahead, logging road will wind its way through the clear-cut and intersect the STS in 0.5 mi.]
2.8	Pass Blue Diamond #6. Trail flattens briefly approaching top of chair lift. Views E across Elm Hollow.
3.0	Top of "Avalanche" at chairlift. Vista of N plateau and Ninemile Valley. Here turn left down "Sidewinder", ski area service road to the bottom of the hill.
3.85	Bottom of chairlift at "Avalanche". Pond on left is source of water for snowmaking. Brown building on left is the pump building (air and water), maintenance building ahead left. Cut across lawn and across south side of lodge.
4.1	At bottom of chairlift and Elm Hollow, follow logging road, ascending easily along east side of Elm Hollow. Logging road will cross a path that ascends a small hollow on left.
4.55	Grassy grade joins this road from acute right. Cross a hollow on the left and turn left on an old logging road that goes up the hollow. (Blue diamond points up that road.)

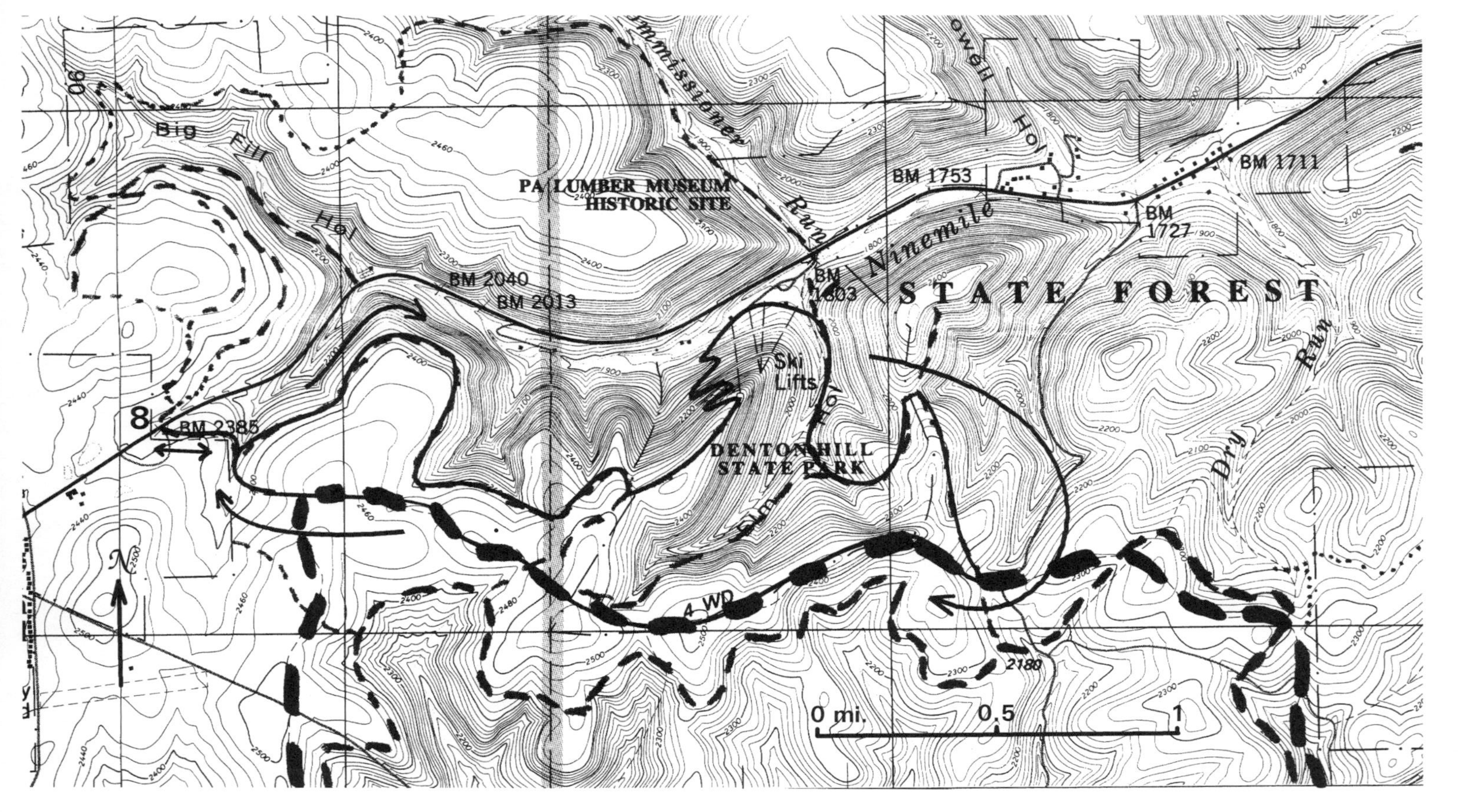

90
Big
Fill
Hol
PA LUMBER MUSEUM
HISTORIC SITE
Commissioner
Run
Nwell
Hol
BM 1753
BM 1711
BM 1727
Ninemile
BM 1803
BM 2040
BM 2013
STATE FOREST
Dry
Run
Ski
Lifts
Hol
DENTON HILL
STATE PARK
Elm
8
BM 2385
4 WD
2180
0 mi.
0.5
1
N

4.85 Turn left at intersection of logging grade (blue diamond #7), rising moderately and bending sharp left shortly.

5.05 Logging road bends right, flattening.

5.25 Bend left at top of hollow, passing flagstone rock quarry.

5.5 Intersect logging road that parallels Thompson Hollow. Turn right, rising gently past views down Thompson Hollow to Route 6. [The road to the left at this intersection rises and deadends in about 0.25 mi.] In 1.1 miles the grassy logging road will begin to descend to the STS.

6.2 Turn right onto orange-blazed STS at yellow/black wooden gates.

6.5 Blue-blazed trail to vista, 200' right.

7.65 STS passes blue diamond (#4) which marks the top of Elm Hollow and then enters clear cuts(1984/85 to the left of STS; 1993/94 to right of STS) along 100 ft. wide buffer zone.

8.9 After passing STS trail register, follow blue-blazed access trail back to District Forestry Office parking area in 0.5 mi.

9 SPLASHDAM/BINKY HOLLOWS

FEATURES: flagstone quarries, beaver ponds, northern hardwoods
DISTANCE: 12.6 miles
TIME: 6 hours
ELEVATION: 1820 - 2540
TERRAIN: moderate old grades; easy bushwhacking
BLAZES: orange (STS), blue (access trail); otherwise none
PARKING: District Forest Office
COMMENTS: Fairly easy to follow

Flagstones are composed of sandstone of similar grain size which readily splits along its horizontal bedding planes in a uniform manner (i.e., in layers of similar thickness, or "parallel stratification"). This characteristic is a result of changes in the size, amount, direction or speed of sediments at the time they were deposited - these changes disturbed the uniformity of the sediments being deposited and changed the bonding or cementing pattern. This effect is associated with rapidly moving water currents, most commonly occurring in streams or along coastlines.

In this region, flagstones are normally associated with gray sandstone. The most likely place to find this sandstone is where the hilltops are flat (sandstone is often just below the surface), or where there are benches or ledges in the hillsides (also caused by erosionally-resistant sandstone).

Sandstone surfaces, or "bedding planes" tell us about the early environment at the time the sediments were deposited. Ripples indicate relatively slow water with gentle back-and-forth movements, like in tidal pools. Current lineations are linear, ribbon like ridges raised slightly from the surrounding smoother rock surface, and they are parallel to each other - these indicate currents (and current direction) that brought the sediments in. Crossbedding, a sudden change in the horizontal angle of the sediment beds, are believed to indicate the presence of sand dunes or river deltas, where sediments dropped out in response to changes in speed (i.e., on the leeward side of the dune, or when moving water enters a quiet body of water).

Geologists classify the deposits as beach or stream using a number of clues. Beach deposits are usually more uniform in particle size, contain little shale or conglomerate, may contain fossils, may show crossbedding in two directions, and parallel stratification extends for a much longer distance parallel to the beach (perpendicular to the direction of flow indicated by current lineations).

Flagstones are sometimes referred to as "slate", but slate is actually a metamorphic rock, not a sedimentary rock.

The flagstone quarries in Binky Hollow are mostly gray sandstone, show linear parting lines in a WNW-ESE direction, contain some layers of unconsolidated sandstone and some shale, and contain some seashell fossils in the upper layers.

TRAIL DESCRIPTION:

This route follows the blue-blazed access trail from the District Forest Office on Denton Hill Summit to the orange-blazed STS. Just before Thompson Hollow Road you will exit the STS along a grassy logging road, then turn right onto the ATV Trail. From the top of Binky Hollow you will bushwack briefly through open woods, then follow an old railroad grade. When the grade becomes rough, you can bushwhack your way along the edge of the hollow to an old road - this road leads up to the old flagstone quarries and down to Lyman Run Road. After following Lyman Run Road west you exit left onto the Splashdam Trail, an easy old grade (after crossing part of a beaver pond) to the STS, which will rise moderately, bringing you back to the blue-blazed access trail and District Forest Office.

Miles	Description
0	Follow road from Forestry Office past gate.
0.14	Trail turns right (blue diamond #1), leaving logging road.
0.42	Trail intersects STS (orange blazes), where you turn left and pass trail register.
1.15	Trail passes through clear-cuts (1984-85 cut to right; 1993-94 cut to left) along 100 ft. wide trail buffer zone.

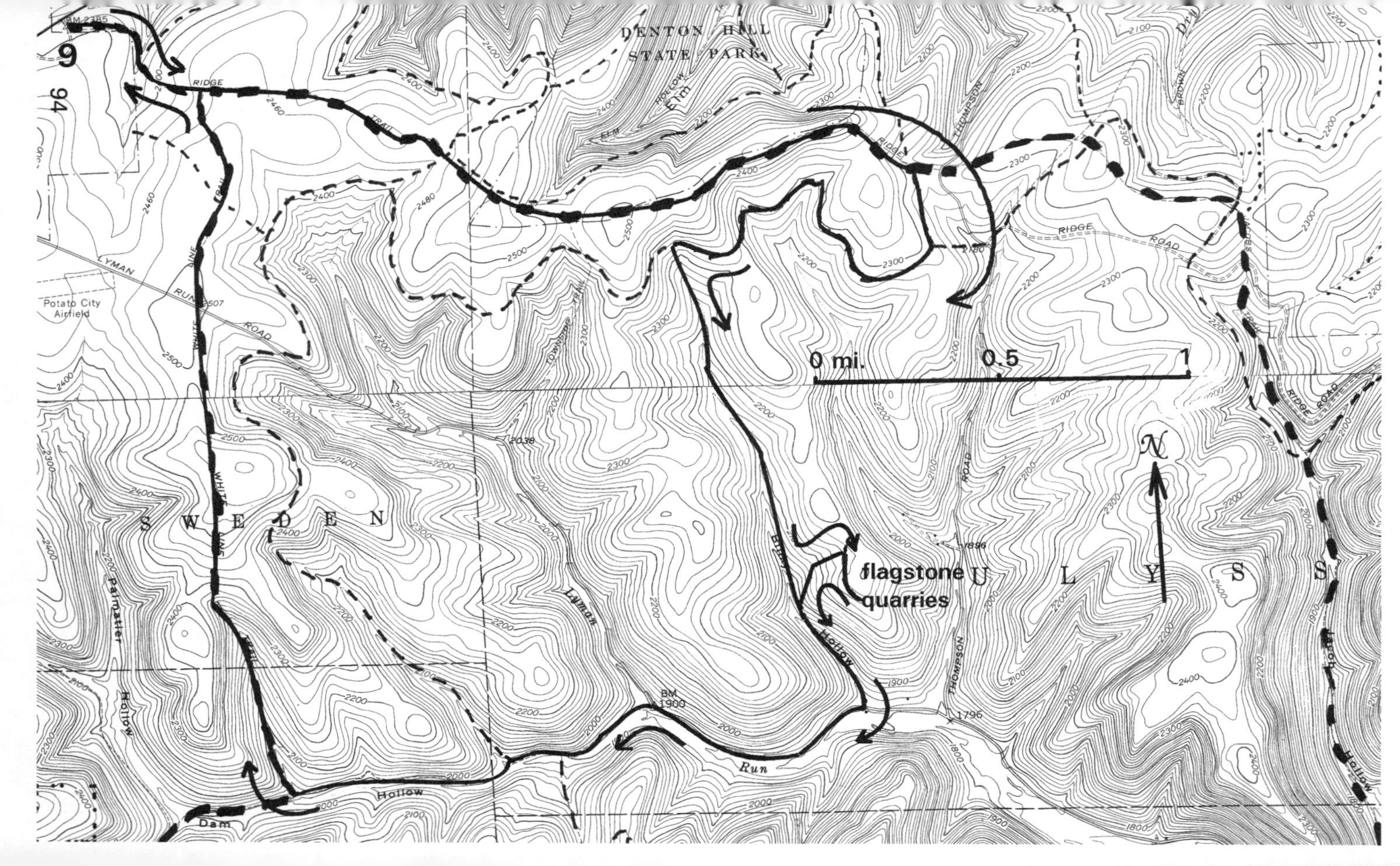
9
DENTON HILL
STATE PARK
SWEDEN
ULYSSES
flagstone
quarries
0 mi.
0.5
1
N
Potato City
Airfield
LYMAN RUN ROAD
WHITE LINE TRAIL
RIDGE TRAIL
RIDGE ROAD
THOMPSON ROAD
TOWNSHIP TRAIL
Lyman Run
Bliss Hollow
Elm Hollow
Palmatier Hollow
Jacob Hollow
Dam
BM 1900

1.55 Trail leaves clear cuts, reentering forest along narrow path. Elm Hollow on left (no sign) leads to Denton Hill Ski Area.

2.75 Blue-blazed trail to vista, 200' left.

3.0 Turn right onto grassy road at yellow fences, leaving STS.

3.15 Grassy road intersects ATV Trail at a sign that says "Denton Hill 4 miles" to the right. Turn right here onto ATV Trail. Watch the contours to your left as you swing around the top of an unnamed hollow and then across a flat. The next hollow is Binky Hollow.

4.4 Drop down Binky Hollow from ATV Trail (easy bushwack, following hollow). In the next 0.25 miles you will pick up an old grade in the bottom of Binky Hollow (old railroad grade - you can see where the ties used to be). Follow it down past a series of open areas.

5.05 After passing a small grassy meadow with apple trees the grade will get rougher. At this point it is best to travel along the open flat area above left, paralleling the bottom of Binky Hollow, to avoid wet areas, rough areas and blowdowns.

5.4 Hollow enters on right - in about 0.1 miles, follow the bottom of the hollow along the old grade again.

5.75 Small hollow enters on left. [A road up this hollow (about 0.25 mi. long) bends right and leads to several flagstone quarry pits at the top of the hollow.] Continue down Binky Hollow after this side trip.

7.15 After following driveway past Binky Hollow Camp (white), turn right on Lyman Road.

8.05 Turn left off Lyman Run Road onto Splashdam Trail. A downed tree to the right of the former logging road will get you across the area flooded by beavers.

8.5 Splashdam Trail joins ATV Trail briefly (ATV Trail exits right) before resuming as an old grade.

9.5 Turn right at intersection of STS (orange blazes), following White Line Trail (STS) up hollow.

10.3 After rising along a moderate to steep grade, STS reaches top of plateau and levels, passing the highest elevation along the STS (2,545 feet).

11.0 STS intersects grassy road, crossing diagonally left.

11.3 Trail crosses Lyman Run Road and becomes wet as it passes clear-cut area on right of trail.

11.9 Trail becomes gentle downhill, then crosses ATV Trail and meanders along easy grade through large cherry.

12.15 STS bends right in small clearing to join Ridge Trail, which runs E. Exit left just before the trail register box, following blue-blazed trail to District Forestry Office (about 0.4 miles).

10 ROCK RUN ROAD VISTA/LOSEY RUN

FEATURES: view
DISTANCE: 13 miles
TIME: 7 hours
ELEVATION: 1710 - 2440
TERRAIN: moderate old grades; some bushwhacking
BLAZES: none
PARKING: Susquehannock Lodge
COMMENTS: Not hard to follow with average bushwhacking skills. Logging (1995 - 1998) may necessitate detours in upper Losey Run.

In 1810, Samuel Losey settled on 2,000 acres along Pine Creek in Potter County. He lived to be 106.

Billy Brown homesteaded the area around Dry Run and built the farmhouse that Wil and Betty Ahn converted into the Susquehannock Lodge, which is presently operated by Ed and Carol Szymanik. The Susquehannock Lodge has provided lodging and meals for hikers and skiers since 1963.

Although people refer to the "mountains" of Potter County, there are no mountains here. The area is part of the Allegheny Plateau, an ancient sea floor that rose an estimated 200 million years ago, producing a giant tableland. The bedrock looks almost horizontal, but is gently folded, providing natural drainage channels. Erosion over the years has produced the steep-sided, narrow valleys, carving the tableland into a dramatic landscape. The Valley of the Ninemile, part of the Pine Creek watershed, is along a syncline (the bottom of one of these troughs), while the Ridge Trail follows an anticline (the top of the bedrock wave). The side valleys, including Losey Run, are secondary erosional features.

Although you will climb no mountains on this hike, you will walk out of the steep-sided valleys of Dry Run and Losey Run. The rest of this hike is over the rolling level top of the plateau, which you will see from the Rock Run Vista.

TRAIL DESCRIPTION:

This route follows the Billy Brown Trail south from the Susquehannock Lodge and along the edge of an old clear-cut. A short bushwack from the clear-cut is necessary to connect with an old grade along the top of the ridge before descending quickly to Losey Run. At the Losey Run Hunting Camp you follow the driveway briefly to an old grade up a small hollow - an easy bushwack near the top and along the edge of the plateau will get you to Rock Run Road and the Rock Run Vista. From Rock Run Road follow Ridge Road west. At a split in the road another short bushwack will get you to an old grade that descends the hollow. That grade will disappear, necessitating another easy bushwack to a former logging grade and back to the Losey Run Hunting Club. Losey Run Road parallels the stream, which you cross on a grassy, old logging road up Dramater Hollow. At the top of the hollow a brief bushwack will get you going down a hollow, where an old grade will return you to the Billy Brown Trail.

Miles	Description
0	From Susquehannock Lodge follow Billy Brown Trail S past barn and W side of Dry Run. Just beyond the barn is sign for the trail, which is marked with blue diamonds (x-country ski trail)
1.6	Intersection of Switchback Trail. Continue straight, following blue diamonds left into ferned, grassy clearing.
1.9	Trail bends right, enters clearing, then turns left along edge of clear-cut on grassy grade.
2.0	T intersection - here turn left, following skid road briefly toward Forestry boundary near large hemlocks. 50 yds in from clear-cut is a grassy grade which you follow uphill, parallel to edge of clear-cut briefly before it bends left (E) onto Ridge Trail. State Forest acquired this land in 1994.
2.6	Grade enters on acute left. Ridge Trail winds gently downhill SE, then E, then S and descends along left side of hollow along moderately steep grade.

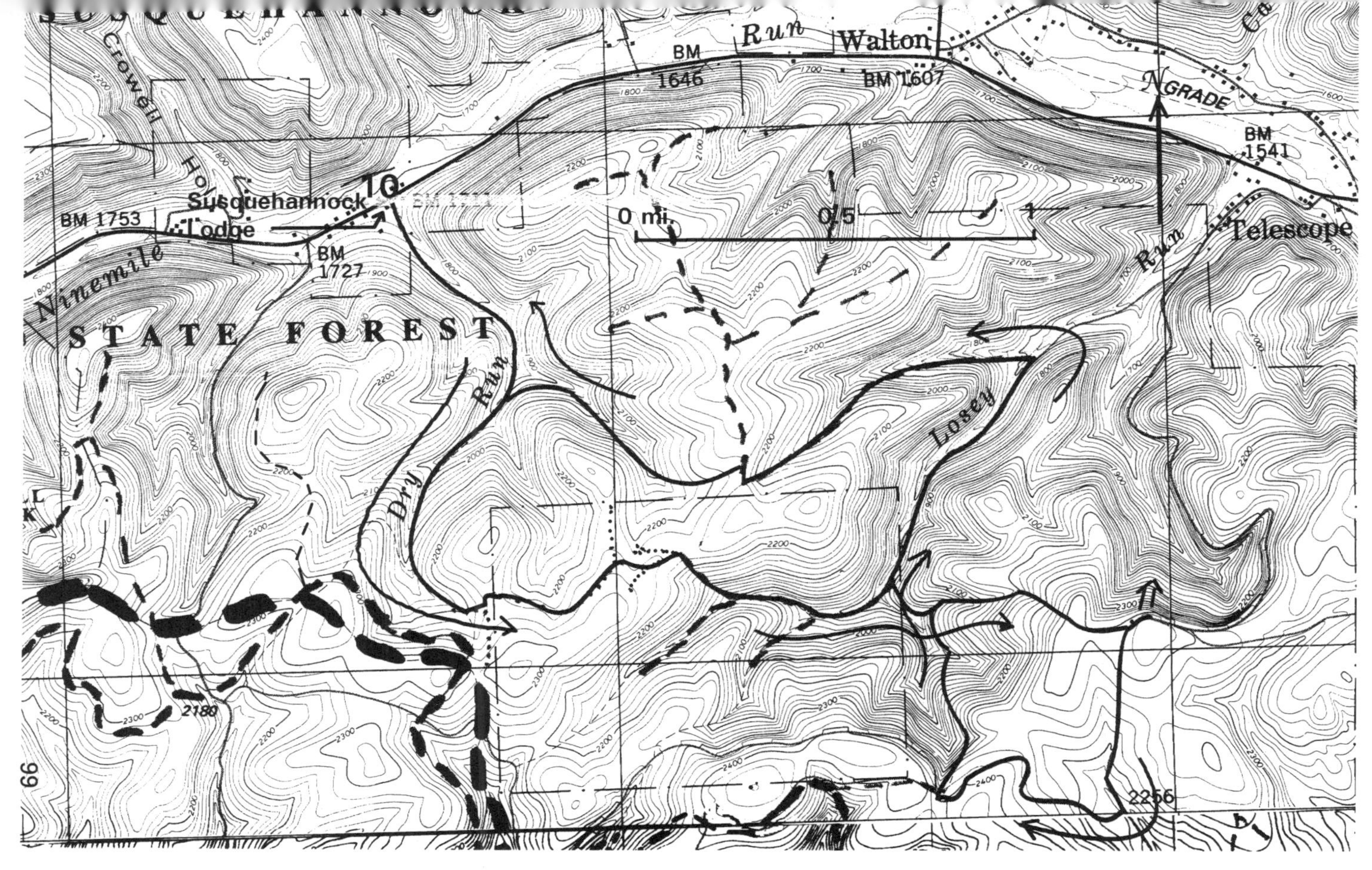

Walton
Run
BM 1646
BM 1607
GRADE
BM 1541
Telescope
Run
Crowell
Ho
Susquehannock
Lodge
BM 1753
BM 1727
10
0 mi.
0.5
1
Ninemile
STATE FOREST
Dry
Run
Losey
2180
2256

3.1 Logging road enters from right. Continue downhill.

3.55 Cross to right of Losey Run at Losey Run Hunting Camp. Turn right on driveway, pass buildings, cross to left side of stream and follow old skid trail up left side hollow.

3.85 Grade enters from acute right behind and trail begins to deteriorate - follow right side of drainage, rising moderately.

4.3 Trail disappears - continue straight in easy bushwack to top.

4.4 At top the trail is difficult to find - cross to the N side of the flat and bushwack your way E, paralleling the top edge of the hollow on your left (an easy bushwack)

4.85 Turn left on Rock Run Road to north plateau vista 0.1 mi N. Backtrack S on Rock Run Road and either retrace route back to Losey Run Hunting Camp (and pick up route description at m.p. 8.65 below) or continue S along Rock Run Road to Ridge Road.

5.65 Turn right on Ridge Road (sign), a gated logging road.

7.45 Split in road at top of hollow at sign on left for Daggett Trail. Turn right down hollow and pick up old grade on right side - the top of it may have a few blowdowns, but generally clears quickly and descends (easy/moderate).

7.85 After leveling, trail starts to drop down at moderate rate. When the trail gets lost, bend left and bushwack your way toward bottom of the hollow.

8.15 Where two top branches of hollow join, pick up grade on the right side of the hollow (as you descend).

8.4 Grade ends (m.p. 3.85 above). Follow hollow down to Losey Run, picking up an old grade near bottom right. Drop to stream and cross near turkey feeder.

8.65 Bear right at Losey Run Hunting Camp, following driveway parallel to Losey Run, crossing old Forestry boundary.

9.55 After gate turn left on Drumater Hollow logging road, which crosses Losey Run.

10.25 Hollow splits in Y. Logging road bends left.

10.55 Grassy logging road crosses to right side of hollow.

10.85 At top of Drumater Hollow road bends sharp right, levels. Within the next 0.25 miles, bushwack your way left (W) (easy) and begin to drop down into hollow to Dry Run. The slope will steepen as you drop down hollow but become easier after the top two branches of the hollow join. Generally descend along the left side of the hollow.

11.8 Hollow enters on right. Follow skid trail along left side.

12.1 Cross Dry Run on remains of old stone bridge, then turn right and follow Billy Brown Trail N 0.85 miles to Susquehannock Lodge.

11 LYMAN RUN NORTH

FEATURES: streams; lake
DISTANCE: 8.2 miles
TIME: 4 - 4.5 hours
ELEVATION: 1600 - 2430
TERRAIN: moderate grades
BLAZES: blue (Beehive Trail), orange (STS) and blue (Lake Trail); none elsewhere
PARKING: Lyman Run State Park
COMMENTS: Fairly easy to follow

Lyman Run State Park was once the site of a Goodyear lumber camp and engine terminal, constructed in 1905, a Civilian Conservation Corps (CCC) Camp in the 1930s, and a German Prisoner of War facility in 1945. The park contains 595 acres and a 45-acre lake. The dam was completed in 1951, and now the park is used primarily for recreational activities: camping, swimming, fishing, and picnicking. The 35-mile ATV Trail passes through the park, and in winter it is used for snowmobiling.

A 4.8 mile section of the stream (from the Lake to above Splash Dam Hollow) is protected by special selective harvest fishing regulations. 6 - 9 inch native brook trout and 10 - 12 inch brown trout are common. In the lake and downstream, trout are stocked.

Because there are not any natural lakes in the area, a manmade lake provides a unique environment that can add to the biodiversity of the forest. On the down side, impoundments allow the water to warm in summer, which can stress cold water fish populations, such as trout, downstream. Unless they are dredged of accumulated sediments, all lakes are doomed to fill in, progressing to pond, marsh, wet meadow, and eventually forest. Lyman Run, compared to similar lakes that contain development and soil disturbance above them, will take longer to fill because undisturbed forest above it creates relatively small amounts of sediment.

TRAIL DESCRIPTION:

This route follows the Beehive and ATV Trail up Daggett Hollow and then down into Jacob Hollow to the orange-blazed STS. Across Lyman Run leave the STS at the B & S Trail turn, following blue blazes back down to an old railroad grade along Lyman Run. As the grade approaches the lake, the new trail parallels the south side of Lyman Lake and crosses the dam crest, fording Lyman Run below the spillway back to the ATV and Beehive Trails to Daggett Run.

Miles	Description
0	From Lyman Run State Park main parking area follow road N toward Daggett Campground.
0.15	Turn right onto Beehive Trail at sign, then turn left onto ATV Trail up Daggett Hollow. Near the top of the hollow the ATV Trail will make a series of hairpin turns.
2.05	Logging road joins ATV Trail from right and trail makes a sharp left turn, heading W.
2.45	Bear left at fork (right fork is grassy).
2.55	Pass intersection of logging road on left. The ATV Trail then bends right and begins a winding descent to the bottom of Jacob Hollow.
3.75	Turn left onto orange-blazed STS in Jacob Hollow, descending Jacob Hollow along a frequently wet trail.
5.45	STS crosses Lyman Run Road, following the Fish Trail across Lyman Run. The STS will then follow Lyman Run downstream and bear right.
5.8	At intersection of B & S Trail (sign marks intersection) turn left, leaving STS, following blue blazed trail across hollow and down toward Lyman Run, joining old railroad grade.
6.5	Trail leaves old railroad grade as it approaches Lyman Lake, rising about 75 ft above lake.

7.0 Trail turns left and crosses crest of dam. Near spillway the trail turns right, following maintenance road down and fording Lyman Run below spillway.

7.25 Cross Lyman Run and turn left onto ATV Trail, which rises and crosses Lyman Run Road. At Rock Run Road ATV Trail turns left, passing parking area.

7.55 ATV Trail turns sharp right at Forestry gate near outhouse and switches back along moderate slope.

8.05 Turn left onto Beehive Trail and descend to Daggett Camping Area road, where you turn left and return to your vehicle in 0.15 miles.

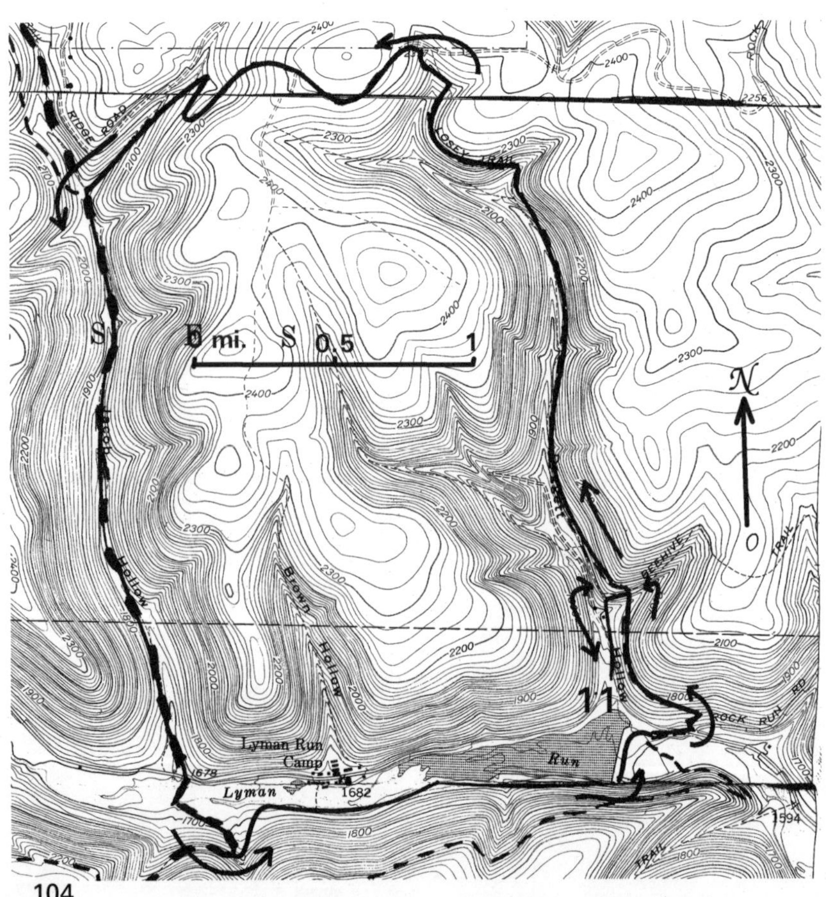

12 LYMAN RUN STATE PARK

FEATURES: CCC Camp, lake, view, old flagstone quarry
DISTANCE: 6.85 miles
TIME: 4 hours
ELEVATION: 1600 - 2430
TERRAIN: moderate grades
BLAZES: orange (STS) and blue (lake trail); none elsewhere
PARKING: Lyman Run State park
COMMENTS: Fairly easy to follow

In 1933 the Civilian Conservation Corps established a camp at Lyman Run. The CCC, a Great Depression workfare program, was established by Franklin Delano Roosevelt to put unemployed men to work in rural areas - parks were built, trails were cut, trees were planted, and former logging railroad grades were converted to roads. The program was administered by the Department of the Army - it also provided a corps of men who could be pressed into service quickly when the U.S. entered World War II. In Potter County the CCC employed 562 men.

On April 8, 1945, 250 German prisoners of war arrived at the Lyman Run CCC Camp and were employed as woodcutters. The wood was used by chemical plants to make charcoal for war production, and the prisoners were paid eighty cents a day. One of the German POWs was killed by a falling tree. Another escaped and committed suicide at the close of the war after learning that he was to be deported back to Germany.

The former CCC camp is at the bottom of Brown Hollow, and this hike passes the buildings that still remain.

TRAIL DESCRIPTION:

This route follows the relocated (late 1995) Left Daggett Trail (with a side trip to the old flagstone quarry) over the mountain and down Brown Hollow past the former CCC Camp. From Lyman Lake Road take the orange-blazed STS (Fish Trail), across Lyman Run to the

B & S Trail turn. Here blue blazes will lead you back down to an old railroad grade along Lyman Run. As the grade approaches the lake the trail parallels the south side of Lyman Lake and crosses the dam crest. Ford Lyman Run below the spillway, and the ATV and Beehive Trails will lead you back to Daggett Run.

Miles	Description
0	From Lyman Run State Park main parking area follow road N through Daggett Camping Area and near stream, passing bottom of Left Daggett Hollow.
0.5	Take left branch of fork in trail, crossing Daggett Run and following grade along easy uphill grade, which shortly bends left and rises along left side of hollow.
0.75	After meeting the bottom of the hollow the grade will make a left hairpin turn, rising to an old flagstone quarry. At the quarry is a view down Daggett Run. Watch out for snakes! From quarry follow thin neck toward mountainside.
1.0	As slope ahead along mountainside begins to get steeper, follow the contour off to the left into Left Daggett Hollow. A grade will shortly bring you to the Left Daggett Trail along the left side of hollow.
1.33	Left Daggett Trail turns sharp left onto an old woods road, following it up the mountainside briefly at a moderate rate.
1.65	Trail passes large, moss-covered, gray sandstones with quartzy conglomerate, following contour, then bends right after passing large gray/brownish sandstones that exhibit various erosional features due to different rock hardnesses. From these rocks the trail will head S, then bend W across the top of the plateau. As you approach mountain laurel, the trail will bend right (N) to avoid it.
2.65	Trail turns left at Brown Hollow, following it downhill. Evenutally the trail will become a skid trail on left side.
3.6	Pass old CCC Camp site and turn right on Lyman Lake Road.

4.1 Turn left onto STS at bottom of Jacob Hollow, following STS across Lyman Run. The STS will then follow Lyman Run downstream and bear right, following the Fish Trail.

4.45 At intersection of B & S Trail (sign marks intersection) turn left, leaving STS and following blue blazed trail back toward Lyman Run and onto on old railroad grade.

5.15 Trail leaves old railroad grade as it approaches Lyman Lake, rising about 75 ft above lake.

5.65 Trail turns left and crosses crest of dam. Near spillway the trail turns right, fording Lyman Run below spillway.

5.9 Cross Lyman Run and turn left onto ATV Trail, which crosses Lyman Run Road, turning left past parking area.

6.2 ATV Trail turns sharp right at Forestry gate near outhouse and switches back along moderate slope.

6.7 Turn left onto Beehive Trail and descend to Daggett Camping Area road, which you retrace to start.

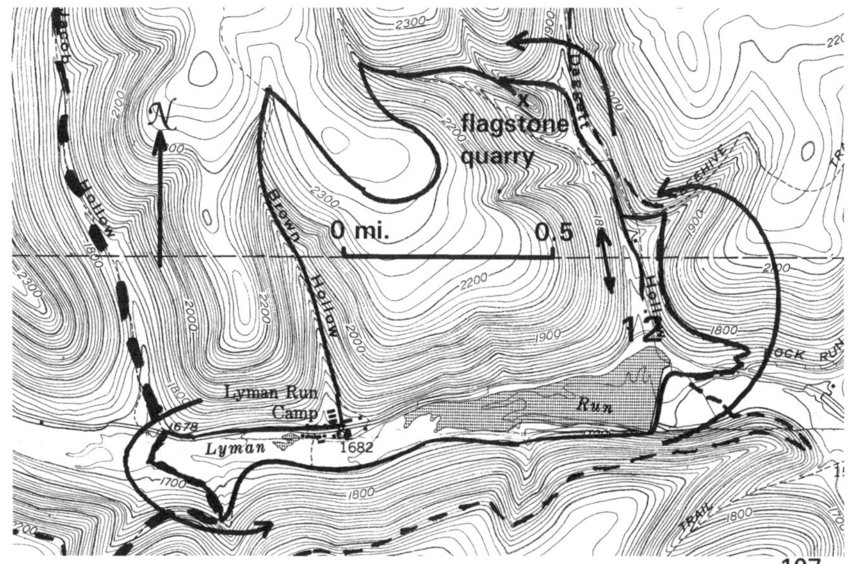

13 LYMAN RUN STATE PARK: BEEHIVE/ WILDCAT TRAILS

FEATURES: forest types, view, rock formations
DISTANCE: 3.95 miles
TIME: 3.0 hours
ELEVATION: 1620 - 2190
TERRAIN: moderate old grades and path
BLAZES: blue blazes
PARKING: Lyman Run State park
COMMENTS: Fairly easy to follow

Along Rock Run Road to the east of Lyman Run State Park is a field of large rocks that give the stream and road its name. These rocks are composed predominantly of sandstone: sand particles were deposited by water and compressed into rock by the weight (heat and pressure) of succeeding sediments. Within the sandstone layers are small pieces of quartz (a metamorphic rock not found naturally in this area of Pennsylvania), transported here by water. Particle size indicates the speed of the water transporting the sediments - faster water transports larger particles. The thickness of the layers of rock is indicative of the time of relatively unchanged environment - a change in sediment size or type, caused by a change in the speed of sediment-bearing water or by a change in sediments being imported, will create the appearance of a new layer. Color of sediment (reddish from oxidized iron, brownish from oxides or plants, black from organic sediments) may also be clues to the environment at the time of deposition. Crossbedding - where rock layers incline at angles different from the relatively horizontal rock strata of the region - indicate that some of the incoming sediments were subject to local current changes as moving water stopped suddenly into quieter water. Plant and seashell fossils tell whether the environment was terrestrial or marine.

These are all clues to help you interpret the environmental history of the area long ago when these sediments were deposited.

They tell of vacillating periods of uplifting outside the area, creating slopes that eroded into this region, and show that the region sometimes was dry land when this occurred.

What caused these rocks to become exposed and take the appearance of boulders? Nearby glacial action cooled the region, creating thermal stress fractures in the bedrock. Subsequent eroding forces (wind, water and ice) began to break the rock apart and carry it away.

TRAIL DESCRIPTION:

This route follows the ATV Trail from Rock Run Road to the blue-blazed Wildcat Trail. After a side trip along Rock Run Road to the rock formation, you will follow the Wildcat Trail to the blue-blazed Beehive Trail and then the ATV Trail back from Daggett Hollow.

Miles	Description
0	From ATV parking area at Lyman Run State Park and bottom of Rock Run Road, follow ATV Trail N.
0.15	Where ATV Trail bends sharp left, exit ATV Trail and follow old grade (blue-blazed Wildcat Trail) along fairly steep grade. The trail will bend right shortly, and the slope will moderate, level and gently descend. As you follow the blazes the grade will become more pathlike.
0.65	As you near Wildcat Run and the bend in Rock Run Road, descend to Rock Run Road (easy bushwhack) and follow it uphill.
1.15	Vista of Lyman Lake.
1.35	Field of large sandstone boulders on right. See what story these rocks tell you about the early regional natural history. After exploring, retrace steps along Rock Run Road to Wildcat Run.
2.05	Exit right off Rock Run Road at bend and Wildcat Run. You will pick up an old grade along the right side of Wildcat Run (and blue blazes) as it bends left, following the main branch

along a fairly steep grade. The rocks you pass along the trail are similar to those seen along Rock Run Road.

2.5 Trail crosses branch of Wildcat Run. The trail will cross a secondary branch shortly as it winds its way through beech and hemlocks.

2.7 Turn left onto Beehive Trail.

3.1 Beehive Trail turns left, descending run along steep, rocky path. The trail will become a more moderate grade along the left side of the stream shortly.

3.45 Turn left at ATV Trail, following it back to start in 0.5 miles.

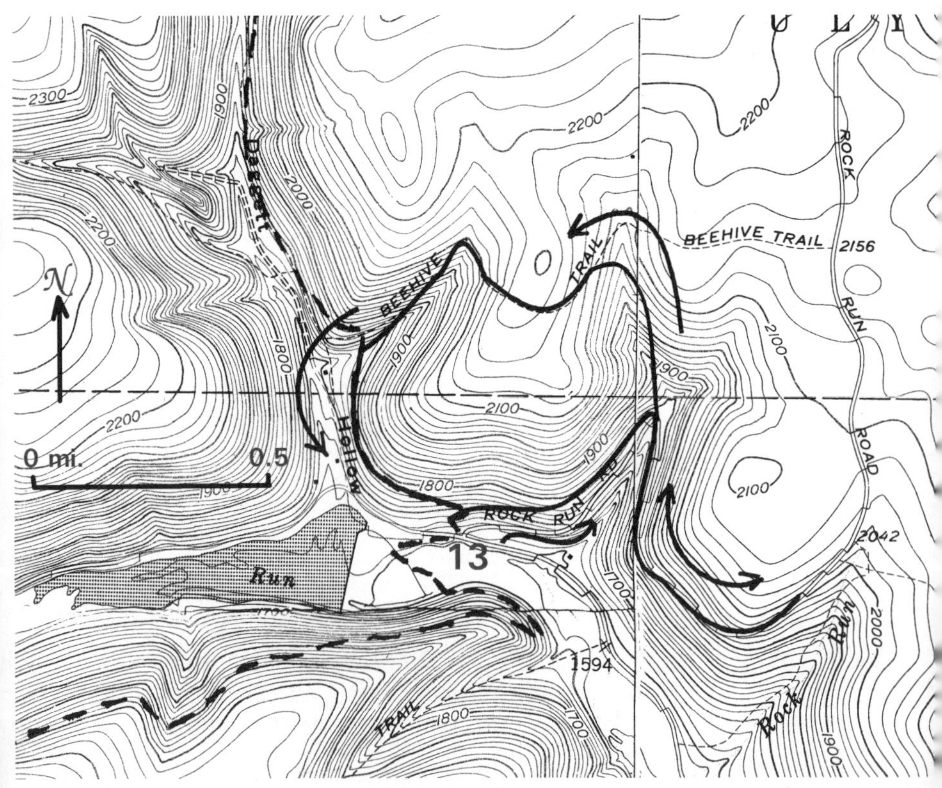

14 LYMAN RUN SOUTH (EWING TRAIL)

FEATURES: northern hardwoods, stream, lake
DISTANCE: 7.8 miles
TIME: 5 hours
ELEVATION: 1600 - 2280
TERRAIN: moderate old grades
BLAZES: orange (STS) and blue (Lake Trail); none elsewhere
PARKING: Lyman Run State Park at Rock Run Road
COMMENTS: Fairly easy to follow

From 1906 to 1908, the Goodyear Lumber Company logged hemlock in the Lyman Run area. At Lyman Run State Park were a camp and an engine terminal - the logging railroad system here contained 10 miles of main line and 30 miles of spur track. Each day five trains of 22 cars each brought hemlock from Lyman Run to the Goodyear Mill in Galeton. At night trains brought hemlock bark to the tanneries and left empty bark cars for the next day's work.

From 1908 to 1910, the Emporium Lumber Company cut hardwoods along Lyman Run, primarily maple for flooring. Its mill in Galeton was located along the West Branch, near today's Patterson Lumber Company. When Emporium was finished, R.J. Gaffney took the remaining small hardwoods to a chemical factory ° mile below the mouth of Lyman Run. The smaller hardwoods (40 - 60 cords per day) were used to make ingredients for gunpowder. The chemical factory was closed in 1916.

The area traversed by this hike contains a 225-acre tract for which the highest bid ever ($2 million for 1.9 million board feet of State Forest saw timber) was received). This work will be undertaken in 1995 - 1998. Cherry, sugar maple, red maple, beech and mixed hardwoods will be cut. Hemlock, blue beech, serviceberry and den trees will be left standing to preserve "biodiversity". No-cut buffers around the STS, wetlands, and spring seeps will be maintained.

Today the forest is managed to maintain a sustainable timber yield and to provide for other uses besides timber. According

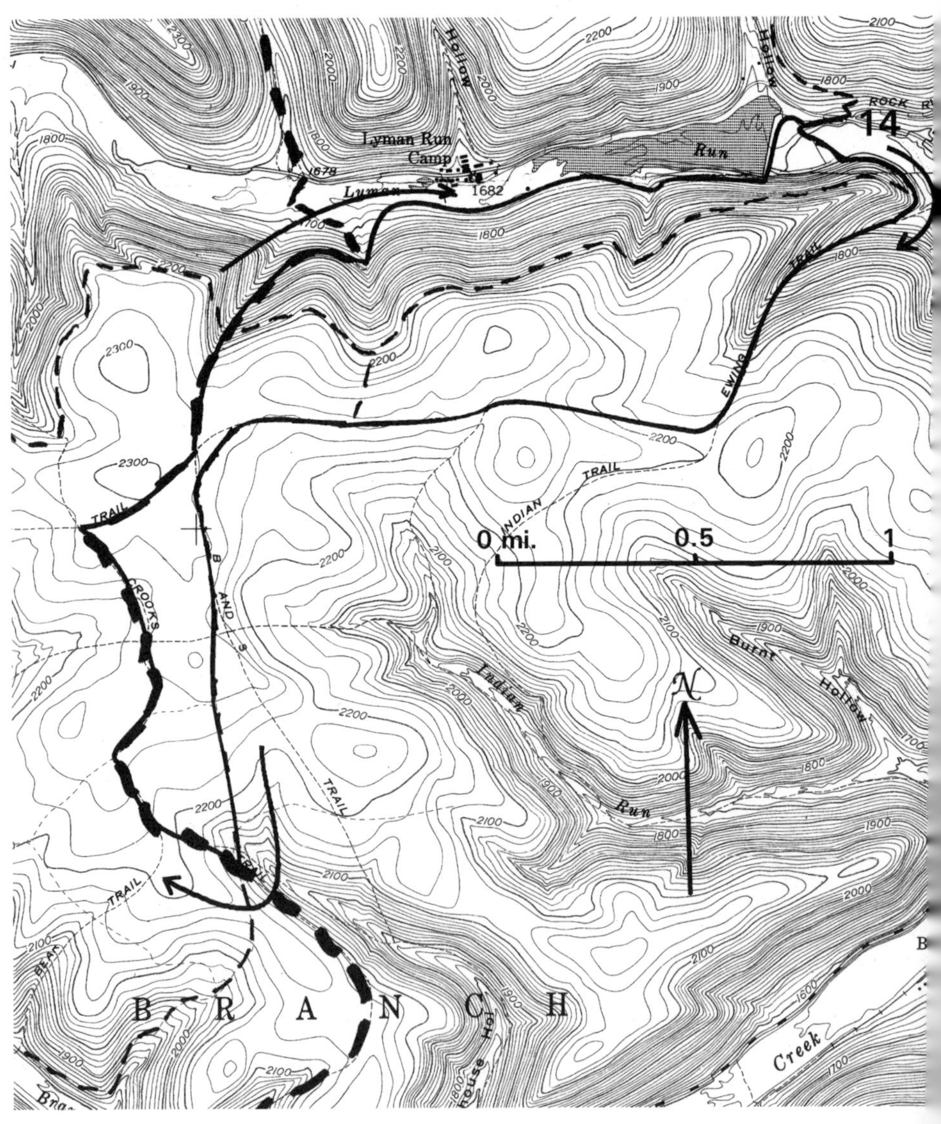
Lyman Run
Camp
1682
1678
Lyman
Run
Hollow
ROCK
14
EWING
TRAIL
INDIAN
TRAIL
0 mi.
0.5
1
CROOKS
B AND S
Indian
Run
Burnt
Hollow
TRAIL
BEAR
B R A N C H
Creek
N

to theory, the forest will recycle itself every 100 years. Like any theory, however, field evidence indicates that a living, dynamic forest environment cannot always be controlled by man.

Deer damage is a major factor in determining which tree species will regenerate successfully. To limit deer damage electric fencing is now placed around new clear-cuts to discourage deer from browsing until forest regeneration has had a head start. The fence is then dismantled and moved to another location. The clear-cut at the top of the Ewing Trail, just before it joins the ATV Trail, was protected by an electric fence after it was clear-cut in 1993/94. Of course, I saw a half dozen deer jump **through** the fence at a full run (counting was easy: the fence "twangs" each time one jumps through). What I found surprising is that the deer did not jump **over** a fence only 4 - 5 feet high!

TRAIL DESCRIPTION:

This route follows the ATV Trail across Lyman Run to the bottom of the Ewing Trail. There an old grade brings you up the hollow, across the flat plateau, and along the edge of a (1993) clear-cut to the ATV Trail. Follow the ATV Trail south to the orange-blazed STS (Crooks Trail/Ewing Trail/B&S Trail) back across the plateau and down near Lyman Run. The new blue-blazed Lake Trail leads you parallel to the south edge of Lyman Lake, across the top of the dam and across Lyman Run. You hook back onto the ATV Trail near Lyman Run Road.

Miles	Description
0	From Rock Run & Lyman Lake Roads, follow ATV Trail down toward Lyman Run below spillway of dam.
0.2	ATV Trail crosses Lyman Run on wooden bridge.
0.5	ATV Trail bends sharp right at a Y in the trail. Here leave the ATV Trail, following grassy grade left, across and up left side of Ewing Hollow. In 0.4 miles the grade will begin to rise more steeply and the trail will become severely eroded.
1.2	After leveling, the trail will split in a Y (the left branch is the top of the Indian Trial). Continue following the level Ewing

Trail along the right fork. The level trail will cross several wet areas.

1.7 Trail will enter and follow left (S) edge of clear-cut.

2.2 At corner of clear-cut, turn left onto ATV Trail, which makes a quick right and winds its way W then bends S.

3.75 Turn right onto orange-blazed STS, leaving ATV Trail and following STS (Crooks Trail) NW and N.

5.05 STS turns right (E) onto Ewing Trail, leaving Crooks Trail.

5.4 STS turns sharp left, following B & S Trail N.

5.75 STS crosses ATV Trail and descends steeply, passing vista of Lyman Run Valley.

6.3 At intersection of B & S and Fish Trails (sign marks intersection) leave STS and follow blue blazed trail toward Lyman Run, joining old railroad grade parallel to Lyman Run.

7.0 Trail leaves old railroad grade as it approaches Lyman Lake, rising about 75 ft above lake.

7.5 Trail turns left and crosses crest of dam. Near spillway the trail turns right and fords Lyman Run below spillway.

7.75 Turn left onto ATV Trail, which rises to intersection of Rock Run and Lyman Lake Roads and parking area.

15 WETMORE RUN

FEATURES: northern hardwoods, stream
DISTANCE: 6.6 miles
TIME: 3.5 hours
ELEVATION: 1520 - 2165
TERRAIN: moderate old grades/logging roads
BLAZES: none
PARKING: room for 1 vehicle along Rock Run Rd. at Wetmore Run, 2.6 mi N of Lyman Lake Rd.
COMMENTS: Fairly easy to follow

74% of Pennsylvania's forested lands are privately owned, primarily by individuals and farmers. 2% of the total forest lands are owned by municipalities, and 5% are owned by the forest industry. This hike traverses mostly land owned by the forest industry (Patterson Lumber Company) and Galeton Boro for municipal water.

Unlike the lumber companies of the late 1800s, lumber companies today utilize forest management plans to enhance timber quality and forest regeneration, and they must comply with regulations designed to protect the natural environment.

47% of Pennsylvania's forests are mixed oak, and 38% are northern hardwoods. In this region almost 70% of the forest is northern hardwood. Over the years the forest has been maturing: over half of it is now mature, about a third is middle-aged, and about 15% is young growth. In Potter County trees are maturing at more than three times the rate of cutting, particularly among black cherry, red oak, sugar maple, hemlock, and ash. If current trends continue then old growth hardwoods will increase and begin to dominate the forest. Timbering can help achieve a more stable tree age distribution and greater environmental diversity within the forest.

Forest management (or the lack of it) will have a great impact on the forest of tomorrow. Although 75% of Pennsylvania's forests are in the hands of private individuals, only 3% of them have written forest management plans, yet over half of them have harvested timber! If you own part of Penn's Woods, you should seek advice on good forest stewardship and the PA Tree Farm program. Contact The Pennsylvania Forestry Association (56 East Main St., Mechanicsburg, PA 17055; phone: (717) 766-5371) or your local Bureau of Forestry Office for more information.

Owen Wetmore settled at the mouth of Wetmore Run in the 1830s, giving the stream its name.

TRAIL DESCRIPTION:

This route follows an old grade from Rock Run Road along upper Wetmore Run. A logging road will bring you to an old grassy grade, which descends along Wetmore Run to the Galeton Waterworks/ Reservoir. Follow the road to the Right Branch of Wetmore Run and then a grassy grade up the Right Branch past another reservoir. The grassy grade becomes a dug grade which ascends the Right Branch, and the logging road at the top brings you back to the top of Wetmore Run, where you then retrace your steps.

Miles	Description
0	From Rock Run Road (parking for 1 car), cross Wetmore Run on footpath and follow left side of run downstream along old grade. This grade will cross Forestry boundary and bend left, leaving hemlock.
0.6	Grade bends right, crosses hollow, and rises to logging road. Turn right onto logging road.
0.95	Pass logging road on right (it crosses Wetmore Run over large culvert). In about 50 yds. turn right onto grassy grade toward Wetmore Run, which it soon parallels, shortly passing through field of large gray, quartzy sandstones.
1.75	Cross white blazed boundary. Trail will soon begin to descend in moderate/easy slope, approaching Wetmore Run.
2.25	Bending left at bottom, grade becomes less distinct.
2.5	Cross white blazed boundary. After entering open area the

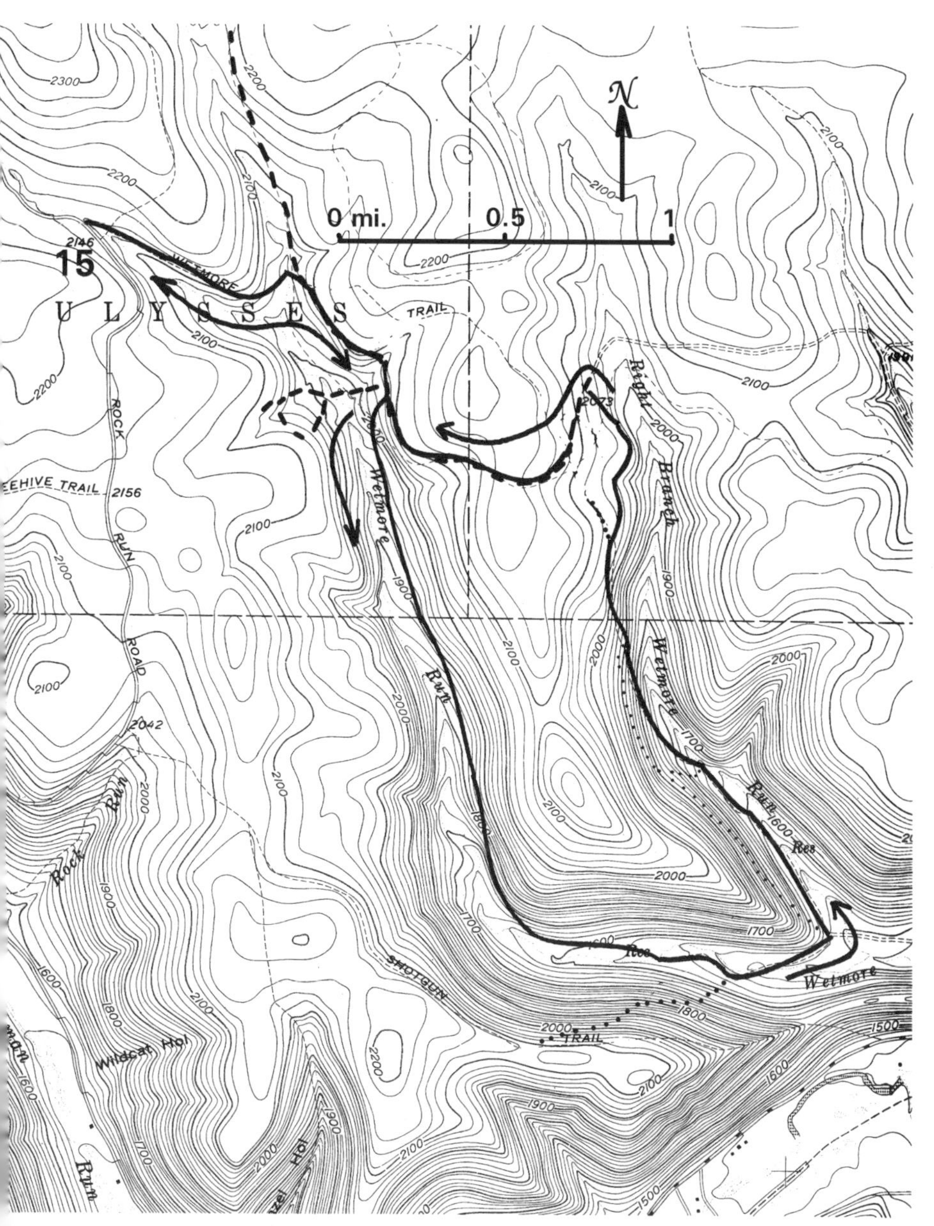

N
0 mi.
0.5
1
15
ULYSSES
WETMORE
TRAIL
Right Branch
Wetmore
Wetmore Run
Wetmore Run
Res
Wetmore
ROCK RUN ROAD
EEHIVE TRAIL
2156
2146
2042
2073
Rock Run
SHOTGUN
TRAIL
Wildcat Hol
Run

grade will disappear: continue to parallel Wetmore Run.

2.75 Top of old Galeton Reservoir. Cross on upstream side of it and pick up grade on opposite side. Just ahead skirt right side of newer Galeton reservoir and follow road.

3.05 Grassy grade (to top of Shotgun Trail) comes in on right shortly before you cross wooden bridge over Wetmore Run. Continue along road.

3.3 After bending sharp left the road will approach a bridge. Turn left onto old woods road just before crossing bridge, following it past concrete impoundment.

3.75 Shortly after a steep trail enters on acute left, cross open area. Grade then begins to rise more noticeably and another steep grade comes in on the left.

4.1 Pass large boulders. Trail becomes somewhat steeper, washed out and rougher/stonier. Views down Right Wetmore periodically when the leaves are down.

4.25 Y in trail (right branch blocked by blowdowns). Turn left, rise steeply for 50 yds., then turn right at another intersection (left goes gently downhill). Rise moderately but briefly before leveling. Views across Right Wetmore.

4.55 As old, overgrown trail goes off to the left, skirt cut area along right edge (hill drops off quickly to right).

4.85 Turn left on newer logging road (very wide) at top of Right Wetmore Run. In about a mile you will pass the grassy woods road on left where you descended Wetmore Run (m.p. 0.95 above).

6.0 Y in road. Go left on older, smaller of the two, descending briefly to cross Wetmore Run, then bending left on older woods road, following grade back to Rock Run Road.

16 BEECH FLATS: TOM CABIN HOLLOW

FEATURES: hemlock swamp; forest & stream environments; old reservoir; view
DISTANCE: 9.25 miles
TIME: 5.5 hours
ELEVATION: 1400 - 2400
TERRAIN: wet, rocky, steep, and rough in places; moderate old grades
BLAZES: none
PARKING: Game Commission parking area (go 2.8 mi N of Rt. 6 on Rock Run Rd. and follow gravel road 1 mi. E to parking area)
COMMENTS: BUSHWHACKING SKILLS A MUST - route can be DIFFICULT to follow, and it is EASY TO BECOME DISORIENTED in the flat hemlock swamp.

Sphagnum moss can hold 15 to 25 times its own weight in water. Sterile acidic conditions slow the process of decay, and great quantities of dead plant material accumulate. Sphagnum moss was once used as a surgical dressing instead of cotton because of its natural sterility and its ability to absorb moisture. Today we are more familiar with its more common name, peat moss.

Sphagnum moss is usually associated with bogs, but may also be found in marshes and swamps. There greater amounts of dissolved oxygen and bacterial activity keep the lower parts of its hummocks in a state of decay, while new growth continues above.

At the source of Beech Flats Run water from springs, seeps, and rainfall collects, only slowly running off. Hemlock grows in this cool, moist environment, and you may experience sphagnum moss's amazing capacity to store water if you don't watch where you step.

TRAIL DESCRIPTION:

This route follows grassy forest breaks through State Game lands #64 and a short bushwack across the top of Tom Cabin Hollow to an old woods road. The woods road disappears in mountain laurel, forcing a bushwack through a hemlock swamp and wet areas where you can sink to your knees in sphagnum moss. Those possessing a poor sense of direction and novice bushwhacking skills can become disoriented easily in the "flats". The Beech Flats drainage is followed across an open field to a logging road, which will bring you up to the top of the flat again. A grassy path leads to the top of a hollow that empties N toward Pine Creek - a rough, rocky descent which gets easier near the bottom of the hollow. A logging road parallels Pine Creek and bends up Tom Cabin Hollow, which it crosses and then becomes a dug grade. The trail becomes faint at the top - a compass bearing and short bushwhack get you back to the Gamelands logging roads and back to the start.

Miles	Description
0	From State Game Land 64 parking area off Rock Run Road head E on logging road (leftmost road as you face E), quickly passing a grassy logging road to Martin Hollow, then turning right on skid road (15A at head of it), gently descending SSE.
0.35	Y intersection. Bend left, fairly level.
0.85	Y in road. Continue ESE on right fork.
1.1	T intersection of grassy logging roads. To get to Tom Cabin Trail turn left, then turn right in about 100 ft. along semblance of old grade, which disappears in hemlock - bushwack E through hemlock and turn right at ravine, following it to main hollow.
1.35	After crossing main hollow turn left and follow the ferny road parallel to hollow (ESE). This old logging road crosses an open, ferned area and swings right, rising then leveling.
1.85	The logging road gets very wet, then is blocked by mountain laurel - detour left in hemlock swamp (watch wet areas), paralleling Beech Flats drainage. Before making this detour it is a good idea to take a compass bearing along the road - with the many wet areas and flat terrain it is very easy to become disoriented here.

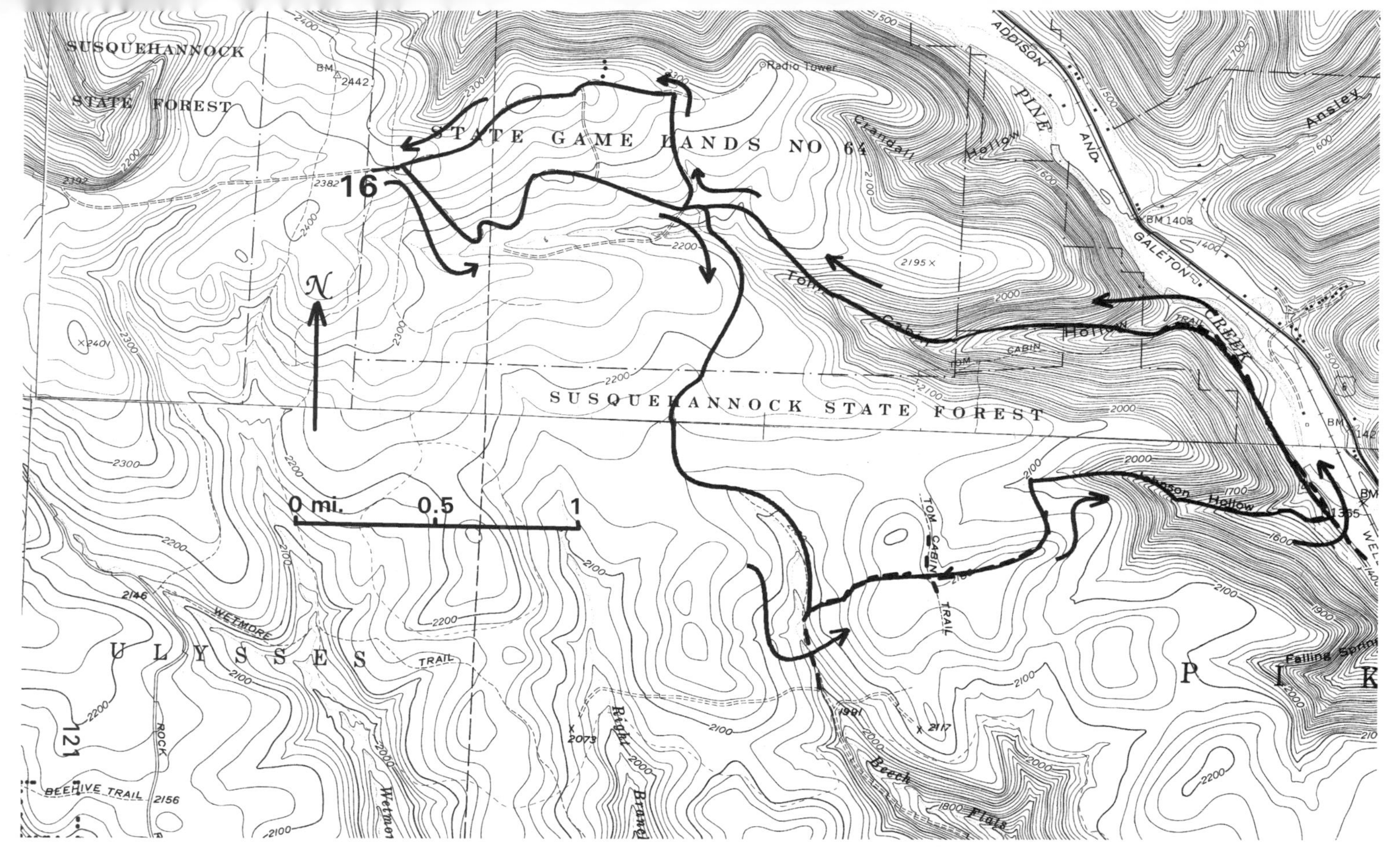
SUSQUEHANNOCK STATE FOREST
STATE GAME LANDS NO 64
16
N
0 mi.
0.5
1
Radio Tower
Crandall Hollow
ADDISON AND GALETON
PINE CREEK
Ansley
Tom Cabin Hollow
SUSQUEHANNOCK STATE FOREST
TOM CABIN TRAIL
Johnson Hollow
Falling Spring
WETMORE TRAIL
ULYSSES
PIKE
Right Branch
Beech Flats
BEEHIVE TRAIL
ROCK

2.15 Regain grade along left side of stream. Many wet areas.

2.25 Grade crosses to right, then to left side where drainage bends sharp left. After crossing to the left the drier route is to follow this side of the drainage rather than to follow the grade.

2.55 Enter a long, open, wet meadow, bushwhacking your way along. Halfway across the meadow two drainages will join. Cross field to far end toward old stumps.

3.0 At far end of field on left side you will pick up a road. There is an old hunting camp on right side across hollow.

3.2 Turn left on intersecting logging road, rising gently.

3.6 After bending right and flattening at the top, an old grade comes in on the right (old Tom Cabin Trail) and you come to a Y in the road. Take right branch (straight ahead on newer grade). At next Y just ahead, bend right.

3.75 Smaller grade enters on acute left - continue on main logging road, which bends left in cut.

3.9 Pass old woods road goes off right (SSE) - continue on main logging road gently downhill, heading E. The main logging road will become a grassy woods road just ahead, bending left and heading NE. This grassy road will quickly split - take left branch - and will bend left more sharply, descending more steeply NNE, then flatten.

4.3 At bottom of drainage turn right to descend Johnson Hollow along right side. The path down will turn into a rough bushwack as you scramble down the hollow. Eventually pick up a rocky, washed-out trail on left side of hollow. Trail will become a grade as you descend.

5.2 Cross to right side of stream along ferny logging road.

5.45 Turn left at intersection of grassy logging road: this is the Tom Cabin Trail (right branch of this intersection descends to Pine Creek near former railroad bridge). The logging road (Tom Cabin Trail) heads W, paralleling Pine Creek. Exercise caution in crossing the washout just ahead.

6.05 Trail enters hemlock, bending left up Tom Cabin Hollow.

6.25 Y in road - take the right fork, descending and crossing to right side of hollow, where you rise quickly to an old grade.

6.5 Trail passes above a laid-up stone retaining wall (old dam for Galeton reservoir). 10" steel/iron pipe in bottom of hollow.

7.15 Hollow on left. Grade gets a little steeper and you come to a Y (right bends sharply & steeply uphill, going up hollow on right) - continue along main grade. Hollow on right has a lot of large, moss covered, gray, quartzy sandstone.

7.5 Trail becomes rolling level. After passing large gray sandstones to right trail rises steeply but briefly, then flattens and becomes less distinct.

7.8 When trail disappears, head due W, crossing two gullies.

8.0 Emerge from hemlock at intersection of Tom Cabin Trail and Game Commission Logging Road. (m.p. 1.1 above). Turn right, following logging road N.

8.4 Turn left on logging road in wide grassy area.

8.7 Foot trail to right leads to view (in 50 yds.) to opposite side of Route 6, looking up the Genesee Fork of Pine Creek and along the plateau north. After this side trip, continue on logging road, passing intersecting road on left and then a road on the right (to a pit where Game Commission dumps road kills).

9.25 Back at Gamelands parking area.

17 SPLASHDAM HOLLOW

FEATURES: beaver ponds, northern hardwoods
DISTANCE: 6.3 miles
TIME: 3.5 hours
ELEVATION: 1905 - 2520
TERRAIN: mostly easy to moderate grades, 1 fairly steep grade
BLAZES: orange (STS), blue directional arrows on ATV Trail
PARKING: Sunken Branch Road at STS crossing E of Billy Lewis Rd.
COMMENTS: fairly easy route

Beavers build dams to hide from predators along shallow, narrow streams and to protect their lodges. Beavers do not build watertight dams - although sticks and mud make a watertight dam difficult, the passage of some water through the dam relieves the water pressure behind it - otherwise the beaver would spend a major portion of his time repairing the dam.

The beaver is a browser. The small branches and twigs on the upper portions of trees are too high for the beaver to reach, and the beaver does not know how to climb. But the beaver has sharp teeth and an instinct to cut down trees, primarily to reach his food. Most trees he cuts down will fall toward the stream because that is usually the more open, sunnier side - the side on which trees produce more branches.

By cutting down trees, the beaver opens the shoreline to additional sunlight, encouraging willows, birch, and aspen (the preferred food of the beaver) to proliferate. This also removes the forest canopy, allowing the under story to grow, accelerating the natural progression of the forest.

Nineteenth century loggers copied the beaver by constructing log dams filled with stones and mud, creating ponds on small streams. Logs were brought to the pond, and when it was time to float the logs to the mill a gate would be raised, releasing the water and logs. These "splashdams" allowed loggers to transport their logs along smaller streams and tributaries which usually lacked the depth and flow to float timber.

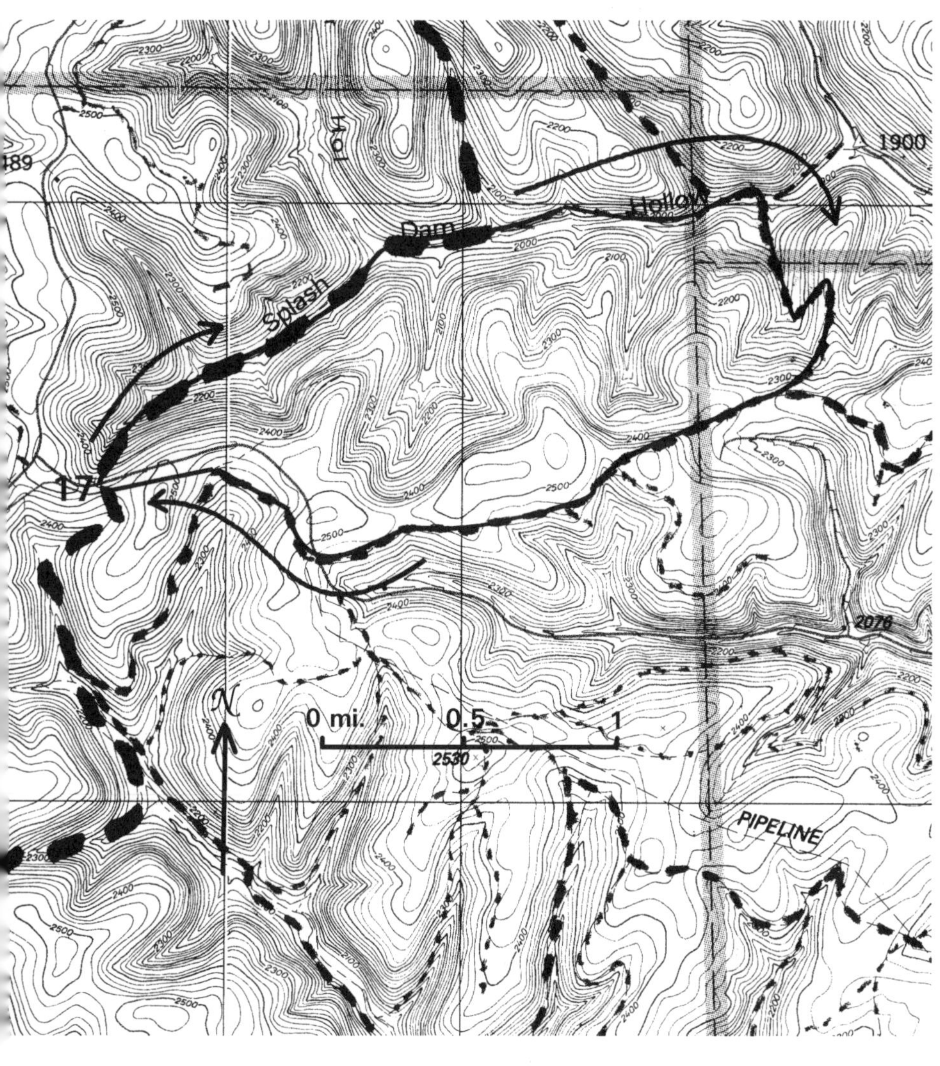
Splash
Dam
Hollow
1900
17
0 mi.
0.5
1
2530
2076
PIPELINE
N

TRAIL DESCRIPTION:

This route follows the orange-blazed STS and an old grade down Splashdam Hollow from Sunken Branch Road. Cross Splashdam Hollow along the ATV Trail, following it up a fairly steep slope, then past a clear-cut and across Sunken Branch Road. From the ATV Trail the grassy Captain Shelton Trail returns you to the start.

Miles	Description
0	From STS crossing at Sunken Branch Road, follow STS NE from road down Splashdam Trail (moderate slope).
0.5	After crossing stream and bearing right in meadow with apple trees, STS crosses Splash Dam Run and continues easy descent of hollow along left side, passing meadows and beaver dams along Splashdam Run.
1.7	STS turns sharp left onto White Line Trail to leave Splashdam Hollow. Here continue straight, leaving STS and follow Splashdam Run along footpath, then grade.
2.5	After joining ATV Trail (logging road) that descends from hollow on left, follow ATV Trail as it turns right, crosses Splashdam Hollow, and begins to rise on S side of hollow. The trail will bend sharp left, then sharp right as it rises along a moderate grade.
3.6	ATV Trail joins Sunken Branch Cutoff at “#8" post. Bear right at this intersection, following it easily uphill past a series of clear cuts to Sunken Branch Road.
5.25	Cross Sunken Branch Road and bear right, continuing to follow ATV Trail along Captain Shelton pipeline. The pipeline is exposed in eroded areas.
5.95	ATV trail will bend sharp left - here continue straight along grassy grade, crossing grassy crossroads.
6.25	Turn right on STS, dropping down to Sunken Branch Road.

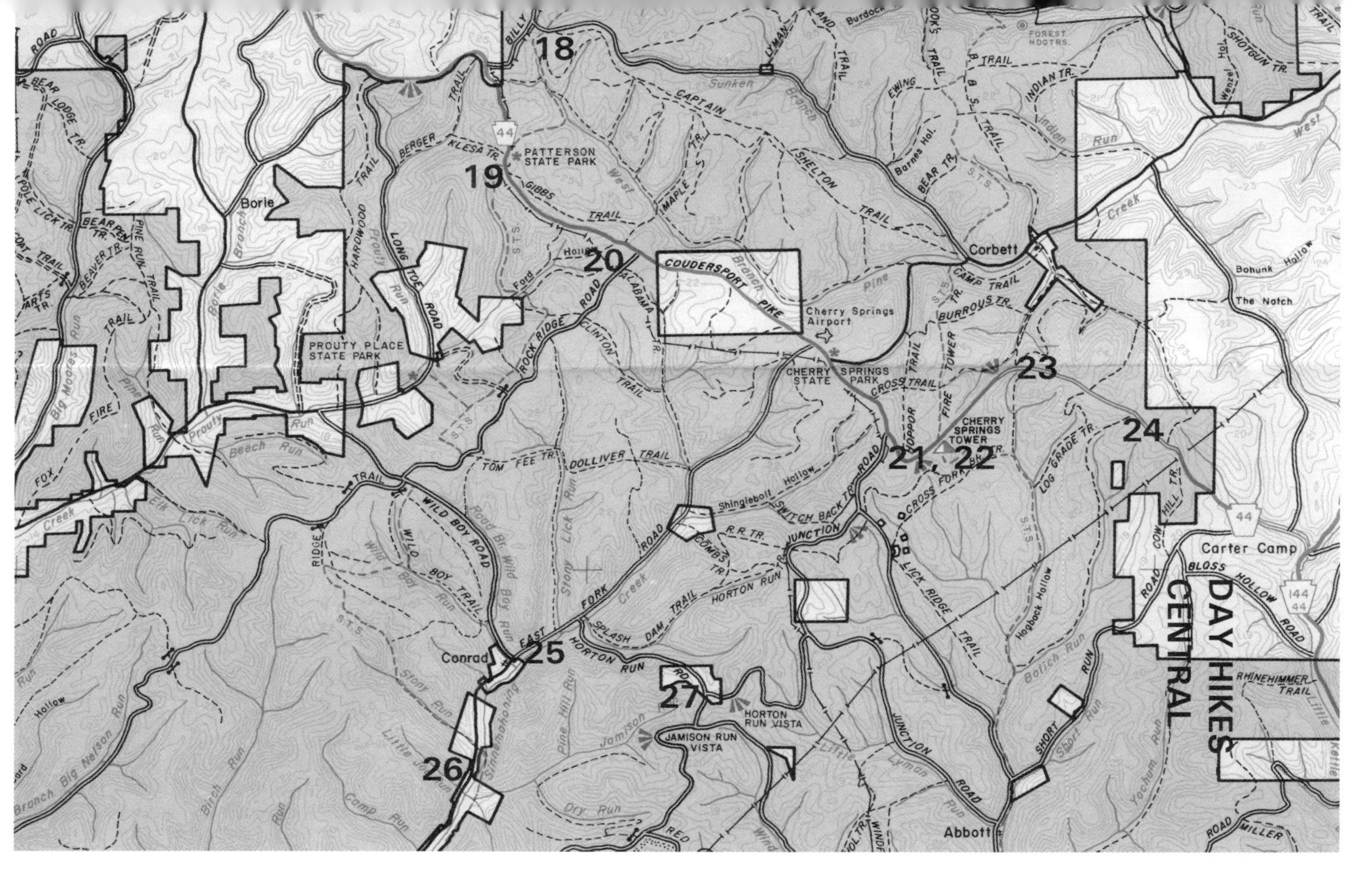

DAY HIKES CENTRAL
18
19
20
21
22
23
24
25
26
27
Corbett
Carter Camp
Abbott
Conrad
Borie
The Notch
PATTERSON STATE PARK
PROUTY PLACE STATE PARK
CHERRY SPRINGS STATE PARK
Cherry Springs Airport
CHERRY SPRINGS TOWER
HORTON RUN VISTA
JAMISON RUN VISTA
COUDERSPORT PIKE
BLOSS HOLLOW ROAD
COW HILL TR.
LICK RIDGE TRAIL
JUNCTION ROAD
SHORT RUN ROAD
EAST FORK ROAD
WILD BOY ROAD
WILD BOY TRAIL
LONG TOE ROAD
ROCK RIDGE ROAD
HARDWOOD TRAIL
PINE RUN TRAIL
BEAR LODGE TR.
FOREST HDQTRS.

18 CAPTAIN SHELTON TRAIL

FEATURES: Pine Creek, northern hardwoods, beaver ponds
DISTANCE: 11.9 miles
TIME: 6.5 hours
ELEVATION: 1760 - 2510
TERRAIN: moderate grades
BLAZES: orange (STS), some snowmobile directional arrows, otherwise none
PARKING: Sunken Branch Road at STS crossing, E of Billy Lewis Road
COMMENTS: Easily followed with average bushwhacking skills. Several options for shorter routes.

On August 27, 1859, Edwin Drake discovered oil in Titusville, PA. By 1864 oil wells near Bradford, PA extended 40 miles up and down the Allegheny River. Getting the product to market from this remote area was expensive and dependent on railroads. John D. Rockefeller's increasing monopoly of oil production, transportation, and refining under his Standard Oil Company and his influence on the railroads placed other producers under severe economic disadvantages.

The independent oil producers, looking to avoid the burdensome railroad fees, formed the Tidewater Oil Company to join the Bradford oil field to the Reading Railroad in Williamsport, a distance of 109 miles. Despite the engineering difficulties and Rockefeller's efforts to prevent the pipeline, the project was successful. Oil from the Bradford field began to flow through the two six-inch steel pipes, the first major oil pipeline in the U.S., on May 29, 1879. The Captain Shelton Trail is part of the pipeline. Eventually it was extended another 241 miles to Bayonne, NJ.

The successful pipeline was a threat to Rockefeller's oil monopoly, so he bought a controlling interest in the company. By 1883 his Standard Oil Trust owned or controlled 90% of American refineries and pipelines.

The pipeline is now used for fiber-optic communications.

TRAIL DESCRIPTION:

This route follows the rolling Captain Shelton Trail (sections of which are shared by the ATV Trail) from the STS across the top of the plateau. There are several options for loop routes: the Beech Hollow Trail (3.7 mile loop), the Maple Hollow Trail (6 mile loop), the Old Cabin Trail (8.25 mile loop), and an unnamed snowmobile trail to the West Branch, used here (11.4 mile loop). The West Branch Trail (and a portion of the ATV Trail) is used to return to the STS, which leads you back to the start of the Captain Shelton Trail.

Miles	Description
0	Follow STS S from Sunken Branch Road and quickly turn left (E) on grassy right-of-way
0.3	Cross grassy crossroads and intersect ATV Trail, which shares the Captain Shelton Trail here. Parts of the steel pipeline are exposed along the ATV Trail.
0.7	Grassy crossroads goes off to right, then ATV trail exits sharp left to road. Captain Shelton Trail continues straight ahead on grassy trail through selective cut.
1.1	After crossing top of two hollows on the left, Shelton Trail crosses grassy logging roads at top of Beech Hollow. A grassy road parallels the Shelton Trail 50' off to the right. [ALTERNATE ROUTE (3.7 mi. loop): turn right onto the second logging road. Turn right in 50 yds. onto ferny logging road, which gradually descends BEECH HOLLOW. Near bottom of hollow logging road will bend right, ending at the intersection of West Branch/ATV Trails in 1.0 mile (m.p. 10.2 below).]
1.25	Enter clear-cut. View to N across Sunken Branch Hollow
1.6	Climb small rise and cross grassy logging road in clear-cut.
1.8	Orange diamond directs snowmobiles down Maple Hollow (on right). The Captain Shelton Trail continues due SE.

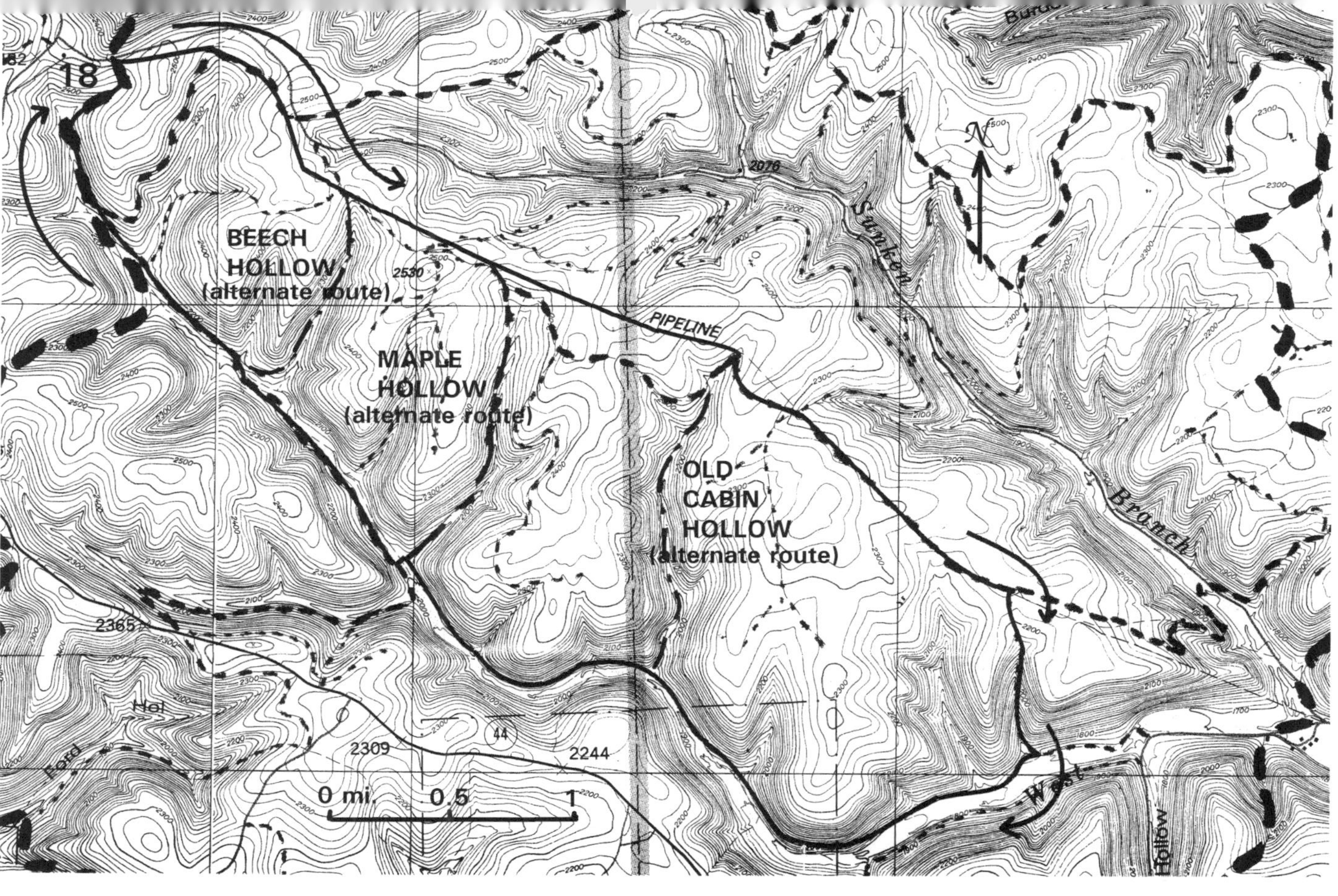
18
BEECH HOLLOW (alternate route)
MAPLE HOLLOW (alternate route)
OLD CABIN HOLLOW (alternate route)
PIPELINE
Sunken
Branch
West
Hollow
Ford
Hol
2530
2076
2365
2309
2244
44
0 mi. 0.5 1

[ALTERNATE ROUTE (6 mi. loop): Turn right, following the snowmobile sign down MAPLE HOLLOW. Bend right at the outhouse shortly ahead, descending along the ATV Trail 1.3 miles to the West Branch Trail (m.p. 9.0 below).]

2.05 Leave clear-cut. Detour around blowdowns, wet spots.

2.8 At the second small branch at the top of Old Cabin Hollow you will see ATV Trail 100 ft to right. From here follow ATV Trail E to avoid blowdowns.

[ALTERNATE ROUTE (8.25 mi. loop): Follow the ATV Trail S from this point 0.25 miles, and exit left on old logging grade, which descends right side of OLD CABIN HOLLOW In a mile the logging road disappears - follow a deer path along the E side of the hollow for 0.2 mi. to West Branch Trail (m.p. 7.75 below).]

3.2 Intersection of Shelton and ATV Trails (you may also see a sign for the Blackberry Trail (logging grade that heads N from here). Continue along the ATV Trail, crossing a gully here. The Shelton Trail follows the ATV Trail on the other side of the gully.

4.3 ATV Trail bends off left; Capt. Shelton Trail sign straight ahead; to right is blue paint for snowmobile trail. Turn right onto snowmobile trail , descending hollow to West Branch.

5.4 Turn right at bottom of hollow onto West Branch Trail.

5.9 Trail crosses hollow. Here trail disappears briefly, so just continue following the West Branch upstream along base of mountain. In 0.25 mi. you will pick up the trail again just above base of mountain.

6.4 After passing a small hollow, trail crosses onto private property (white blazes) passing additional beaver ponds and meadows. Trail becomes a footpath along mountain base.

7.15 After passing old beaver pond, trail crosses small grassy hollow with running water. There is a grassy grade which descends left into the meadow at this point, but you follow a worn path along base of mountain.

7.75 West Branch Trail descends, crossing Old Cabin Trail at bottom of hollow. Trail becomes intermittent, difficult to follow - if you lose it bushwack along base of the mountain.

9.0 West Branch Trail crosses Maple Hollow (ATV Trail). From here either continue following an intermittent path near the base of the mountain OR turn left onto ATV Trail across West Branch of Pine Creek and along S side of stream.

9.95 Beech Hollow enters from right on N side of stream.

10.2 ATV Trail crosses to N side of stream at Beech Hollow Trail (grassy logging grade). Follow ATV Trail, paralleling stream on N side.

11.2 Leave ATV Trail where it turns sharp right to leave West Branch, continuing straight. There is a grassy fork here - the left will join the STS on the other side of West Branch, the right (straight) fork will intersect the STS on this side of West Branch.

11.4 Turn right onto STS on north side of West Branch of Pine Creek, following STS up small hollow 0.5 miles to start.

19 FORD HOLLOW/PATTERSON PARK

FEATURES: forest/stream environments
DISTANCE: 11.5 miles
TIME: 6.5 hours
ELEVATION: 1780 - 2520
TERRAIN: moderate grades
BLAZES: orange (STS); none otherwise
PARKING: Patterson Park
COMMENTS: Not hard to follow

"Northern hardwood forest" best describes the Susquehannock State Forest, though there are additional forest types scattered about, and there are more specific designations based on specific species associations. Sometimes called a "transition forest", it shares some species common to the northern "Boreal Forest" and some with the southern "Oak-Hickory Forest".

The northern hardwood forest is dominated by Sugar Maple, American Beech, and Yellow Birch, with an understory (when it has one) of Striped Maple or ferns. Hemlock and pine may be present, especially in wetter areas and ravines. Northern Red Oak and Basswood may be common. Cherry, Gray Birch, Ash, Red Maple, White Birch, Quaking Aspen, and Bigtooth Aspen may be found on sites that were disturbed by logging, farming, or fire.

The Beech-Maple relationship is called a "frequency-dependent selection": young Beech grows best under a canopy of Sugar Maple, and young Sugar Maple grows best under Beech, so over time they trade places in the canopy and understory and then repeat the process.

Black Cherry is a very important wood for furniture and fine cabinetry, and the cherry growing in the Susquehannock State Forest is among the world's finest. Pennsylvania is the world leader in the production of high-quality Black Cherry lumber - if you have any cherry furniture, the cherry probably originated in Pennsylvania and most likely grew in or near the Susquehannock State Forest. You will see some of this high-quality black cherry on this hike.

TRAIL DESCRIPTION:

From Patterson Park this route follows the orange-blazed STS across the West Branch of Pine Creek to the Captain Shelton Trail. The Captain Shelton Trail will join the ATV Trail, which you follow down Maple Hollow, then up to Route 44. On the other side of Rt. 44 a gas line brings you to the top of the Rock Ridge Trail at Ford Hollow and Rock Ridge Road. The Rock Ridge Trail (a grassy logging road) goes down Ford Hollow to the orange-blazed STS, leading back Patterson Park.

Miles	Description
0	From Patterson Park follow STS across Rt. 44. STS turns left (N) onto Plantation Trail, paralleling Rt. 44 (W), then bends right (N) and descends hollow.
0.9	STS bends left at old logging railroad junction near West Branch of Pine Creek, paralleling the West Branch.
1.4	STS crosses W Branch of Pine Creek, approaching driveway of blue camp, continuing to parallel W Branch.
1.85	STS turns right (NE) and begins ascent of hollow.
2.15	STS bends left (N), then turns left and levels.
2.3	Just before Sunken Branch Road, turn right onto grassy path (Captain Shelton Trail), leaving STS.
2.6	Cross grassy crossroads and join ATV Trail, which shares Captain Shelton Trail.
3.0	ATV Trail exits sharp left to Sunken Branch Road. Here continue straight along Shelton Trail through selective cut.
3.5	After crossing logging roads, trail enters clear-cut.
4.1	Turn right onto snowmobile route, following it 75 yds. to ATV Trail by outhouse and down Maple Hollow.

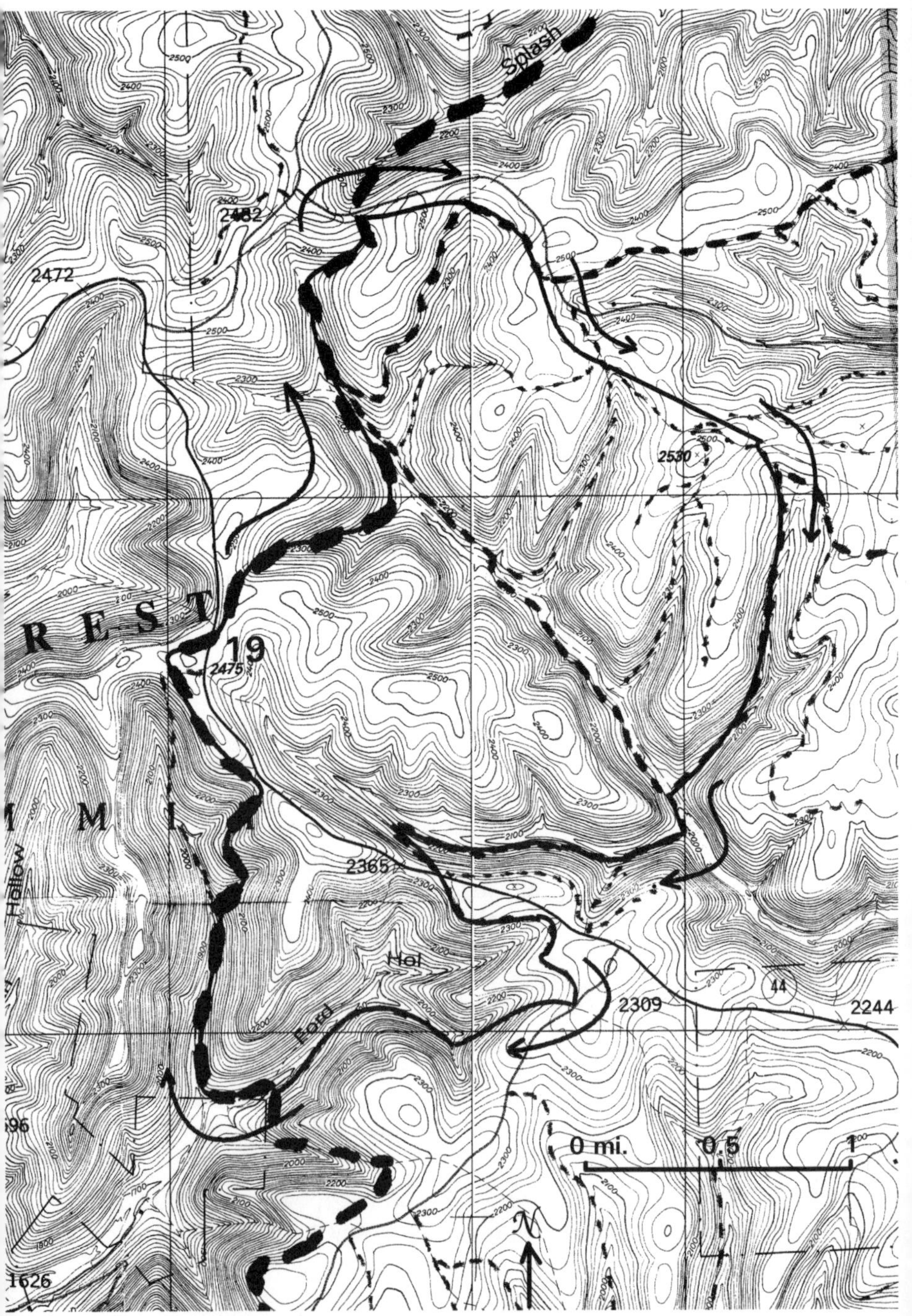

Splash
2482
2472
2530
R E S T
19
2475
M M I
Hollow
2365
Hol
Ford
2309
44
2244
0 mi.
0.5
1
1626

5.4 At bottom of Maple Hollow follow ATV Trail across West Branch, turning left (E), then right, passing hunting camp. This is the bottom of the Gibbs Trail.

5.7 Pass Forestry gate off left (Kuhn Trail).

6.85 ATV trail bends sharp left, leaving Gibbs Trail and rising to Route 44. [NOTE: If you wish to shorten your hike, you can follow the Gibbs Trail drainage back to Patterson Park in 1.0 mi. The Gibbs Trail is intermittent.]

7.15 Cross Route 44 and bend left at gas line.

7.9 Intersection of Rock Ridge Road, gas line, and Rock Ridge Trail. Turn right and follow the Rock Ridge Trail (grassy logging road) toward Ford Hollow.

8.8 Rock Ridge Trail bends left at main stem of Ford Hollow, becoming an easily followed footpath.

9.4 Turn right on STS at bottom of Ford Hollow. The Rock Ridge Trail may degrade somewhat before this intersection, but it is hard to miss the orange-blazed STS. The STS will cross Ford Hollow, then bend right, ascending toward Patterson State Park along a grassy logging road.

10.4 STS turns right (NE), leaving grassy road along moderate grade.

11.3 STS crosses logging road, then turns right (NE), meandering back to start in about 1/4 mile.

20 EAST FORK - SINNEMAHONING/FORD HOLLOW

FEATURES: view, streams
DISTANCE: 6.35 miles
TIME: 3.5 hours
ELEVATION: 1785 - 2360
TERRAIN: moderate grades; some bushwhacking and rocky areas
BLAZES: orange (STS), some snowmobile directional arrows, otherwise none
PARKING: Rock Ridge Road at Rock Ridge Trail/gas line intersection, 0.3 mi SW of Rt. 44
COMMENTS: Not hard to follow with average bushwhacking skills

On March 26, 1804, the Pennsylvania Legislature created Potter County. Originally it was proposed to call the new county "Sinnemahoning", a Native American word for "stoney lick", the name they gave to the stream. Instead the Pennsylvania Senate named it in honor of General James Potter of Northumberland County, who had served under Washington in the American Revolution. While he must have had connections in the Pennsylvania Senate, he had no connection to the place that bears his name.

TRAIL DESCRIPTION:

This route follows the Alabama Trail down the upper East Fork of Sinnemahoning Creek and up the Clinton Trail to Rock Ridge Road. After following Rock Ridge Road about ° mile, a bushwack down Card Hollow leads to the orange-blazed STS. The STS will follow a rolling level path past a vista and a very rough, rocky area before dropping down to Ford Hollow, where the route then swings up the Rock Ridge Trail back to the start.

Miles	Description
0	From intersection of gas line, Rock Ridge Road, and Rock Ridge Trail (0.25 miles SW of Rt. 44), follow gas line S for 30-40 yds., turning left off gas line onto Alabama Trail (grassy path at the third large tree from the gas line gate).
0.15	Trail begins to drop more noticeably. View down E Fork - Sinnemahoning across clear-cut.
0.25	Cross logging road. Orange snowmobile diamonds lead you down the hollow, descending more steeply.
0.5	Go left at fork in trail, descending along left side of hollow.
0.75	At trail crossing, go straight ahead on grassy trail (orange diamond points left here for snowmobiles). Trail will cross an open area and follow a well-defined path 20 ft. above right side of stream.
1.1	After entering along right edge of open area, cross gas line.
1.85	Turn right in pines where hollow enters on right, following Clinton Trail (grassy path) up right side of hollow.
2.0	At Y continue straight, ascending easily.
2.2	At Y descend along left branch, crossing stream and bending right in grassy open area along a semblance of a logging road. The grade will bend left and become more easily followed as it rises.
2.4	Grade turns sharp right, becoming ferny logging road.
3.0	Trail bends left, then right, and levels.
3.2	Bear right on Intersecting logging road.
3.5	Turn left, following Rock Ridge Road about 0.5 mi., then turn right, bushwhacking down Card Hollow (on right side, with drainage pipe under road).

4.1 Turn right on STS. The STS will pass large rocks of quartzy conglomerate.

4.25 Trail crosses between two large sandstone rocks and steps up a ledge of conglomerate.

4.5 Vista of plateau. STS then passes a blowdown area, crosses over large boulders, and bends left, descending Hockney Hollow.

5.5 Near bottom of Hockney Hollow follow STS right (NW) leaving the Hockney Hollow Trail, moderately uphill.

5.75 STS turns left and descends moderately.

5.85 At Ford Hollow turn right, leaving STS, along old trail on right side of Ford Hollow - the Rock Ridge Trail.

6.45 At first fork of Ford Hollow, Rock Ridge Trail bends right and becomes a grassy logging grade ascending right side.

6.35 Intersection of Rock Ridge Road, gas line, and Rock Ridge/ Alabama Trails.

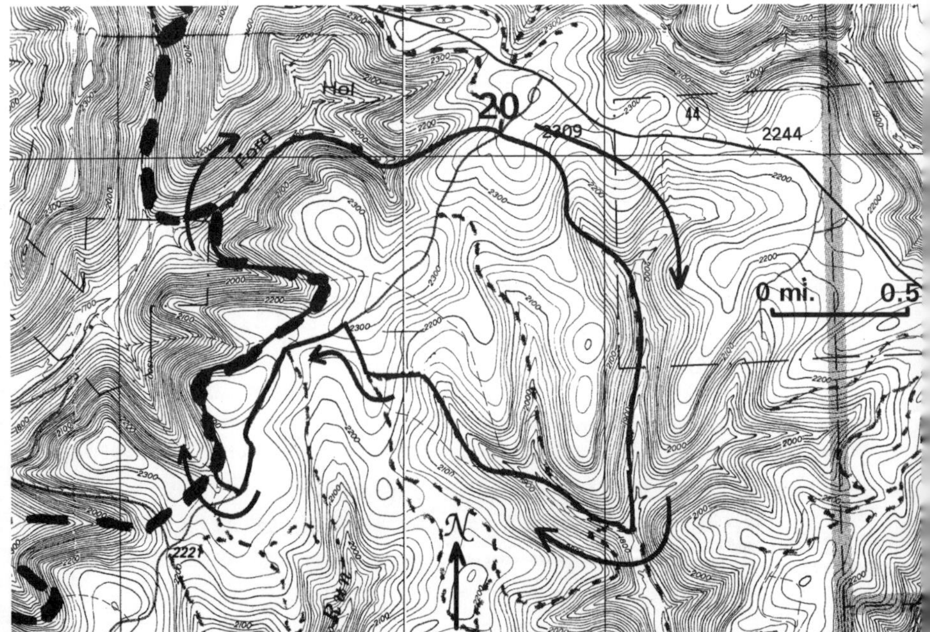

21 WATER TANK HOLLOW

FEATURES: views, old railroad grade, forest types
DISTANCE: 8 miles
TIME: 4.5 hours
ELEVATION: 1760 - 2470
TERRAIN: some steep old grades; some bushwhacking
BLAZES: orange (STS), otherwise none
PARKING: Cherry Springs Fire Tower off Rt. 44
COMMENTS: The Burrous Trail can be difficult to follow over the flatter top of the hollow near the STS

In 1895 Frank and Charles Goodyear extended the Buffalo & Susquehanna Railroad from Hull (Conrad) to Galeton to transport hemlock to their sawmill on the east side of the town. The railroad had to get over the plateau near Cherry Springs - a tunnel was too expensive, so switchbacks were constructed at the top of Shinglebolt Hollow on the Conrad side and in Upper Dry Hollow on the Galeton side. These grades followed an average slope of 2-1/2%, and the switchbacks allowed trains of 15 cars to cross this natural barrier.

A 15-car train was adequate for hemlock logging operations, but proved inadequate when the Goodyears later shifted from hemlock, which was being exhausted, to coal and coke. The constraints of train size, construction costs, distance, and competition from other railroads all contributed to financial problems that forced the B & S into receivership in 1910 and the Goodyears' loss of control over the railroad.

There are several places in the region called "Water Tank Hollow", and each one derives its name from the water tanks that were constructed in them to provide water for railroad steam engines. The Burrous Trail, also followed on this hike, was used by George Wayne Burrous, who commuted from his cabin at the bottom of Upper Dry Hollow to his job as a fire spotter at the Cherry Springs Fire Tower.

TRAIL DESCRIPTION:

This route follows the STS S from Cherry Springs Fire Tower, then E along the B & S grade at the top of Hogback Hollow across Rt. 44 and down into Upper Dry Hollow. At the bottom of Water Tank Run an easy bushwhack across the hollow and up the Burrous Trail brings you to the STS. Top of the Burrous Trail can be difficult to follow. Orange-blazed STS crosses plateau back to the fire tower.

Miles	Description
0	From Cherry Springs Fire Tower follow orange-blazed STS (SE) downhill, curving left (NE).
0.2	STS turns left, levels, then starts downhill along easy grade, passing vista of Hogback Hollow and surrounding plateau.
0.6	Shortly after passing STS register box, STS passes Cherry Springs Hunting Club. Here turn left onto driveway (former B & S grade), leaving the STS.
1.8	Cross Route 44 following old railroad grade, gently downhill. Occasional glimpses down hollow. The grade was cut and filled to maintain an even grade.
2.6	View back up hollow to Rt. 44
3.7	Grade switches back left in Upper Dry Hollow.
4.5	Grade crosses wet drainage. Gas line crosses grade.
5.0	Switchback right at intersecting grade at bottom of Water Tank Run. After following the grade a short distance (about 0.1 mi.), descend bank wherever convenient and cross Water Tank Hollow to small hollow entering on opposite side. There is an old skid trail along the right side of this small hollow - the Burrous Trail. Follow it uphill.
5.6	Burrous Trail flattens out and becomes a path that is sometimes difficult to pick out - so watch carefully for it or use a compass and map.

5.9 Trail bends somewhat right

6.0 Trail bends right somewhat again.

6.1 Trail crosses drainage area and bends somewhat right once again.

6.3 Turn left on orange-blazed STS at large stump, following STS south over rolling terrain.

7.2 STS passes sign for Cross Trail.

7.95 STS crosses Route 44 to fire tower.

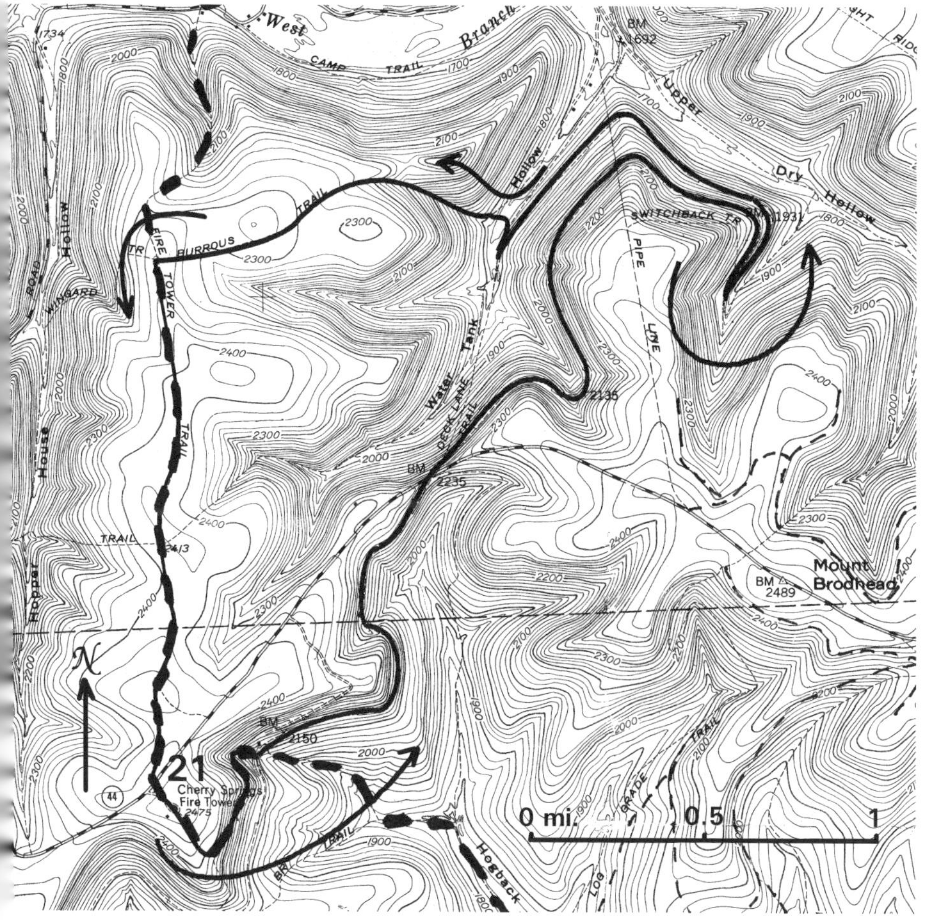

22 B & S GRADES

FEATURES: old railroad grades, views
DISTANCE: 13.7 miles
TIME: 7 hours
ELEVATION: 1540 - 2470
TERRAIN: steep & rocky in one area, some bushwhacking
BLAZES: orange (STS); otherwise none
PARKING: Cherry Springs Fire Tower off Rt. 44
COMMENTS: Easy to follow grades, but good bushwhacking skills needed between Combs Trail and Horton Run logging road, a fairly rugged area.

The Goodyears constructed the Buffalo & Susquehanna Railroad (B & S) from Warton to Hull (Conrad) in 1893. The line was extended to Galeton after they purchased a sawmill there in 1895, then was extended to Westfield and Ansonia in Tioga County and to Addison and Wellsville, NY.

By 1902 the Goodyears had acquired all the remaining uncut hemlock in Potter County and began to diversify their operations in Pennsylvania to include coal and iron-making. Unfortunately, the B & S route proved to be a costly way to move coal and iron, and in 1910 the B & S was unable to meet expenses. The line was reorganized, and the Goodyears lost control of it. A section of the line in NY was sold, and the Pennsylvania Railroad was contracted to carry coke and coal to Buffalo from Driftwood, PA.

The B & S repair shops in Galeton, located where Patterson Lumber Company is today, were dismantled in 1912. By 1914 the B & S became profitable once more. It was sold in 1932 to the Baltimore & Ohio, and the tracks were removed.

In the past when old rail grades were abandoned, ownership usually reverted to the adjacent landowners and the rights-of-way were often lost forever. Today federal law allows the Interstate Commerce Commission to "railbank" grades proposed for abandonment. Railbanking preserves them for future use, avoids their loss to reversionary rights, and allows their use as interim greenways and trails. For more information contact the Rails-to-Trails Conservancy, Suite 300, 1400 Sixteenth St., NW, Washington, D.C. 20036 or the Rails-to-Trails Conservancy of PA, 105 Locust St., Harrisburg, PA 17101.

The Goodyear railroads were constructed to bring hemlock to market - other uses were incidental, including passenger service. According to one local story a woman riding the B & S complained to the conductor that she could walk faster than the train was moving. When the conductor invited her to do so she replied, "I would, but my relatives aren't expecting me that soon." You will zip right along on these easy B & S grades, too.

TRAIL DESCRIPTION:

This route follows the STS from the Cherry Springs Fire Tower S, then turns down an unblazed grade to the former B & S grade. In Shinglebolt Hollow at the top of the Combs Trail, leave the B & S grade and bushwack your way up a steep, rocky side hollow, across open woods on the flat, and down through a moderately steep route through open woods to Horton Run. After bushwhacking part way down Horton Run follow a logging road down the remainder of the hollow to the old B & S grade which brings you back N along East Fork of Sinnemahoning Creek to Shinglebolt Hollow, where you switch back along the grade to the top and back to the STS.

Miles	Description
0	From Cherry Springs Fire Tower, follow STS south.
0.3	At fork in trail turn right, leaving STS along unblazed grade.
0.4	Turn right (W) on former B&S grade. There is one brief detour in another mile to traverse a grade washout.
1.75	B&S grade crosses Boone Road.
2.65	After passing red hunting cabin, B&S grade crosses Junction Road. There are two grades on the other side of Junction Road - the left rises, the right descends. Take the right grade, descending into Shinglebolt Hollow.

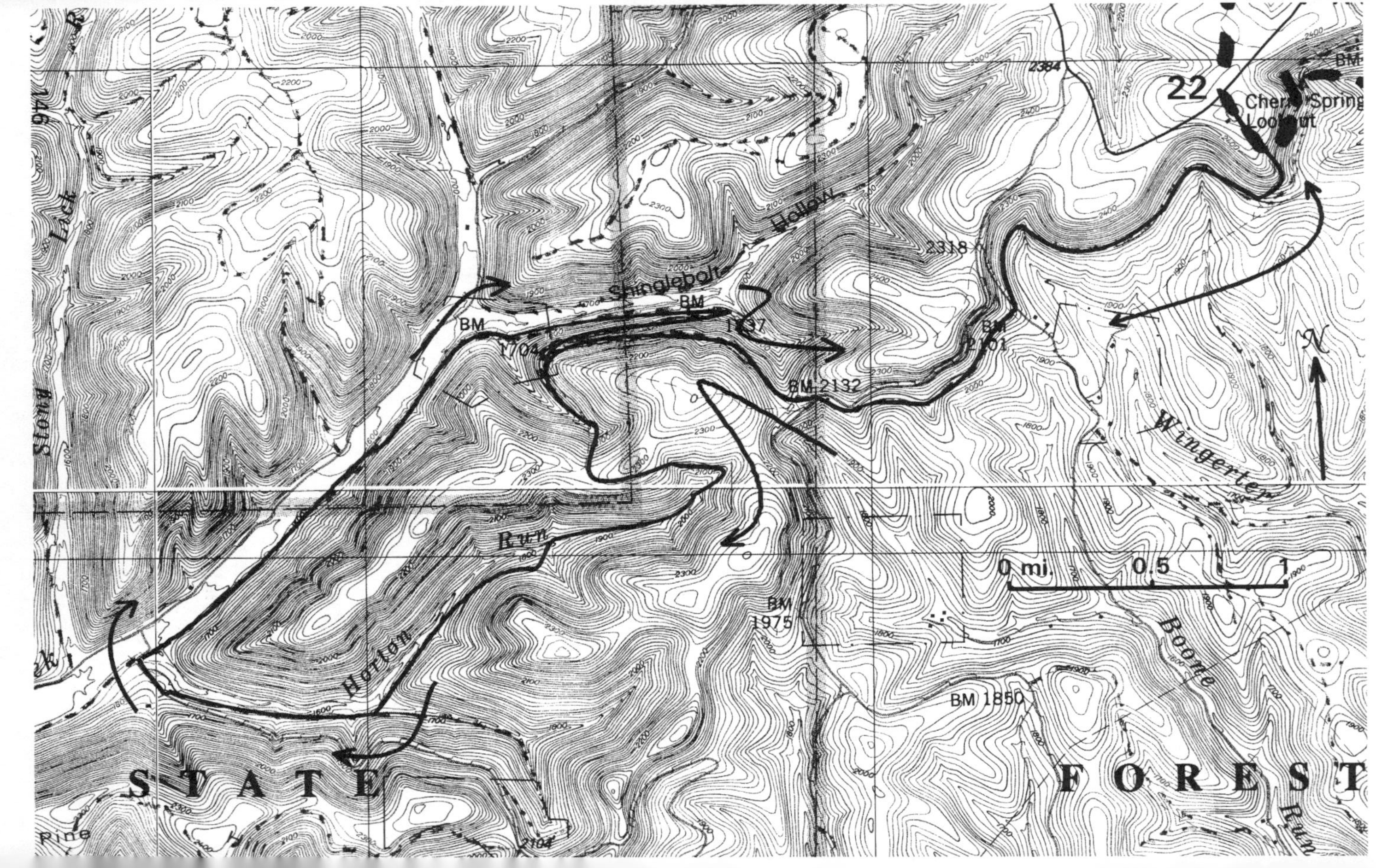
22
Cherry Springs Lookout
2384
2318
Shinglebolt
Hollow
BM
1704
BM
1737
BM 2132
BM 2101
N
Wingerter
Horton
Run
BM 1975
0 mi.
0.5
1
Boone
BM 1850
Stony
Lick
STATE
FOREST
Run
Pine
2104

3.9 B&S switches back to the right, continuing descent into Shinglebolt Hollow, but you continue along the main grade another 0.2 miles. Where the grade abruptly ends, climb the right-hand bank and ascend a steep, faint foot trail along the right side of Combs Hollow.

4.4 At top cross ridge (100 yds. wide) and turn left, following south side of ridge east and dropping down into Horton Run when slope allows. There is no trail to follow here. At the bottom of Horton Run is an old logging grade along the right side of the hollow. The grade sometimes follows the stream bed which may be wet.

5.5 Exit diagonally left where hollow enters on the left, rising along a moderate slope (no trail) to a logging road about 100 yds. above and on left of Horton Run, following it down Horton Run.

6.25 Pass yellow and black forestry gate, continuing along former logging grade past four hunting camps to Horton Run Road.

6.5 Turn right on Horton Run Road, then right shortly onto B&S grade, following it upstream along East Branch Sinnemahoning Creek.

8.05 B&S grade bends right shortly after entering field at bottom of Shinglebolt Hollow, crossing through private property.

8.25 You will need to detour from the grade to cross the grade washout where the Combs Trail would enter on the right.

9.05 Turn sharp right, ascending a switchback grade.

9.75 Turn sharp left at switchback (m.p. 3.9 above) and retrace route back to Cherry Springs Fire Tower.

23 MT. BRODHEAD

FEATURES: old railroad grade, northern hardwoods
DISTANCE: 7.4 miles
TIME: 4 hours
ELEVATION: 1720 - 2470
TERRAIN: some moderate to steep grades; some bushwhacking
BLAZES: orange (STS); otherwise none
PARKING: Route 44 at top of Deck Lane Trail
COMMENTS: Average bushwhacking skills needed for trail between Deck Lane Trail and STS and for Log Grade Trail; Good bushwhacking skill needed to follow top of Switchback Trail.

In 1779, in response to Iroquois raids in the Wyoming Valley of Pennsylvania, George Washington sent General John Sullivan up the Susquehanna into the heart of Iroquois Territory in southern New York. He was to rendezvous with Gen. James Clinton, arriving from the Mohawk Valley of New York, and Colonel Daniel Brodhead, arriving from Fort Pitt, at the confluence of the Chemung and Susquehanna Rivers. They were then to sweep through southern NY, engaging the Iroquois, burning Iroquois villages, and destroying crops.

In view of the impracticality of an unsupported, sustained march across the Allegheny highlands, however, Washington changed the plan and ordered Brodhead up the Allegheny and back to Ft. Pitt, destroying whatever villages he encountered. In August 1779, Brodhead, with 605 men and 20 Indian scouts, destroyed several Indian villages, destroyed 500 acres of corn, and engaged a war party of 40 Indians, killing five and wounding others at no cost to his men before he returned to Ft. Pitt. He never entered Potter County, but this ridge is named in his honor.

Sullivan and Clinton, meanwhile, razed villages, and destroyed enough crops to earn Sullivan the name "Corncutter" by the Iroquois, who were driven to the British Fort Niagara for food. The Iroquois never completely recovered from this campaign, whose major casualty was their food supply.

TRAIL DESCRIPTION:

This route follows a dug grade and path from Rt. 44 into Hogback Hollow, and the STS to the Log Grade Trail. The Log Grade Trail is an easy bushwack, then a path that empties into a cut area. Bushwack through the cut area to Rt. 44 and west 1/4 mile to a gas line. The gas line heads toward the Switchback Trail, which may be difficult to find (if you miss it you can descend steeply along the gas line to the B & S grade in Water Tank Hollow). The Switchback Trail becomes easier as you descend to the B & S grade in Upper Dry Hollow. From the B & S grade in Water Tank Hollow, rise to Rt. 44 along the Deck Lane Trail, a fairly steep old grade.

Miles	Description
0	From Route 44 just east of Deck Lane Trail and driveway, drop over bank to an old grade below south side of highway.
0.2	Trail bears right at bottom of hollow.
0.5	"Y" - take right branch. Trail bears right, becomes less distinct, then turns left, descending hollow.
0.9	Cross stream - grade resumes on other side, continuing along right side of main hollow. As you near the STS the trail will become less distinct.
1.33	Turn left (S) onto orange-blazed STS.
1.7	Turn left at sign for Log Grade Trail, leaving STS. There isn't much of a trail here - follow right side of the drainage. In 0.2 mi. you will follow a path that skirts the left (N) edge of a logged area.
2.4	After leaving cut, trail continues along right side of drainage.
2.7	Trail bears right up right fork and meets bottom of hollow. Very shortly turn sharp left up skid trail, rising moderately.
3.1	Skid trail turns sharp right.

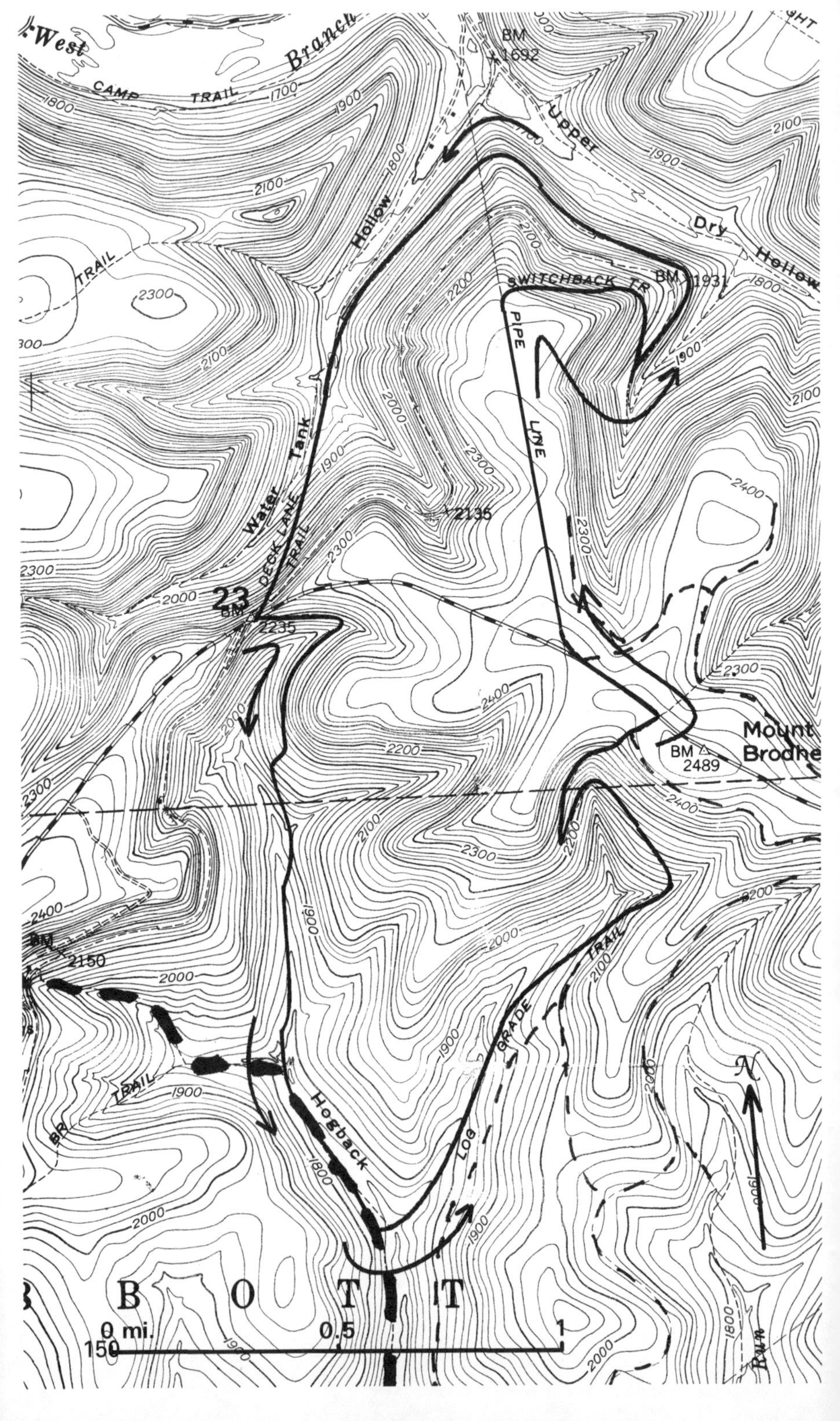

West Branch
CAMP TRAIL
BM 1692
Upper
Dry Hollow
Hollow
TRAIL
SWITCHBACK TR
BM 1931
PIPE LINE
Water Tank
DECK LANE TRAIL
23
BM 2235
2135
Mount Brodhe
BM 2489
GRADE TRAIL
Loe
Hogback
TRAIL
BR
BM 2150
Run
N
B O T T
0 mi.
0.5
1

3.4 At top, skirt left side of opening and bushwhack through young beech briefly to Route 44, where you turn left (W).

3.75 0.2 mi west of Log Grade Trail cross Route 44 at gas line and logging road and follow petroleum line/fiber optics right-of-way (grassy grade, sometimes overwhelmed by blowdowns and small growth).

4.6 Turn right on Switchback Trail - this intersection, in an area of clubmoss just before gas line descends, is difficult to find here, and top portion has several blowdowns, but Switchback Trail becomes easier to follow as you descend. [If you miss this turn the gas line will begin to descend steeply ahead - you can then backtrack to search for this faint grade or you can follow the gas line (steep downhill) to the former rail grade and turn right on it.]

5.2 Intersection of Switchback Trail and former rail grade. Follow the grade as it switches back left and continues down Upper Dry Hollow.

6.0 Grade crosses wet drainage. Gas line crosses grade.

6.6 Pass switchback on right, continuing S on grade up Water Tank Run.

6.95 Exit left where grade comes down. The 8' wide grade (Deck Lane Trail) rises at a moderate to steep rate to Route 44 in 0.4 miles.

24 HOGBACK HOLLOW

FEATURES: wetland environments
DISTANCE: 8.85 miles
TIME: 5 hours
ELEVATION: 1480 - 2420
TERRAIN: easy/moderate grades; some bushwhacking
BLAZES: orange (STS); otherwise none
PARKING: Rt. 44 at top of Bolich Run Trail
COMMENTS: Average bushwhacking skills a help. Hike can be very wet, so it is best to forego this hike during high water/wet periods.

This hike passes a wide variety of environments among the most beautiful in Pennsylvania: springs and seeps with a number of different plant types, hemlock and shrub swamps, floodplains, streams, beaver ponds, cattail marshes, sedge meadows, fields, pine and hemlock forests, and northern hardwoods.

Besides preventing downstream flooding and recharging groundwater supplies, wetlands are particularly efficient oxygen producers (a byproduct of photosynthesis), convert polluting nitrates into inert nitrogen gas, and give off methane (a byproduct of anaerobic, wet, oxygen-poor soils), which helps regulate the ozone layer. Different habitats associated with various types of wetlands provide diversity in the forest and support many different species.

The diversity and beauty of the Hogback and Bolich Run may slow you down, but it is time well spent.

TRAIL DESCRIPTION:

This route follows a logging road from the top of Bolich Run to the Log Grade Trail, which descends to the STS in Hogback Hollow. The orange-blazed STS descends Hogback Hollow and crosses Bolich Run. A logging road up and back across Bolich Run provides a dry route to the base of the mountain, where you can either continue up Bolich Run on the logging road or take the scenic route: bushwack your way through the hemlock to an old railroad grade, a path, and a logging road up Bolich Run. Near the top of Bolich Run is another opportunity to complete the hike along a logging road or to continue along an intermittent grade along the bottom back to the start.

Miles	Description
0	Top of Bolich Run Trail (forestry gate/sign/limited parking) at Rt. 44. Bear right immediately at "Y" in logging road. Logging road will quickly branch again - far right ascends steeply (gas line), left descends Bolich Run (logging road), middle (well-defined grade, ascending moderately): take the middle route. Area will be logged (1995/96).
0.65	End of logging road at cul-de-sac. Follow left edge to (NW) corner and pick up semblance of a trail (Log Grade Trail). Trail will become more discernable shortly, following the right side of the hollow, descending moderately.
0.95	Trail abruptly stops ahead and switches back to the acute left. Prior to this you **may** see signs of other trails entering from the left, but ignore them.
1.25	Shortly after bending right along the hollow, you may see a "Y" in the trail - continue right down the hollow, descending at a moderate rate. Keep a sharp eye for the trail here - it becomes easier to follow as you descend.
1.4	Trail turns sharp right, following bottom of hollow briefly before exiting to the left along fairly gentle grade.
1.7	Skirt right (N) edge of clear-cut as the trail descends.
2.2	Exit clear-cut, crossing small hollow, continuing straight ahead along a grassy path, which will become harder to follow near the bottom of the hollow.
2.4	After crossing Hogback Hollow, turn left (S) onto orange-blazed STS at sign for Log Grade Trail. The STS begins to get wetter shortly, passing over periodic seeps and springs. Along the route are beaver dams, ponds, and wet meadows.

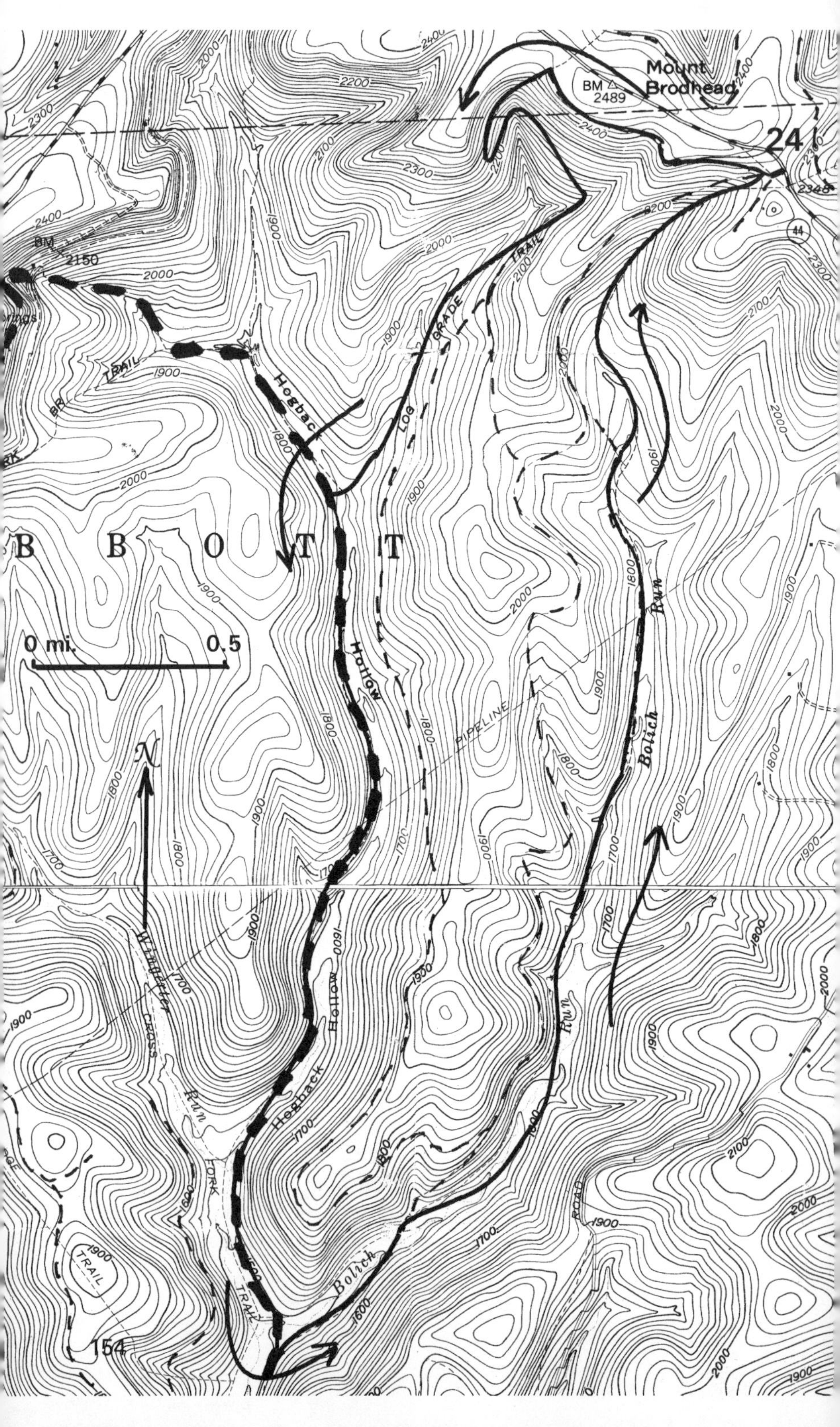
Mount Brodhead
BM 2489
24
BM 2150
TRAIL
Hogback
Log Grade Trail
B B O T T
0 mi. 0.5
N
Hollow
Pipeline
Bolich Run
Cross
Run
Fork
Hogback Hollow
Bolich
Trail
Road

3.3 STS crosses gas line ROW and rises along dug trail (1994 relocation) until about 50 ft above old STS. Relocation avoids many wet areas along original trail.

4.0 Relocation rejoins old STS, descending through pines, crossing wet meadow on cordwood, and crossing to left (E) side of Hogback Hollow. Beaver activities in the vicinity may necessitate temporary detour to cross Hogback Hollow - look for drier crossing just upstream in that event.

4.9 STS crosses Bolich Run on stones, crosses open area and turns onto old, grassy road. Turn left at grassy logging road intersection, ascending hollow gently uphill along S side of Bolich Run.

5.35 Grassy logging road crosses Bolich Run. [If you continue here on the logging road it will return you to the start in 3.75 miles.] This hike follows the more scenic route: after crossing the stream turn right at base of hill, leaving logging road. There is no easily followed trail here - continue along near the base of the hill, through a small hemlock swamp, keeping the main branch of Bolich Run to your right.

5.65 Hillside to the left steepens, forcing you to cross to right side of Bolich Run into a small stand of hemlock. After crossing to other side of these hemlocks, pick up grade with a deer trail on it along right side of Bolich Run.

5.9 Enter clearing with a fire ring. At far side drop down and cross to left side of Bolich Run, where you will pick up an old grade. The grade becomes a path at the base of the hill just to the left of hemlock stand.

6.3 Ascend to dry, easily-followed grassy logging road above left. You will pass another intersecting logging road above beaver pond in 0.25 miles.

6.9 Bend left to avoid washout area.

7.25 Gas line crosses. Grassy area with apple trees ahead right. Logging road will cross to right side of Bolich Run in another 0.25 mi.

7.6 Logging road crosses to left side of Bolich Run and begins to ascend. At this point, you can either take the easy route, ascending the logging road 0.35 mi. and continuing up Bolich Run on main logging road to start in another mile

OR

you can take the scenic route along the bottom right of the hollow where you will shortly pick up traces of an old grade or path. This grade will bend left at the next hollow on the right (0.25 mi.), then become increasingly difficult to find, more overgrown with young striped maple, and occasionally blocked by blowdowns - just follow the bottom of the hollow. The route will become steeper as you rise.

8.7 Trail leaves bottom of hollow, going off to the left along path which ascends to intersect logging road. Turn right on logging road, which then splits left to Route 44. If you miss this turn at the bottom of the hollow, continue ascending hollow, which will intersect the logging road at a water-filled ditch where the logging road splits left to Route 44.

25 WILD BOY NORTH - STONY LICK RUN

FEATURES: views, old railroad grades, stream environments
DISTANCE: 12.75 miles
TIME: 7 hours
ELEVATION: 1475 - 2280
TERRAIN: steep grade; some easy bushwhacking, stream crossings
BLAZES: orange (STS), otherwise none
PARKING: East Fork Road at bottom of Stony Lick Run (0.2 mi. S of Horton Run Road)
COMMENTS: Not hard to follow with average bushwhacking skills. Not recommended in high water or during wet periods.

In 1836 Lewis Stevens, 11 years old, ran away from his alcoholic parents in Toms River, NJ. Picking up whatever work he could, he wandered through the countryside until he came to Potter County. There, at age 17, he built a cabin along Wild Boy Run and lived off the land. He left in 1845 to fight in the Mexican War and again at the start of the Civil War to join the 46th Pennsylvania Regiment. His independent life in Potter County, however, made him ill-suited to the Army in some ways - his years of independence and social isolation fostered a dislike of mindless drilling and marching, of being told what to do, and of living in close quarters with others. He refused to salute officers and eventually deserted. Other than these brief instances in which he left Potter County, he lived a solitary, subsistence existence in his cabin along Wild Boy Run, several miles from his nearest neighbors, with whom he had only minimal contact. His neighbors knew little about him and referred to him as "the wild boy".

You can still find Lewis Stevens' independent spirit alive in Potter County today, and there are many people that may eke out a subsistence living in the countryside, but you will find no trace of his cabin along Wild Boy Run.

This area was originally logged by the Goodyears in 1904/05.

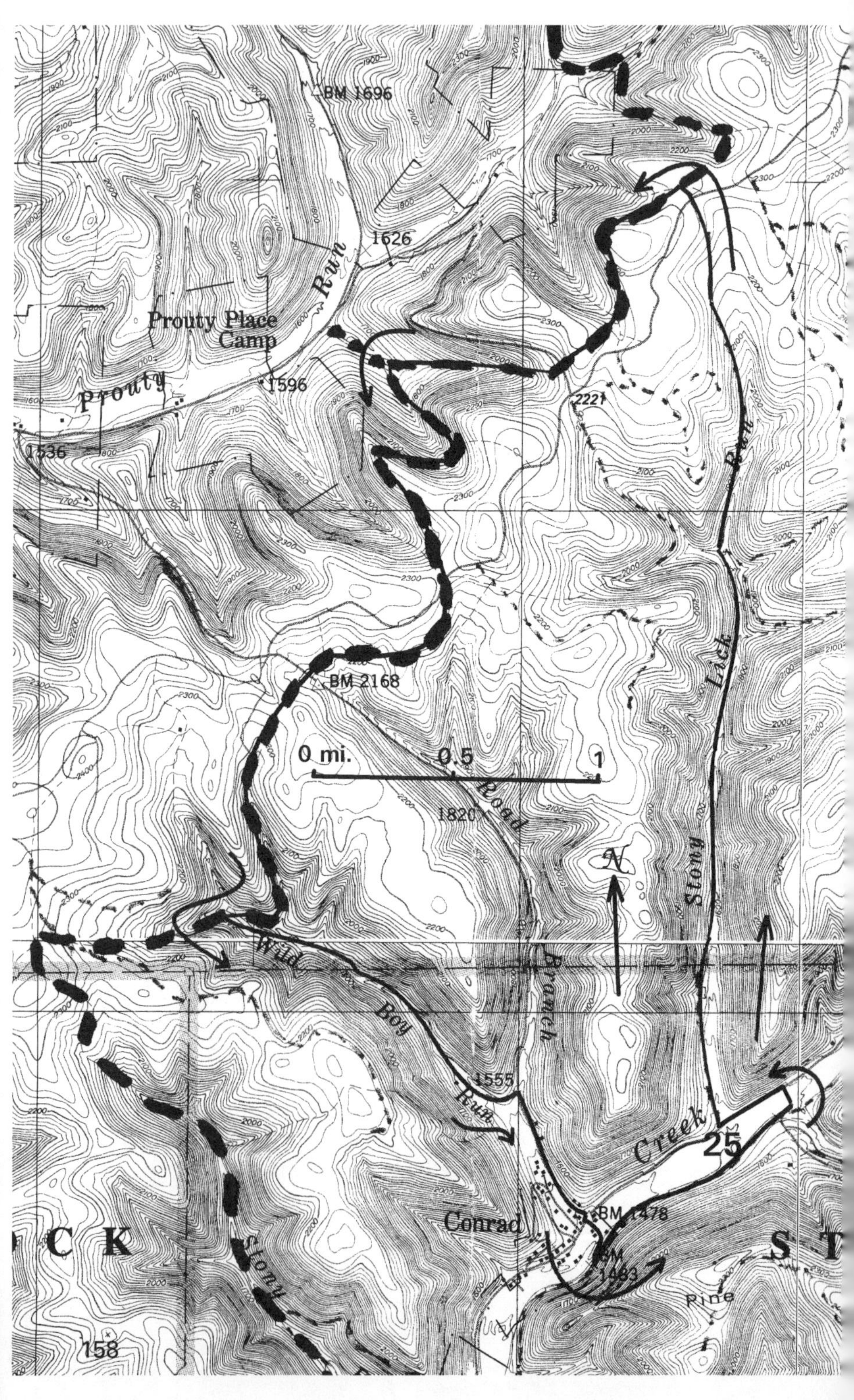

BM 1696
1626
Run
Prouty Place
Camp
Prouty
1596
1536
2221
Run
Lick
Stony
BM 2168
0 mi.
0.5
1
Road
1820
N
Wild
Boy
Run
Branch
1555
Creek
25
BM 1478
BM
1483
Conrad
C K
S T
Stony
Pine
158

TRAIL DESCRIPTION:

This route follows an old grade, an old railroad grade, and a former logging road up Stony Lick Run to Rock Ridge Road. After crossing Rock Ridge Road, bushwhack your way to the STS (short & easy), and follow the orange-blazed STS south to Wild Boy Run. Where the STS ascends the left branch of Wild Boy Run, leave it and follow an old grade down the main branch of Wild Boy Run. A couple of stream crossings are required before you follow Wild Boy Road to Conrad, cross East Fork Road, and follow the former B & S grade back to Horton Run and Cross Fork Roads.

Miles	Description
0	From bottom of Stony Lick Run (East Fork Road, 0.2 mi. S of Horton Run Road) ascend the driveway toward the Blue Ribbon Gun Club, exiting along the jeep trail at bend in driveway, ascending left (W) side of Stony Lick Run. In about ° mile the jeep trail will descend to Stony Lick Run and become harder to pick out (generally follows left side of the hollow). The trail will also make several wet crossings as it ascends Stony Lick Run.
2.5	Tom Fee Hollow enters on the left. Continue along Stony Lick Run, and pick up a ferned logging road that crosses Stony Lick Run. Follow the logging road along the left (W) side of Stony Lick Run to Rock Ridge Road.
4.0	Cross Rock Ridge Road and bushwack north 0.1 mi. to the orange-blazed STS, where you turn left, heading W over a number of large sandstone boulders.
4.5	Vista of plateau. In about 1/4 mi. the STS will pass between two large sandstone rocks, step down a ledge of conglomerate, and cross Card Hollow.
5.3	STS crosses Prouty Lick Road descends Prouty Lick Run.
6.0	STS crosses Prouty Lick Run at blue-blazed trail access trail and ascends Prouty Lick Trail along a fairly steep slope.

6.8 View down Prouty Lick Hollow.

6.95 STS turns sharp left, ascending moderate to steep Fanton Hollow Trail past clear-cut (1990/91).

7.15 STS crosses Rock Ridge Road and winds through beech.

8.05 STS crosses Wild Boy Road and jeep road.

8.35 At old railroad junction, STS crosses Wild Boy Run, following a logging road along the right side of the hollow.

9.15 After bending right near the bottom of Wild Boy, STS crosses branch of Wild Boy Run to old grade on opposite side. Here leave STS and turn left on grade down Wild Boy.

9.45 Grade crosses to left side of Wild Boy Run.

9.95 Cross to right side of Wild Boy Run, following a path. [If you continue to follow the grade several wet crossings will be required. Staying right minimizes the number of crossings.]

10.35 Cross back to the left side of Wild Boy Run, following grade as it enters grassy, open area with apple trees.

10.6 Approach white camp (Davidsburg Hunting Club), cross stream and follow grade to driveway. The driveway will cross Wild Boy Run (wet crossing).

10.9 Turn right on Wild Boy Road, following it 0.5 mi. to East Fork Road in Conrad. At East Fork Road, turn right and then turn left, following a road across the East Fork of Sinnemahoning Creek to the B&S grade on the other side.

11.55 Turn left at B&S grade.

12.45 After passing a former railroad siding, turn left on Horton Run Road, crossing bridge to East Fork Road, then turning left to vehicle - about 0.3 mi. from Horton Run Road/B&S grade intersection.

26 WILD BOY SOUTH - STONY RUN

FEATURES: flagstone quarries, stream/forest environments
DISTANCE: 8.5 miles
TIME: 4.5 hours
ELEVATION: 1390 - 2360
TERRAIN: moderate grades; old railroad, stream crossings
BLAZES: orange (STS), otherwise none
PARKING: Harold B. Williams residence on East Fork Road at Jamison Run
COMMENTS: Easy to follow. Stream crossings required.

In 1893 the Goodyears extended the B & S Railroad from its mill at Wharton to Hull (now known as Conrad). Hull was one of four villages in the East Fork - Sinnemahoning watershed.

From 1899 to 1914 the Emporium Lumber Company operated a barrel stave mill in Hull. Barrels were made of either red oak or white oak, depending on what was kept in them. Red oak was used for barrels that held dry goods - its open pores made it unsuitable to hold liquids, but dry red oak has no odor or taste that might be transferred to flour or sugar. White oak, also called "stave oak", was used for barrels that held liquids - the red-brown gum in its pores made it watertight, and it was used extensively for casks, wooden pipes, and wooden ships.

TRAIL DESCRIPTION:

This route follows the orange-blazed STS up Stony Run, past several flagstone quarries. Near the top of Stony Run the path becomes steeper, then levels. After passing the "Old Stove" the STS follows an old grade downhill. Where the STS turns to cross Wild Boy Run leave the STS, following an old grade down Wild Boy Run. After several wet stream crossings, turn onto Wild Boy Road, following it to Conrad. Cross East Fork Road and follow the B & S grade S to Jamison Run and the STS back to start.

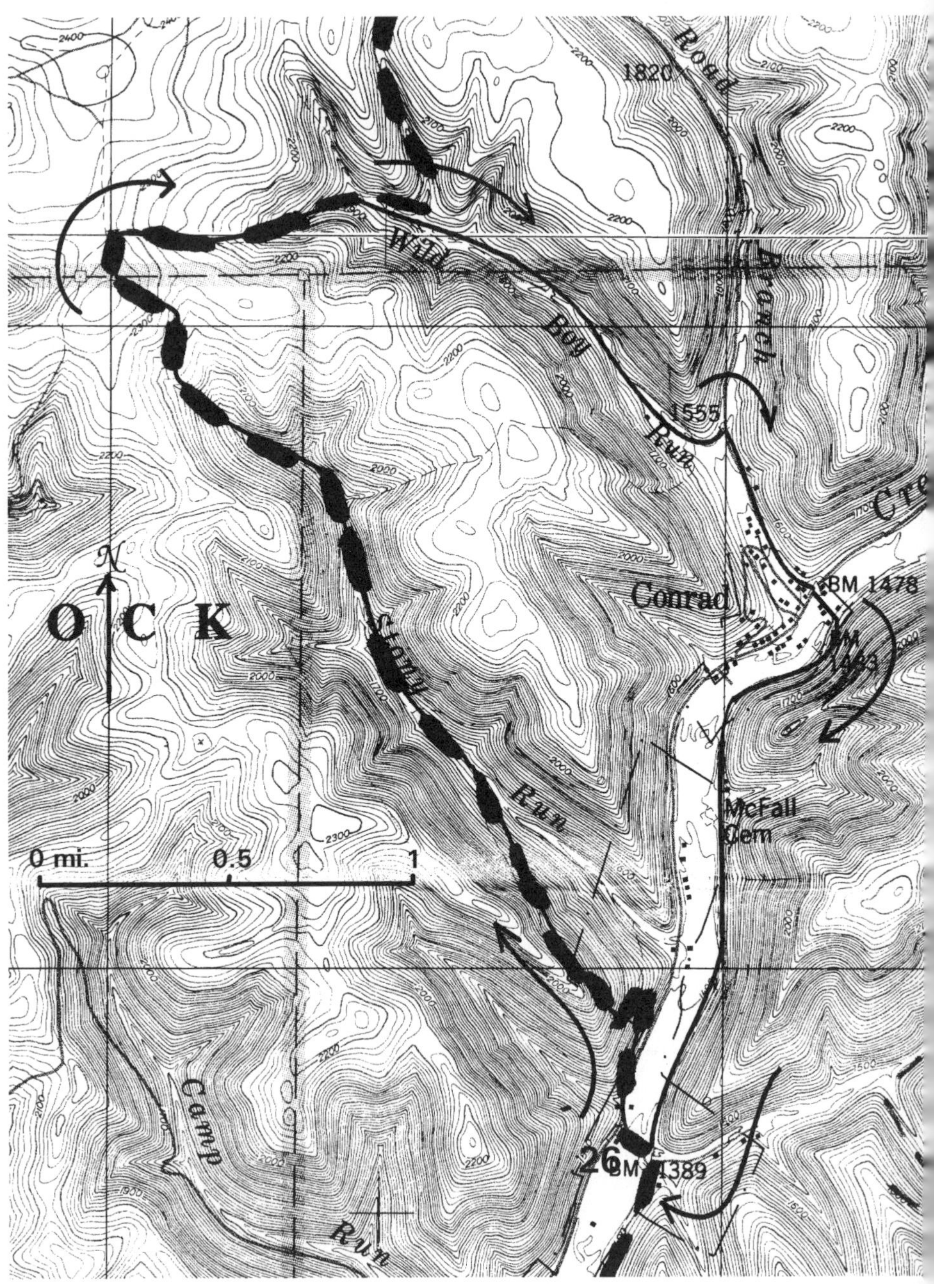
Road
1820
Wills
Branch
Boy
1555
Run
Cre
BM 1478
Conrad
O C K
N
Stony
Run
McFall
Cem
0 mi.
0.5
1
Camp
26
BM 1389
Run

Miles	Description
0	From Harold B. Williams residence on East Fork Road at Jamison Run, follow STS north up steep path.
0.35	Follow STS left at fork in trail near edge of meadow, paralleling it steeply uphill, then turning left on old railroad grade and following it S.
0.5	STS turns right (NW) at grade switchback, passing three flagstone quarries.
1.4	STS intersects old woods road, bearing left, gently rising parallel to Stony Run. Trail shortly leaves the old grade, following a footpath and crossing Stony Run several times.
2.45	STS bears left at a fork, following a skid trail uphill.
2.75	STS crosses over top of Stony Run along fairly steep uphill grade, passing moss-covered, gray sandstone boulders.
3.0	Trail bends left, then right, becoming gentle uphill and less rocky as trail follows part of old railroad grade.
3.5	Trail turns right and starts to descend.
3.7	Trail passes old barrel in open area at intersection of Ridge and Cairn Trails. Trail here is level. After passing several wet areas the STS tuns right (E) off grassy Ridge Trail and begins to descend and bears right, crossing logging road.
3.85	STS passes the "Old Stove", following an old railroad grade downhill. The trail will wind its way past the edge of a small opening and bear left at an old railroad junction, following a well-defined grade downhill.
4.45	Where STS turns sharp left, leaving grade to cross Wild Boy Run, continue straight, following grade along right side of Wild Boy Run.
4.65	Grade crosses to left side of Wild Boy Run.

5.15 Cross to right side of Wild Boy Run, following a path. [If you continue to follow the grade several wet crossings will be required. Staying right minimizes the number of crossings.]

5.5 Cross back to the left side of Wild Boy Run, following grade as it enters grassy, open area with apple trees.

5.75 Approach white camp (Davidsburg Hunting Club), cross stream and follow grade to driveway. The driveway will cross Wild Boy Run (wet crossing).

6.05 Turn right on Wild Boy Road, following it 0.5 mi. to East Fork Road in Conrad. At East Fork Road, turn right and then turn left, following a road across the East Fork of Sinnemahoning Creek to the B&S grade on the other side.

6.7 Turn right at B&S grade.

7.2 Grade passes Graveyard Hollow and "Cemetery Junction" at McFall Cemetery.

8.2 After crossing narrow wooden bridge across Jamison Run, turn right on the STS, arriving back at East Fork Road (H.B. Williams residence) in 0.3 miles.

27 PINE HILL (JAMISON RUN TRAIL)

FEATURES: old railroad grade, Sinnemahoning Creek, northern hardwoods
DISTANCE: 8.0 miles
TIME: 4 hours
ELEVATION: 1390 - 2100
TERRAIN: some steep bushwhacking
BLAZES: orange (STS); otherwise none
PARKING: Horton Run Road near intersection of McConnell Road
COMMENTS: Easy bushwack down Jamison Run, but very steep.

Indian James Jamison, a legendary hunter, was killed by a panther, or mountain lion, in Potter County about 1810. The panther, it was reported, was also stabbed to death by Jamison.

According to Henry Shoemaker (*Extinct Pennsylvania Animals*, 1917, reprinted by Spencer Kraybill, Pine Creek Historian, Waterville, PA in 1993), the mountain lion was much more common east and south of Potter and Clinton Counties. One of the famous hunters of the time, C.W. Dickinson of McKean County, attributed this to the presence of the gray timber wolf, which was feared by the large cats, in Potter, Clinton, and McKean Counties.

The mountain lion, panther, or "painter" (along with lynxes, wolves, and foxes) was blamed by early settlers for decreasing numbers of elk, deer, turkey, and small game. Bounties were placed on them, and they were eliminated as a species in Pennsylvania in the early 20th century. But as the number of mountain lions decreased game animal populations continued to decline. The decreasing amount of game was not due to mountain lions (who had coexisted with these other species for centuries) but to other factors, primarily human activity: land development destroyed habitats, and excessive hunting sent the numbers of some species plummeting below sustainable levels.

Although the cats did occasionally attack livestock and dogs, Shoemaker claims that mountain lions very rarely attacked people unless they were attacked first. Many tales of early travelers being killed by panthers actually involved a death due to other causes - the mountain lions were scavenging the dead carcasses. Most such accounts were actually tales passed on as "fact" and could never be traced to an eyewitness. The mountain lion was a victim of bad press and of people's imaginations - it was hard to imagine that a large cat, whose loud, piercing cry at night made the hair on your neck stand on end, did not stalk and kill humans.

The last mountain lion in Pennsylvania, it appears, was killed in Mifflin County in 1916. Today, although the PA Game Commission has not confirmed their return, increased sightings of mountain lions by reliable witnesses have been occurring in Potter and Tioga Counties.

TRAIL DESCRIPTION:

This route bushwhacks down Jamison Run from Horton Road. The upper portion is very steep, but then the slope moderates, allowing you to follow an old grade, then a logging road down Jamison Run. After passing the bottom of Dry Run the logging road becomes an old grade, then a path and a bushwhack to a driveway that brings you to the STS at the bottom of the hollow. The STS is followed briefly before the old B & S grade brings you to Horton Run Road, where Horton Run is ascended back to the start via the road, a driveway, a logging road, and a bushwack.

Miles	Description
0	There is a sign for the Jamison Run Trail on Horton Road near McConnell Road, but you want to start this hike from the intersection of Horton Run Road, McConnell Road, and a logging road. Follow the logging road away from the intersection and bushwhack down Jamison Run when convenient (within the first 100 yds.). The first 0.3 miles drop steeply just left along the bottom of the hollow.
0.33	When hollow becomes a little less ravine-like cross to the right side, following a worn grade (or bushwhacking your way if you can't find the grade. A small branch of Jamison Run will enter on the left shortly ahead, and there you will pick up an old grade in the bottom of the hollow. This grade is subject to a number of washouts and wet crossings, but isn't too difficult to follow.

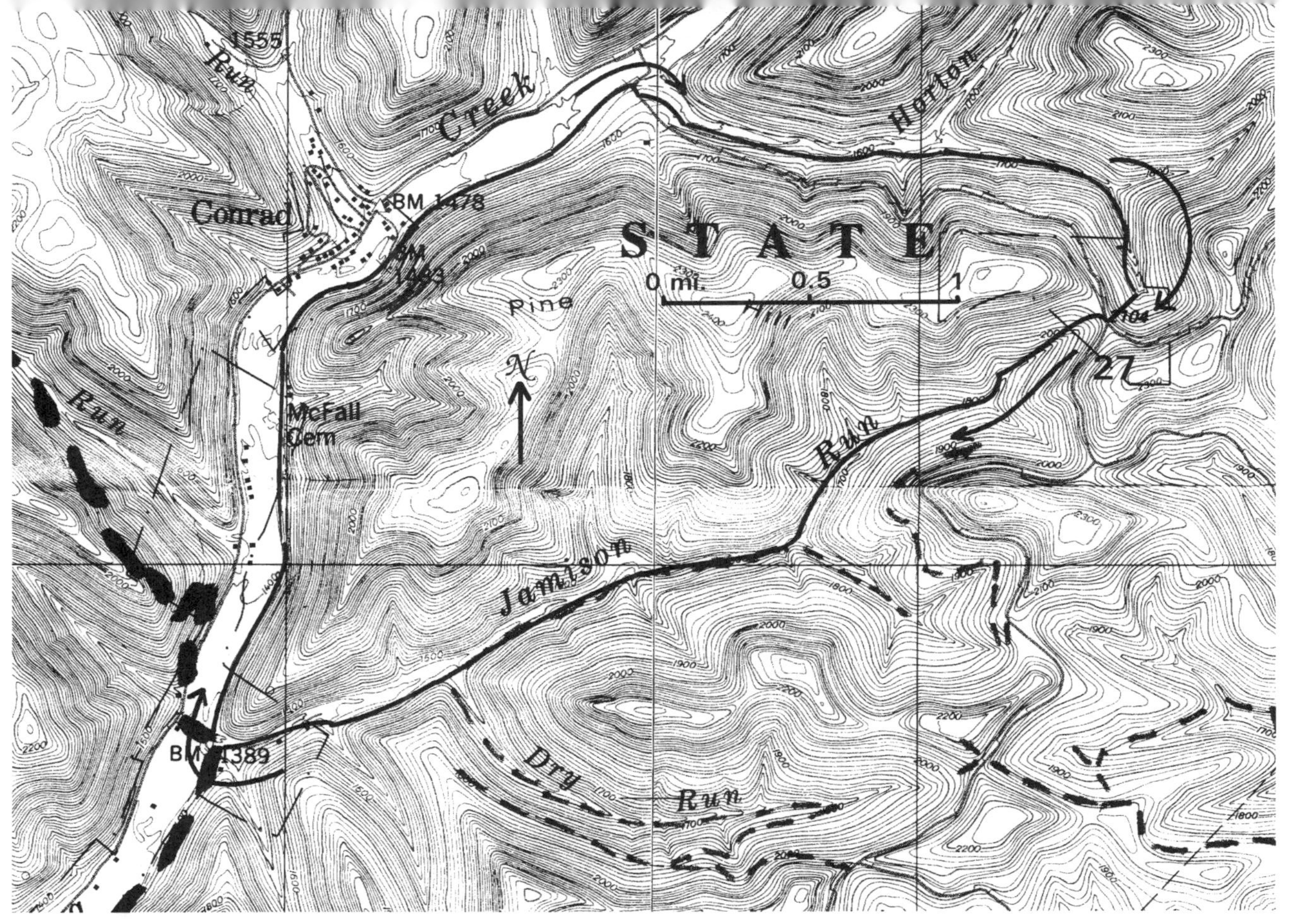
1555
Run
Creek
Horton
Conrad
BM 1478
STATE
0 mi.
0.5
1
Pine
N
McFall Cem
Run
27
Run
Jamison
BM 1389
Dry
Run

1.35 A hollow will enter on the left (this is the second hollow on the left you have encountered in Jamison Hollow). There is a logging road that ascends this hollow and descends along the left side of Jamison Run. Cross here to this road and descend along the left side of Jamison Hollow to avoid frequent washouts and wet crossings.

2.5 Dry Run enters on the left. Here the logging road ascends Dry Run, but you continue to descend along the left side of Jamison Run along a route that quickly assumes the appearance of a trail.

2.7 Descend the right-hand branch of a Y in the trail (both branches are cut grades).

2.8 The cut grade will end, and you head right, following a worn trail that descends moderately steeply, then bears left along the trace of an old worn trail, descending easily. The trail will then disappear in the hemlock.

3.0 On the other side of the hemlock is a mowed, grassy lawn, and a hollow entering on the left. Cross to the other side of this hollow and bear right along a trail on the far side of the lawned area. After passing the beige stucco camp with the yellow brick chimney follow the driveway from this camp.

3.35 After passing a residence at the bottom of Hi Foster Hollow (on left), bear right at the intersecting driveway onto the STS, and right again along the old B&S grade, leaving the STS. Leave the grade to cross Jamison Run on a narrow wooden bridge and rise to the B&S grade again, following the East Fork of Sinnemahoning Creek upstream.

4.3 After passing McFall Cemetery, "Cemetery Junction", and Graveyard Hollow, the B&S grade is used as a driveway for camps from Conrad.

4.9 Driveway veers off left to the village of Conrad - follow the B&S grade off to the right. The grade will become wider.

5.6 Pass old shack on right side of grade - a former rail siding.

5.8 Turn right on Horton Run Road, then quickly turn left, following driveway past four camps along Horton Run.

6.05 After passing the yellow and black Forestry gate, the driveway becomes a grassy logging road, rising easily.

6.75 Grade branches right (left grade continues up the main branch of Horton Run). Follow the right branch, which becomes more narrow.

7.3 At split in Horton Run, logging road branches. Bend right. The grade degenerates quickly and you will have to cross to the left side of the stream bed. In about 1/4 mile you will cross back right at an open area, following a deer trail above the stream bed.

7.75 After a short bushwhack, ascend to an old logging grade high on the right of Horton Run. If you follow the road right you will end up on Horton Run Road, where you can turn left and follow the road back to your vehicle. If you are adventurous, turn left on this logging grade, descending easily to the bend of the hollow. There is a trail from this point to the top along Horton Run Road, but you may not find it, so just ascend steeply, but briefly, to Horton Run Road close to the intersection of McConnell Road.

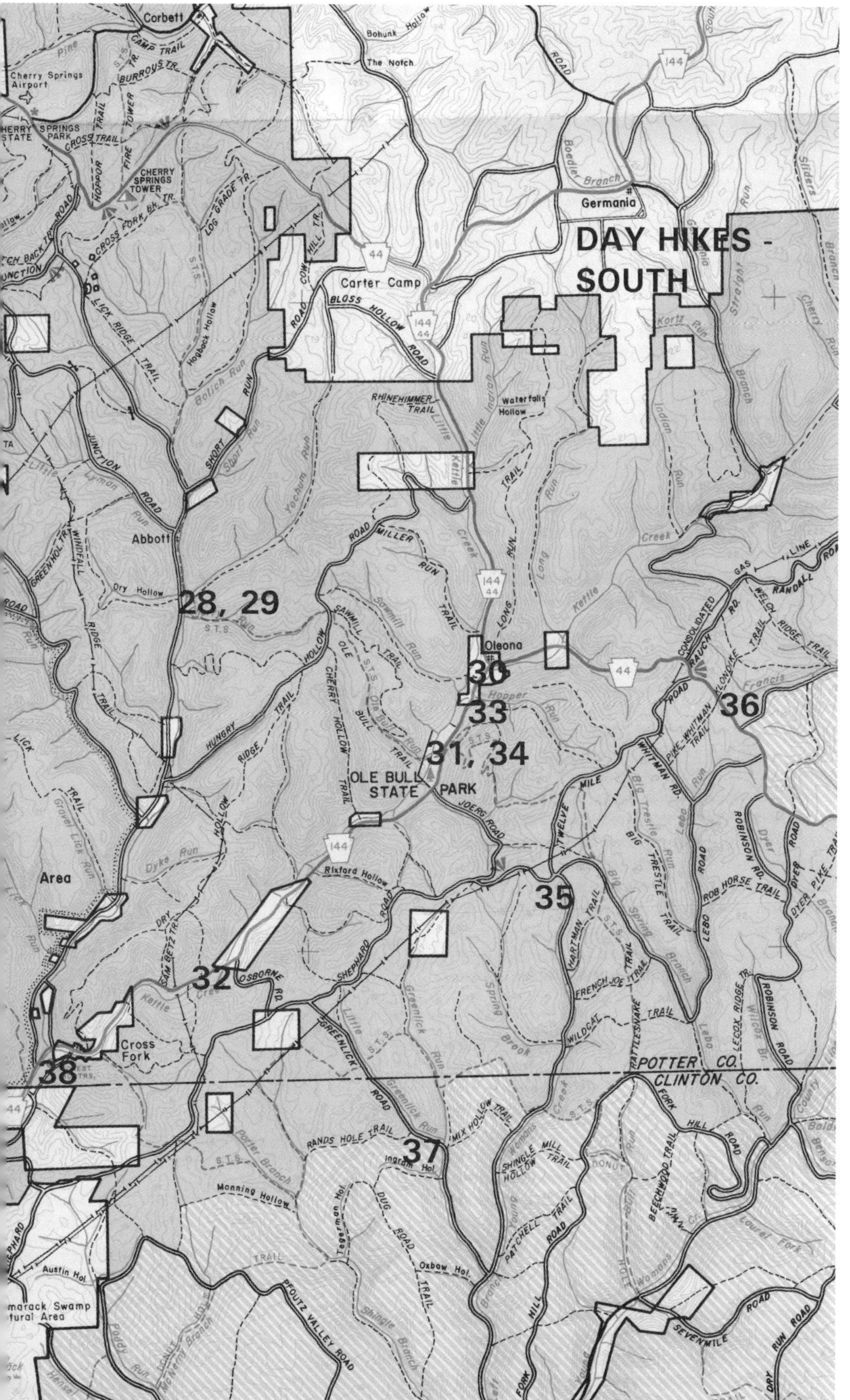
DAY HIKES - SOUTH
Corbett
Cherry Springs Airport
CHERRY SPRINGS STATE PARK
CHERRY SPRINGS TOWER
CAMP TRAIL
BURROUS TR.
CROSS TRAIL
HOPPOR TRAIL
FIRE TOWER
LOG GRADE TR.
CROSS FORK Bk. TR.
LICK RIDGE TRAIL
JUNCTION ROAD
COW HILL TR.
Bohunk Hollow
The Notch
Germania
Boedler Branch
Carter Camp
BLOSS HOLLOW ROAD
Hogback Hollow
Bolich Run
SHORT RUN
RHINEHIMMER TRAIL
Little Indian Run
Waterfalls Hollow
Little Kettle Creek
Kortz Run
Indian Run
Straight Branch
Cherry Branch
Abbott
Lyman Run
Yochum Run
WINDFALL RIDGE TRAIL
GREENHOLLOW
MILLER RUN TRAIL
Dry Hollow
28, 29
SAWMILL TRAIL
Sawmill Run
LONG RUN TRAIL
Long Run
Kettle Creek
GAS LINE
RANDALL
WELCH RIDGE TRAIL
CONSOLIDATED RAUCH RD.
Oleona
30
33
31, 34
36
Hopper Run
OLE BULL TRAIL
CHERRY HOLLOW TRAIL
HUNGRY HOLLOW
RIDGE TRAIL
HOLLOW
OLE BULL STATE PARK
JOERS ROAD
KLONDIKE TRAIL
PIKE-WHITMAN TRAIL
WHITMAN RD.
Francis
TWELVE MILE
BIG TRESTLE TRAIL
Big Trestle Run
Lebo Run
LEBO ROAD
ROBINSON RD.
DYER ROAD
DYER PIKE TRAIL
ROB HORSE TRAIL
Area
Gravel Lick Run
Dyke Run
Rixford Hollow
SHEPHARD ROAD
35
DRY SAM BETZ TR.
HARTMAN TRAIL
Spring Branch
Big Spring Branch
FRENCH JOE TRAIL
RATTLESNAKE TRAIL
32
OSBORNE RD.
Kettle Creek
Little Greenlick Run
Spring Brook
WILDCAT TRAIL
LECOX RIDGE TR.
ROBINSON ROAD
Wilcox Br.
Cross Fork
38
GREENLICK ROAD
POTTER CO.
CLINTON CO.
FORK HILL ROAD
Greenlick Run
MIX HOLLOW TRAIL
Porter Branch
RANDS HOLE TRAIL
37
Ingram Hol.
SHINGLE MILL HOLLOW TRAIL
Monning Hollow
Tegerman Hol.
DUG ROAD TRAIL
PATCHELL TRAIL
HILL ROAD
BEECHWOOD TRAIL
Laurel Fork
Oxbow Hol.
Austin Hol.
Tamarack Swamp Natural Area
PFOUTZ VALLEY ROAD
Shingle Branch
McNerny Branch
SEVENMILE ROAD
DRY RUN ROAD
144
44

28 ROBIN HOLLOW

FEATURES: forest types
DISTANCE: 8.8 miles
TIME: 4.5 hours
ELEVATION: 1320 - 2020
TERRAIN: some steep, rocky slopes; some bushwhacking
BLAZES: none
PARKING: Cross Fork Road at bottom of Dry Hollow/Yochum Run
COMMENTS: Not hard to follow with average bushwhacking skills. On the return, if you do not wish to make the stream crossing on the wire bridge then you can follow Cross Fork Road back from Junction Road instead of following the STS.

The Lackawanna Lumber Company was formed in 1887 by Fenwick Peck and purchased the timber between Little Kettle and Cross Fork Creeks. In 1893 the company bought timber along Windfall Run, Cross Fork Creek, Upper Little Kettle Creek, and Cherry Springs and had the Goodyears build a railroad 13 miles north to Cherry Springs. The deal netted a $1 million profit for Lackawanna. In 1894 the company built two mills in Cross Fork and became third in total lumber production in 1897.

This hike traverses the heart of the hardwoods that were bought by Lackawanna from the Goodyears in 1893. In the late 1960s the area along Green Hollow was timbered again.

TRAIL DESCRIPTION:

This route follows the Dry Hollow Trail (logging road) up the hollow from Cross Fork Road. Exit the logging road near the top of the hollow, bushwhacking along the left drainage to a grade that empties onto the gas line at the top of Windfall Ridge. Cross the gas line and descend Robin Hollow. Turn right on Windfall Hollow Road, following it to Green Hollow, where you turn right and follow an old logging road back to the gas line. Bushwhack down Jordan Hollow on the other side of the gas line, follow a driveway to Junction

Road, then turn right to Cross Fork Road. Exit left after crossing Little Lyman Run, following a driveway to the orange-blazed STS. At Yochum Run cross stream along a two-strand wire bridge and follow the driveway back to your car.

Miles	Description
0	From Cross Fork Road at Yochum Run/Dry Hollow, follow the gated logging road with the sign for Dry Hollow Trail.
1.15	Turn left where logging road makes a sharp right turn in Dry Hollow. Up to now the road has been clear and gently rising - now the grade will become an intermittent trail following the drainage along a moderately steep grade.
1.35	Main drainage bends right. Trail disappears - follow main drainage.
1.6	As terrain levels (about 75 feet in elevation from the top of the hollow), look closely for faint remains of an old skid trail to the right, then bushwack your way to it - it will descend briefly, then tend uphill, becoming more evident.
1.8	Old woods grade enters onto a logging road. Logging road bends left around the hillside, becoming grassy.
2.1	Cross gas line on top of Windfall Ridge to a column of rocks on the opposite side. This rock column marks the top of Robin Hollow Trail: angle to the left behind a pile of slash to a well-beaten woods trail. It will become an old grade soon.
2.95	After a brief, steep descent, turn right on Windfall Hollow Road, following Windfall Road past Mud Lick Hollow Trail, Tobe Hollow, Red Ridge Road, and Ash Tree Hollow Trail.
4.55	Turn right onto Green Hollow Trail (sign), a logging road that ascends the right (S) side of Green Hollow.
5.05	Bear right at a Y in the trail (the left branch descends to Green Hollow). The trail will bend left and cross a drainage, continuing along a moderate to fairly easy uphill grade.

5.7 Bear right at Y in logging road and rise to gas line (Windfall Ridge Trail) just above. Cross the gas line diagonally right (SE) and follow Jordan Hollow drainage down. You will pick up a grassy trail on the left side of Jordan Hollow as you descend. Watch for the trail carefully - if it disappears, look ahead for blowdowns that have been cut to clear the trail or for the trail opening through the trees.

6.55 A road cuts off right - continue downhill and cross Little Lyman Run along an iron footbridge. After passing two hunting camps ascend driveway to road.

6.7 Turn right on Junction Road (there is a sign for the Green Hollow Trail here also).

7.45 Turn right at intersection of Junction Road with Cross Fork Road. You can either follow Cross Fork Road 0.8 miles back to the bottom of Dry Hollow or follow the STS (which will necessitate crossing Cross Fork Creek on a two-strand wire bridge to get back to Dry Hollow).

To follow the STS route: After turning right on Cross Fork Road you will cross Little Lyman Run. Turn left onto a driveway across from the Ashcroft Hunting Lodge and follow it to the STS (orange blazes), which shares the driveway after the right bend.

8.45 STS turns left, crossing creek on wooden footbridge and following old B&S grade.

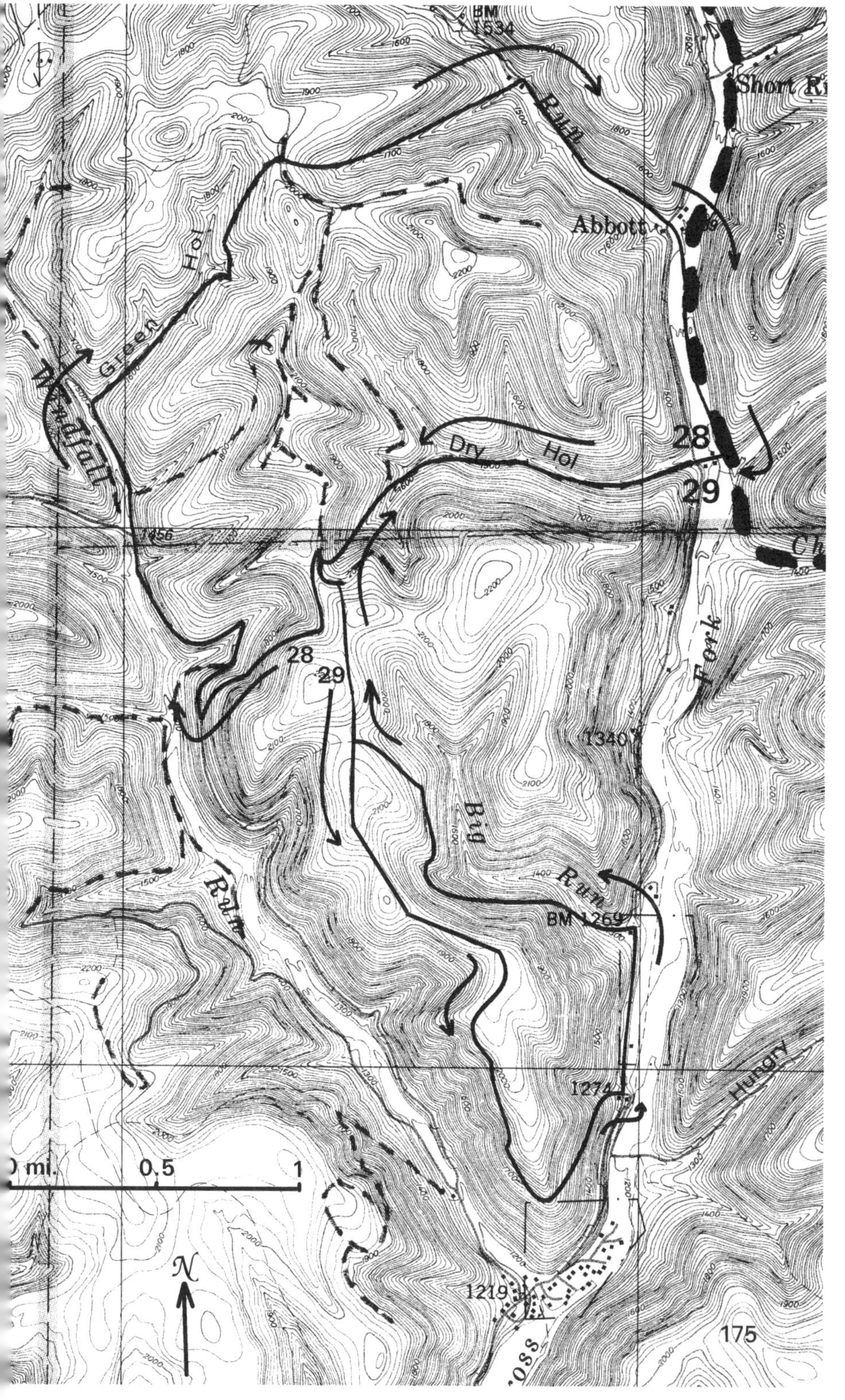
BM 1534
Short Ri
Run
Abbott
Green
Hol
Windfall
Dry
Hol
28
29
1456
28
29
Fork
1340
Big
Run
BM 1269
Run
1274
Hungry
0 mi.
0.5
1
N
1219
Cross

29 WINDFALL RIDGE

FEATURES: views, northern hardwoods
DISTANCE: 10.2 miles
TIME: 5.5 hours
ELEVATION: 1270 - 2160
TERRAIN: moderate old grades; some bushwhacking
BLAZES: none
PARKING: Cross Fork Road at bottom of Dry Hollow Trail
COMMENTS: Not hard to follow with average bushwhacking skills

In 1835, John Wallize, a Polish refugee, sold his shop in Philadelphia to hunt wolves in northern Pennsylvania. He hired a cook and two Indian guides, who guaranteed that the Windfall Run area in Potter County would yield at least 500 wolf hides, 100 black bears, and 100 fox pelts. After constructing a cabin nearby they proceeded to trap with great success.

As winter began, snow accumulated. In one particularly savage storm the snow kept falling, the wind picked up, and the cabin was buried in an avalanche. Trapped inside, their food supplies began to run low. Outside, hungry wolves eventually caught their scent and began to dig through the snow. Hearing the scratching (and, undoubtedly, realizing that the wolf was, in fact, at their door), the men inside took axes and hacked their way through a wall of the cabin, where the wolves then began to enter. The men, using their axes, killed hundreds of the hungry wolves, whose work had liberated them from their snowy prison. They left in the spring with almost a thousand wolf pelts and a thousand more of bear, otter, beaver, fox, and fisher, which proved to be a "windfall" for Wallize, who never trapped again.

Perhaps it is this story that gave Windfall Run its name, or maybe the name is derived from the appearance of the hollow, abundant with hemlock windfalls that allowed so many wolves to hide. On the opposite side of Windfall Ridge is Hungry Hollow, where a somewhat similar story provided the hollow its name.

The Wallize story originated among the Senecas of the

Cornplanter and Allegheny Reservations, but Wallize isn't mentioned among the great wolf hunters of Henry Shoemaker's 1917 classic, *Extinct Animals of Pennsylvania*. That book names Leroy Lyman, who killed 300 wolves in the period 1852 - 1865, as the greatest wolf hunter in Potter County. The last wolf in Potter County was killed about 1890.

There are only occasional claims today of people who have seen evidence of wolves in Potter County. Since the 1970s, however, the eastern coyote (or "Pennsylvania brush wolf") has called Potter County "home".

On this hike you may not see wolves, but you find clubmoss, a Lycopod, in the understory. The name "lycopod" means "wolf's foot" and is derived from its appearance.

You may also see one of Pennsylvania's (state) threatened species, the Eastern Wood Rat. There was a wood rat den along the Big Run Trail when I hiked it: a small cave above the trail with telltale scat piles outside.

TRAIL DESCRIPTION:

This route follows the Dry Hollow Trail (logging road) up the hollow from Cross Fork Road. Exit the logging road near the top of the hollow, bushwhacking along the left drainage to a grade that empties onto the gas line at the top of Windfall Ridge. Turn left, following the gas line to the top of Slip Hollow and bushwhack your way to a dug trail that descends to Cross Fork Road, which you follow N to the Big Run Trail. The Big Run Trail rises back to the gas line, where you then retrace your steps to the start.

Miles	Description
0	From Cross Fork Road at Yochum Run/Dry Hollow, follow the gated logging road with the sign for Dry Hollow Trail.
1.15	Turn left where logging road makes a sharp right turn in Dry Hollow. Up to now the road has been clear and gently rising - now the grade will become an intermittent trail following the drainage along a moderately steep grade.
1.35	Main drainage bends right. Trail disappears - follow main drainage.

1.6 As terrain levels (about 75 feet in elevation from the top of the hollow), look closely for faint remains of an old skid trail to the right, then bushwack your way to it - it will descend briefly, then tend uphill, becoming more evident.

1.8 Old woods grade enters onto a logging road. Logging road bends left around the hillside, becoming grassy.

2.1 Turn left, following gas line (Windfall Ridge Trail).

3.75 Near top of Slip Hollow the gas line will curve right. At the curve, approach the fenced area on the right. Between debris and the fenced area is an old woods lane, which crosses the flat diagonally right and then follows the ridge.

4.0 After crossing the edge of the ridge, trail will bend left, then descends along dug path.

4.55 After crossing the point of the hill, trail will become less distinct and more difficult to follow: look for blowdowns that have been cut and look ahead for the trail opening - the path will become easier to follow shortly as the hillside steepens and the trail becomes a dug grade once more.

5.0 Bear right at a fork in the trail, descending steeply past the camp below. Turn left on Cross Fork Road.

5.7 Turn left at sign for Big Run Trail on S side of Big Run, following Big Run upstream. The sign is just after the Old Reading Deer Club (square-hewn, brown log cabin on left).

5.85 Follow State Forest Boundary (white blazes) left, then turn right on old woods road, ascending left side of Big Run.

6.4 Continue straight ahead (right branch) at Y in trail.

7.5 After leveling and bending left, trail intersects Windfall Ridge Trail (gas line), where you turn right.

8.1 Turn right onto Dry Hollow Trail (opposite rock column on left) and retrace steps 2.1 miles to Cross Fork Road.

30 YOCHUM RUN

FEATURES: stream/forest environments, old graveyard
DISTANCE: 11.6 miles
TIME: 6 hours
ELEVATION: 1250 - 2130
TERRAIN: some steep grades; easy bushwhacking
BLAZES: orange (STS), otherwise none
PARKING: Rt. 144 just S of Oleona
COMMENTS: Not hard to follow with average bushwhacking skills

When the first settlers in Potter County arrived in 1808 - 1810 they found a road already built there. The road contained deep wheel ruts with trees from six to 12 inches diameter growing in them and it extended 130 miles from Warren to Renovo, PA. They called it the "Boon Road", because it proved a "boon" to them, saving them valuable time needed to build and prepare for winter.

Robert L. Lyman, Sr. (*Amazing Indeed - Strange Events in the Black Forest,* 1973) hypothesizes that the road was cut in 1756 by a French expedition of 800 men with four light cannons to attack the English at Fort Augusta (Sunbury, PA). After scouting the fort and deciding that it was too strong for them, they threw the cannon into a pit (called "Cannon Hole") and retreated to Canada. Lyman states that some believe this only as tradition, but the story appears in an 1885 edition of *Otzinachson History of the West Branch,* by J.F. Meginnes, and a July 13, 1757, letter written by Marquis de Vaudreuil mentions the aborted expedition.

The trail down Cherry Run follows part of the "Boon Road".

TRAIL DESCRIPTION:

This route follows a driveway from Rt. 144 in Oleona past an old graveyard and across Little Kettle Creek. At the base of the mountain turn left on Miller Run Trail to Sawmill Run. The Sawmill Run Trail ascends the south side of the hollow. Near the top a short bushwhack and a logging road will bring you to Hungry Hollow

Road. Turn left on Hungry Hollow Road to the orange-blazed STS, which will bring you down Cherry Hollow to Yochum Run. After crossing Yochum Run exit the STS and follow a logging road that gently ascends the north side of Yochum Run. Exit the logging road before it turns up the third hollow, bushwhacking your way and using an old railroad grade to Yaudes Hollow, where an old logging road along the right side will rise to Hungry Hollow Road. After crossing Hungry Hollow Road, bushwack your way down the Miller Run drainage and follow the Miller Run Trail back to the start.

Miles	Description
0	From Route 144 in Oleona, just north of the bridge over Kettle Creek, follow driveway from west side past graveyard. This driveway is below gift shop, next to a fence, and is marked with a "walk-in fishing only" sign.
0.2	Cross Little Kettle Creek on wooden footbridge and turn left onto Miller Trail at the base of the mountain.
0.5	Trail bends right up Sawmill Run. Cross over to left (S) side of Sawmill Run where grades and skid trails will allow you to rise along stream. In about 0.25 mi. You will pick up a fairly well-defined skid trail along this side.
1.85	Y in skid trail: continue along path parallel to Sawmill Run.
2.35	Trail bears left at fork in Sawmill Run, then crosses small hollow on left.
2.6	Trail may disappear - follow flat along left side of hollow.
2.75	Trail crosses to right side of left branch of Sawmill Run and disappears again. Follow drainage to logging road, turning right and follow it to Hungry Hollow Road.
3.2	Turn left on Hungry Hollow Road, passing clear-cuts.
3.7	Turn right at orange-blazed STS (sign), descending Cherry Run along old logging road.

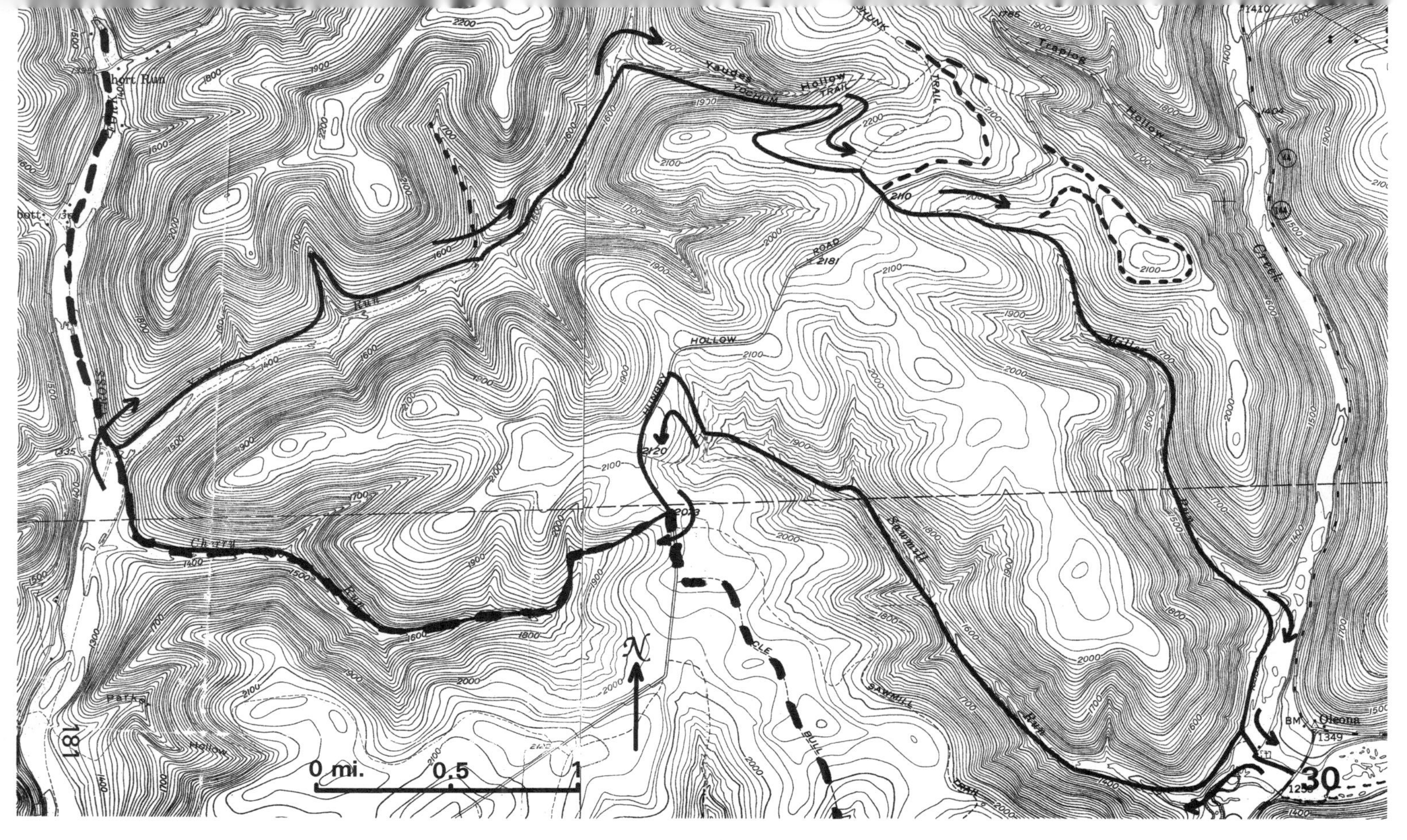

Trapiog Hollow
Yochum Hollow Trail
Creek
Miller Run
Hungry Hollow
Road
Sawmill Run
Sawmill Trail
Bull
Short Run
Cross
Oleona
30
0 mi.
0.5
1

4.3 Logging road crosses to right side of Cherry Run, ending shortly. STS exits right, leaving logging road at the crossing and following skid trail.

5.2 STS crosses Yochum Run. Turn right, leaving STS, and follow logging road on N side of Yochum Run.

6.8 Where logging road begins to bend left up the third hollow, descend to bottom of Yochum Run. Cross to right side of stream and follow old railroad grade.

7.15 Cross small hollow on right, then follow grade to left side of Yochum Run and back to the right side again.

7.45 As the forest on the right side begins to thin out approaching Yaudes Hollow, veer off somewhat to the right, rising slightly. If you don't, then small beech trees will overrun trail and force you to turn right, rising more steeply.

7.55 Turn right up Yaudes Hollow from open area, then turn right again shortly on ferny logging road that rises fairly steeply on right side of Yaudes Hollow.

8.15 Take right branch of Y in trail, which switches back right at another Y just ahead. An old grade entering from acute left will also join it shortly.

8.4 Old grades comes in at acute left and slope becomes easier and begins to bend left.

8.8 Intersection of logging roads. Bear right and cross Hungry Hollow Road, following the Miller Run drainage.

9.4 Cross to left side of hollow after first hollow enters on left. Here pick up a worn skid trail, following it down Miller Run. After trail crosses Miller Run (in 1.25 mi.) it will bend right and parallel Little Kettle Creek.

11.4 Trail descends to bottom by hemlock where you joined at m.p. 0.2 above. Exit left and retrace steps to Route 144.

31 OLE BULL STATE PARK

FEATURES: forest variety
DISTANCE: 3.2 miles
TIME: 2 hours
ELEVATION: 1240 - 1500
TERRAIN: moderate paths
BLAZES: orange (STS) and yellow/brown plastic markers
PARKING: Ole Bull State Park
COMMENTS: Like most State Park trails, the route is easily followed, well-marked, and has strategically placed benches and stairs to help the average American park visitor

From 1843 to 1845 Ole Bornemann Bull, the famous Norwegian violinist, toured the U.S., where he captivated audiences with his dramatic, intense style. He was equally captivated by the New World and returned in 1852 after closing his National Theater at Bergen, Norway. Although the theater closed after only two years, Henrik Ibsen, the famous playwright, was brought to prominence through it.

In 1853 he purchased 11,144 acres in the Kettle Creek area for $10,388 from Williamsport businessman, John F. Cowan. Ole Bull intended to establish a Norwegian colony in America, and almost 150 came and settled at New Bergen (Carter Camp), Oleona, New Norway (1 mile south of Oleona), and Valhalla (Ole Bull State Park). Unfortunately Cowan had withheld 658 acres, containing most of the tillable land, from the property sale. Most of the new colony was with virgin hemlock on steep slopes. Instead of cutting the timber and planting crops, the colonists utilized valuable time removing the roots before cultivating the land. The colony failed, despite the financial assistance that Ole Bull gave it, and after a year most of the colonists relocated to Minnesota and Wisconsin.

With his "castle" uncompleted at Valhalla and his funds dwindling, Ole Bull sold the land back to Cowan for the original purchase price and returned to Norway in 1857. His "castle" was sold at public sale to Dr. Edward Joerg, whom Ole Bull had persuaded to move from Illinois to the ill-fated colony. Joerg used the remains to construct his own home nearby. Joerg's home burned in 1923, and the foundation was used by the state to construct the forest foremen's residence in 1929.

Local legend says that the French army marched past this site a century before Ole Bull tried to settle here. Indians ambushed them, and their fife player was mortally wounded and left to die. Some say you can hear his fife in the late evening when the air is quiet, and that Ole Bull was captivated by its mournful tune.

Ole Bull State Park contains 117 acres and the remains of his unfinished "castle". Bring a tree identification book for this hike to see how many different types of trees you pass along the way.

TRAIL DESCRIPTION:

This route follows the yellow/brown plastic markers over a series of easy/moderate grades and paths up Ole Bull Run, then returns on the orange-blazed STS, with a side trip to the castle ruins. An optional hike on the Beaver Haven Nature Trail is also included.

Miles	Description
0	From parking lot on W side of Kettle Creek, head NW on STS and quickly turn right onto Daugherty Loop Trail, marked with a yellow hiker symbol and arrows on brown plastic. The trail follows a fairly even grade past mixed hardwoods, mixed conifers, Norway spruce, and floodplain.
0.25	Trail bends left, then turns sharp left onto old grade, ascending past dense Norway spruce and mixed hardwoods.
0.6	Park bench along trail. Trail climbs stairs and follows footpath left through Norway spruce, then steepens briefly after bending sharp right at a second park bench.
0.7	Trail rolls after third park bench and is steep or washed out in sections, passing through Norway spruce to the left and a beech-maple-birch forest to the right.
1.05	After leveling and passing a fourth park bench, Daugherty Loop Trail bears left at Y.

1.2 Trail crosses Ole Bull Run on wooden bridge and rises steeply to the STS, which it follows downstream.

1.8 At sign and bench, leave STS, bearing right on trail to "castle ruins". This trail loops around a knoll, past a vista and the "ruins". After retracing your steps, the STS will bring you back to the parking lot.

2.1 From the parking lot, cross road bridge to S side of Kettle Creek, then right at park sign for Beaver Haven Nature Trail. This trail parallels Kettle Creek.

2.55 After crossing wooden footbridge with handrails, the trail splits. Go right, paralleling Kettle Creek. The trail will bend left, looping back through a pine/spruce plantation and past a beaver pond before returning to this spot.

2.85 After recrossing footbridge with handrails, retrace path back to road in 0.35 miles.

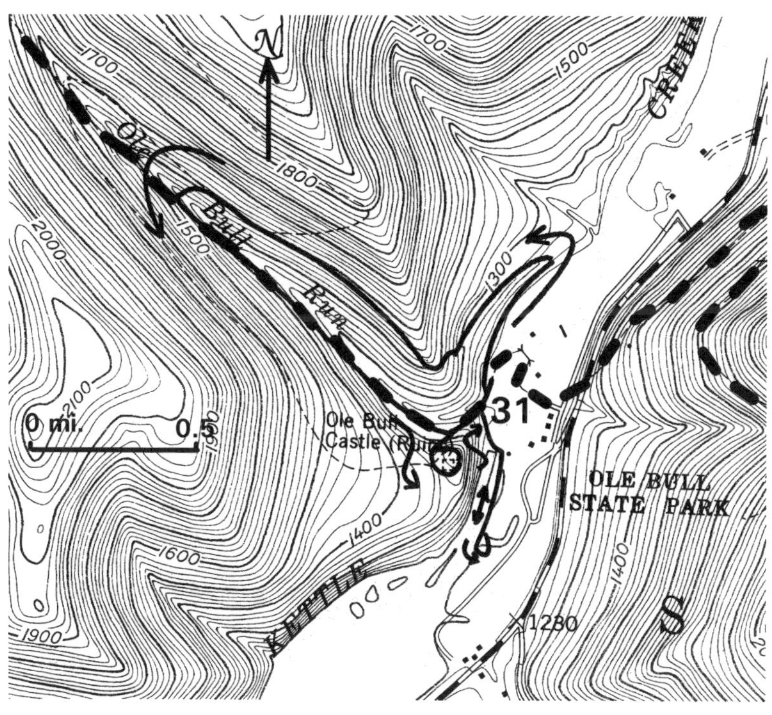

32 BERGSTRESSER HOLLOW

FEATURES: forest types
DISTANCE: 9.1 miles
TIME: 6 hours
ELEVATION: 1120 - 2120
TERRAIN: moderate/steep paths; some bushwhacking & stream crossing
BLAZES: none
PARKING: Fish Commission parking lot on S side of Kettle Creek bridge, S of Ole Bull State Park
COMMENTS: Easily followed with basic map reading/bushwhacking skills

---

The Oleona Railroad was built in 1901 by the Goodyears for the Lackawanna Lumber Company, which timbered the Kettle/Little Kettle Creek area. The railroad was torn up in 1912, and this hike uses part of the old grade along Kettle Creek.

This hike traverses a variety of forest types. Along Kettle Creek are pine and hemlock, wetlands, and a floodplain forest. Bergstresser Hollow has wetlands and a hemlock swamp near the bottom, is predominantly northern hardwoods at the bottom and mixed oak forest with a mountain laurel under story near the top. Dry Hollow Ridge is predominantly mixed oak with mountain laurel, rhododendron, and some sections of birch. The Tubb Hollow Trail has pine/hemlock near the top, then descends through mixed oaks on one side and northern hardwoods on the other.

TRAIL DESCRIPTION:

This route follows an old grade along Kettle Creek to the bottom of Bergstresser Hollow. A skid trail and a short, steep bushwhack near the top gets you up Bergstresser Hollow to a logging road and the Dry Hollow Ridge Trail, which rolls across the top of the plateau (the logging road parallels it to the S a short distance away). Turn left at the gas line and left again along the logging road to the top of Tubb

Hollow. Descend Tubb Hollow along a moderately steep skid trail back to Bergstresser Hollow and to Route 144.

Miles	Description
0	From PA Fish & Boat Commission parking area (S side of Route 144 Kettle Creek bridge below Ole Bull State Park) follow path N along old grade paralleling Kettle Creek. The path may become intermittent, so if you lose it continue along a straight line halfway between Kettle Creek and base of the mountain. The State Forest boundary will parallel it to the right. This section will pass through pine/hemlock in the wetter areas, northern hardwoods along the mountainside, and wetland environments.
0.9	After Rebel Hollow (on left) an old logging road will converge with grade from acute left.
1.0	Cross Pine Tree Hollow. The rock outcrop here is thin-bedded sandstone, heavily iron-stained, with some brachiopod fossils. The grade will become a path.
1.5	Path parallels a back channel where Kettle Creek approaches on right - here follow a steep path rising to the left and join old skid trail up Bergstresser Hollow.
2.1	Just before a small hollow enters on the right, cross to right side of Bergstresser Hollow and follow old trail about 30 ft. above bottom of hollow, continuing up Bergstresser Hollow along moderate grade through mostly northern hardwoods.
3.1	Trail crosses hollow entering on right, continuing up left branch. On the right are mixed oaks; to left is red maple , which will change to aspen-birch forest. After crossing large blowdown ahead you may need to cross over to the left side of the hollow, following skid trails.
3.5	Cross rocky, wet area, veering off to the left. Trail crosses a gully and a small area of mountain laurel. When mountain laurel becomes thick ahead, bushwack left from bottom of steep area to logging road above.

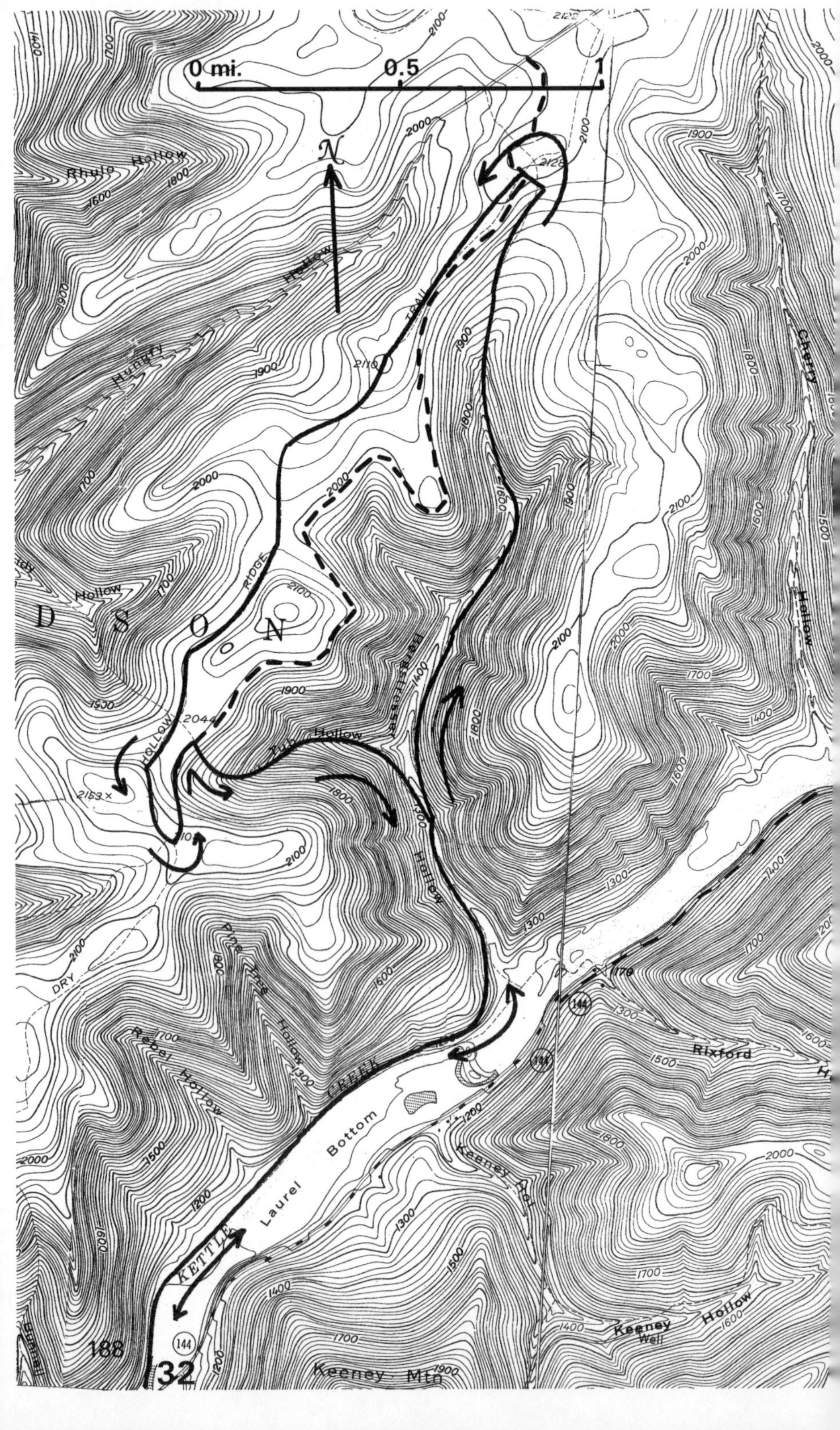
0 mi.
0.5
1
N
Rhulo Hollow
Hungry Hollow
Hollow
TRAIL
RIDGE
D S O N
Bergstresser Hollow
Tub Hollow
Hollow
Pine Tree Hollow
Rebel Hollow
DRY
KETTLE CREEK
Laurel Bottom
Keeney Hol
Rixford
Cherry Hollow
Keeney Well
Keeney Hollow
Keeney Mtn
144
32

3.95 Turn right on logging road, then turn left (SW) in about 0.1 mi. onto the Dry Hollow Ridge Trail, which will pass through white birch and mountain laurel, then open woods of red oak, maple, ash, moss and clubmoss.

[Alternate Route: turn left on logging road and follow it 2 miles to Tubb Hollow Trail, m.p. 6.3 below. There is a plateau vista 0.6 miles before the Tubb Hollow Trail.]

5.1 Trail tunnels through rhododendron, then back into open woods, mostly red oak.

5.75 Surveyors' tape marks Cassidy Hollow Trail crossing. Trail rises, and forest becomes more beech and ash, less red oak. As trail rounds left side of knoll, mountain laurel reappears with chestnut oak on the knoll, with white birch to the left.

6.05 Turn left at gas line and left again at intersecting logging road, following it N.

6.3 Turn right onto Tubb Hollow Trail (white paint on trees mark Tubb Hollow and Cassidy Hollow Trails here). You will pass through hemlocks along a path at a right angle to the logging road and along the left side of Tubb Hollow.

6.9 After descending steeply on the left, cross to right side of Tubb Hollow, descending along skid trail. The left side of Tubb Hollow is mixed oak, the right northern hardwoods.

7.1 Tubb Hollow Trail meets Bergstresser Hollow, which you use to retrace your route to Kettle Creek, then follow Kettle Creek back to your vehicle in 2 miles.

33 HOPPER HOLLOW

FEATURES: forest environments
DISTANCE: 6.5 miles
TIME: 4 hours
ELEVATION: 1250 - 1990
TERRAIN: easy/moderate grades; some bushwhacking
BLAZES: none
PARKING: Rt. 144 at Hopper Run Trail S of Oleona
COMMENTS: Easily followed with basic bushwhacking/map reading skills

The northern hardwood forest, the dominant forest type along this hike, is known for its spectacular fall colors, which is due to reduced chlorophyll production, a function of lower temperature and sunlight angle. Chlorophyll overpowers other pigments, and when chlorophyll production ceases these other pigments become evident, giving leaves their fall colors.

As summer progresses and leaves age, their ability to produce certain hormones is reduced, triggering the movement of nutrients out of the leaf and into storage in the branches and trunk. A layer of corky cells develops where the leaf's stalk joins the twig, walling the leaf off from the tree. Deprived of water, leaf cell sap thickens with sugars. Depending on tree species, various pigments (carotenes, xanthophylls, and anthocyanidins) begin to show through and react with the sugars trapped in the leaf.

The reds and purples of maples, sassafras, sumac, black gum and scarlet oak are due to anthocyanin. The yellows and oranges of beech, birch, some maples, sycamore, poplar, hickory, and honey locust are due to xanthophylls and carotenes.

As the leaf dries out, the cells break down and the colors fade. The leaf breaks off from the stem and falls to the ground, where decomposition adds nutrients to the forest soil.

TRAIL DESCRIPTION:

This route follows the Hopper Run Trail to Twelve Mile Road, and the road north to the Pritchard Trail. At the bottom of Pritchard Hollow a series of skid trails, logging roads, and an old railroad grade parallel Kettle Creek to Route 144.

Miles	Description
0	From Route 144 in Oleona, across from Tom & Kathy's Bed & Breakfast, follow worn trail E from Hopper Run Trail sign along right (S) side of Hopper Run. The trail quickly crosses into State Forest lands.
0.75	Trail descends to Hopper Run, bending right. Ahead a hollow will enter on left at meadow.
1.3	Path rises right to field with gas well. On the other side of the clearing is a gas right-of-way that rises steeply to the right, a gas well maintenance road (which provides a dry route to the top of Hopper Hollow) and a worn path off to the left. Follow the worn path down to Hopper Run, where it crosses to the left side.
1.8	Go right at fork in stream bed.
1.9	Turn left at gas well maintenance road, following road uphill. This road will join a logging road shortly.
2.25	Turn left on Twelve Mile Road.
3.4	Turn left onto Pritchard Trail (unmarked). The Pritchard Trail is located 0.45 miles after the Twelve Mile/Whitman Road intersection at a sharp right bend in Twelve Mile Road. There is a gated Forestry road 50 ft after the Pritchard Trail and on the right side of the road. The Pritchard Trail is a worn path that will begin to descend the hollow shortly.
3.6	Bend left at fork in trail, leaving worn path and following old grade that follows hillside along a moderate descent.

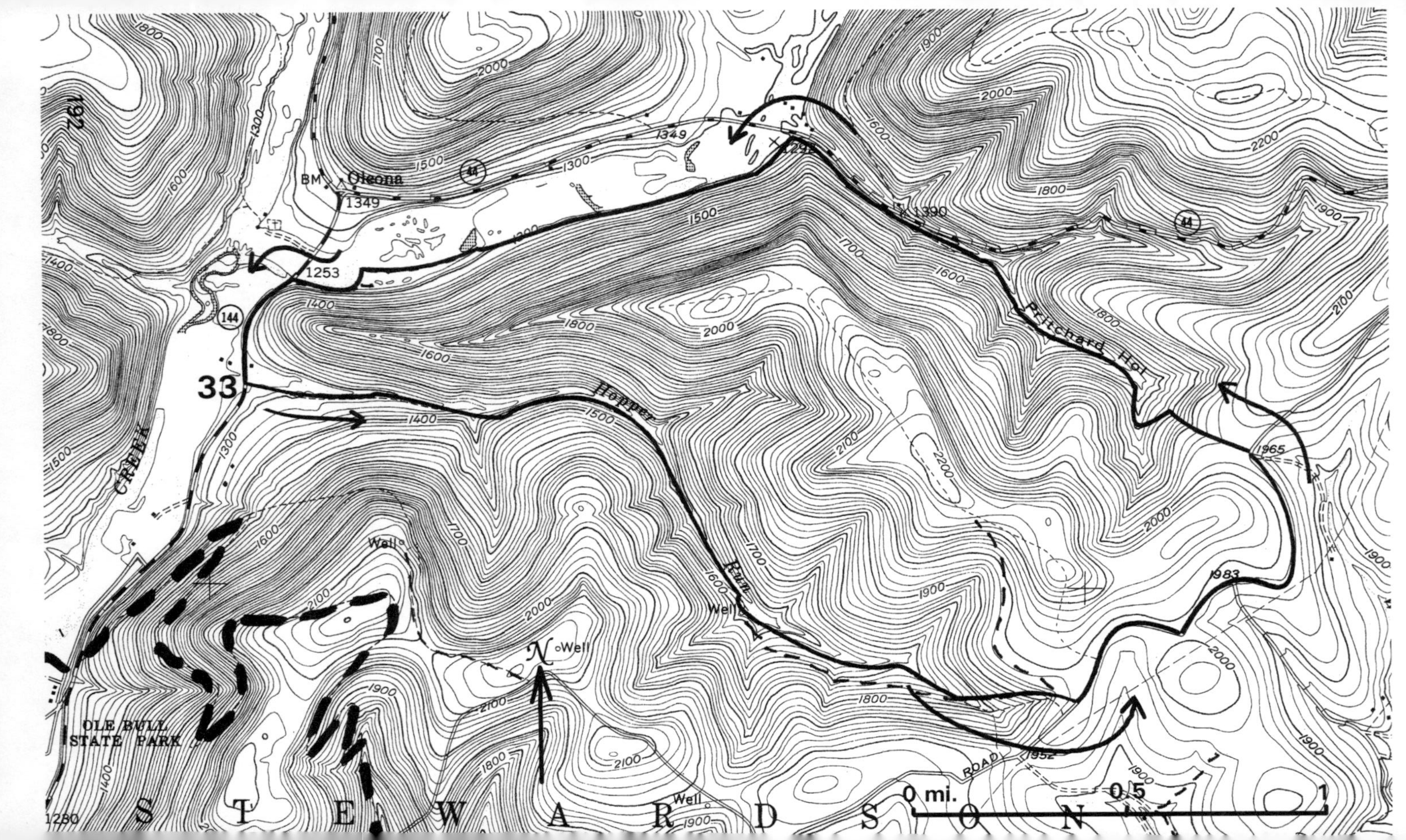

BM
Oleona
1349
1253
144
44
33
CREEK
Hopper
Run
Pritchard Hol
1390
1965
1983
1952
ROAD
Well
OLE BULL
STATE PARK
0 mi.
0.5
1
S T E W A R D S O N

3.8 Bend left at Y intersection, circling hill (the right branch follows the bottom of the hollow).

4.05 Trail descends to rejoin worn path at bottom of hollow where hollow comes in on left. The hollow parallels Route 44 on the opposite side of the stream.

4.4 After crossing a gully you will see a sign below right for the Pritchard Trail. On oppose side of Route 44 is "Hemlock Lodge". Here continue to follow the grade parallel to Route 44 as trail rolls uphill.

4.55 Bear right at Y, following more worn branch downhill. Bear right also at next Y ahead.

4.8 Trail bends left, descending toward Route 44, but before reaching road it bends left and turns left on grassy logging road, rising moderately.

4.95 Logging road meets another grade at a hairpin turn - go right, descending and crossing Forestry boundary in 0.2 mi.

5.55 After descending to bottom of hillside you will find an old railroad grade off to the right. Follow this old grade, continuing along a SW route and passing pond, spruce, and pines along mowed grade past private cabins.

5.95 Bend left, following Kettle Creek along driveway where road splits. The driveway will bend right at base of mountain.

6.25 Turn left at route 144, arriving back at Hopper Run Trail in 0.25 miles.

34 SPOOK HOLLOW

FEATURES: Spook Hollow, views, old railroad grade
DISTANCE: 13.8 miles
TIME: 8 hours
ELEVATION: 1220 - 2180
TERRAIN: easy/moderate grades
BLAZES: orange (STS), blue (North Link Trail), otherwise none
PARKING: Ole Bull State Park
COMMENTS: Easily followed

Plantations usually consist of one species of evergreen planted in a block of closely-spaced columns and rows. As they grow, they block sunlight from reaching the forest floor and the lower branches, which begin to die and self-prune. This results in tall, straight, and relatively knot-free trees when they are cut for timber. Tree diameter grows only slowly.

Before the region was timbered in the mid-to-late 1800s, the dense forest canopy also prevented sunlight from reaching the forest floor, and the wilderness was known by Native Americans as "The Shades of Death". Early pioneers called it "The Black Forest", and most avoided this howling wilderness, with its wolves, panthers, and bears, as much as possible.

Spook Hollow is a pine and spruce plantation that is probably only a "shadow" of the black "forest primeval" that confronted the early pioneers in Potter County. Certainly, they did not encounter Norway Spruce, an introduced species, nor did they have the Susquehannock Trail Club's Tom Fitzgerald and his "Welfare Hollow Sign Shop" (as a forester he was one of the few working people in his Potter County neighborhood) to guide them along in the forest and to help them avoid potential danger. Heed the advice of the signs or recite the inscribed rune while you are walking and Spook Hollow should be a pleasant experience.

A word of caution here: the most dreaded forest animal is the hide-behind. They most frequently inhabit the darker sections of the regional forests and have a well-documented reputation for following people in the woods. No one has ever seen one because they are always hiding behind trees, rocks, and thickets, but the panic they induce as you keep looking back is quite real. Personally, I have found that they will stop following you if you ignore them or if you avoid being the last hiker in line. They are distant cousins of the hide-beyonds, who watch campers at night from just beyond the light of the campfire.

TRAIL DESCRIPTION

This route follows the orange-blazed STS from Ole Bull State Park to Impson Hollow, Twelve Mile Road, through Spook Hollow to Big Springs Road. Here blue-blazed North Link Trail is followed into Big Trestle Hollow to where it crosses the hollow. There the old railroad grade, a trail, and a driveway will bring you to Twelve Mile Road, and the Hopper Run Trail returns you to Rt. 144.

Miles	Description
0	From Southern Gateway parking area at Ole Bull State Park, follow STS SE across route 144, ascending hillside in a series of switchbacks.
1.25	Vista of Ole Bull State Park.
1.75	Trail begins descent into Impson Hollow, crossing grassy logging road, switching back several times during descent.
3.15	After passing leased hunting camp, STS turns left, ascending Impson Hollow. Grade becomes more trail-like after passing hollow on left, passing pine plantation. The trail becomes steeper after the pine plantation.
4.1	STS levels and turns left on Twelve Mile Road, passing gas line road on left.
4.25	STS turns right at grassy lane, then turns right (S) off grassy road into Spook Hollow, passing through plantation. The STS will then cross a gas line and upper Big Spring Branch of Young Woman's Creek. The trail will become a grassy, ferned road in a clearing.

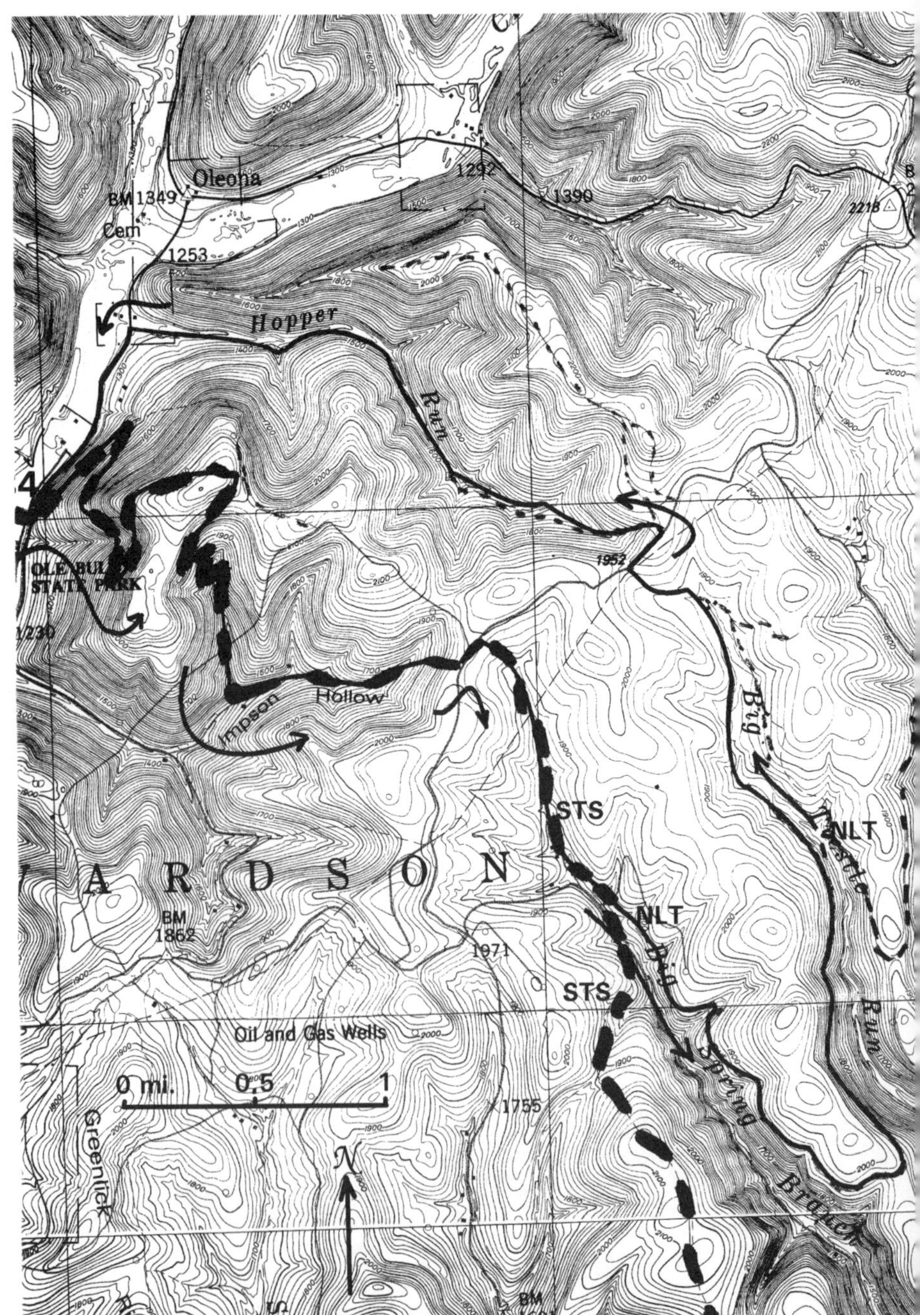
Oleona
BM 1349
Cem
1253
1292
1390
2218
Hopper
Run
1952
OLE BULL STATE PARK
1230
Impson
Hollow
STS
NLT
Big
Trestle
ARDSON
BM 1862
1971
Spring
Branch
Run
Oil and Gas Wells
0 mi.
0.5
1
1755
Greenlick
BM

5.15 After crossing Big Spring Branch, STS exits left, leaving gas line, and follows driveway past Big Springs Hunting Camp. The trail bears left at driveway Y, then exits left off driveway and onto old railroad grade.

5.5 At Big Springs Road cross and leave the STS, following blue rectangles of the North Link Trail through Norway spruce along old grade.

5.85 North Link Trail crosses small hollow, bearing right on old railroad grade (North Bend & Kettle Creek RR) on other side, continuing to parallel Big Springs Branch through predominantly oak forest. North Link Trail will bend into Big Trestle Hollow.

9.0 North Link Trail exits old railroad grade on right. Here leave the North Link Trail, continuing along old railroad grade.

9.55 Cross cindered access road for electric line.

9.75 The grade becomes a trail, which you follow past a hunting camp (Sydertsville Club), then follow driveway.

10.25 Pass Big Trestle Trail sign.

10.5 After crossing gas line, turn right onto Twelve Mile Road.

10.65 Turn left onto grassy logging road at sign for Hopper Run Trail. Bear left at the Y intersection ahead.

11.0 Turn right at Hopper Run Hollow crossing, following right side of Hopper Run Hollow.

11.4 After worn path crosses to left side of Hopper Run, follow it up to clearing for gas well (the grassy logging road you were previously following ends at this gas well). On opposite side of clearing follow worn trail down to Hopper Run and follow it along the left side of Hopper Run.

12.9 Turn left on route 144, following it 0.9 miles back to parking area.

35 SPRING BROOK

FEATURES: old railroad grade; stream environments
DISTANCE: 9.6 miles
TIME: 5.5 hours
ELEVATION: 1440 - 2190
TERRAIN: moderate grades; some bushwhacking & stream crossings
BLAZES: orange (STS), otherwise none
PARKING: Intersection of Twelve Mile, Big Spring, and Spring Brook Roads
COMMENTS: Easily followed with minimal bushwhacking/map reading skills

In 1969/70 the oak leaf roller began to defoliate oaks in the southern section of the Susquehannock State Forest. In 1975 extensive oak mortalities occurred due to this persistent infestation. There is a sign near Spring Brook and Twelve Mile Roads intersection commemorating the nearby planting of the 100,000,000th seedling in the State Forest System to replace these oaks.

Among other insects that have affected the forest are the fall cankerworm (mid-1960s), the elm spanworm (1993/94), thrips, which attack hardwoods, and the gypsy moth (1990/91), which attack oaks. These have been fought with chemicals, fungal agents, and other insects. Sometimes these efforts have been very successful, but at other times the insect infestations are corrected by natural cycles (overcrowding, disease, and predator population increases). Sometimes little can be done to address the problem: chestnut trees have almost vanished from the forest due to blight, elms are gone due to Dutch Elm disease, and beech trees are dying to beech scale disease, caused by an insect and fungus.

Replanting programs are used to address some of these problems and to help the forest become reestablished. Between 1910 and 1924 more trees were planted in the Susquehannock State Forest than in any other in Pennsylvania.

TRAIL DESCRIPTION:

This route follows Big Spring Road to the orange-blazed STS, which follows a route south to Fork Hill Road. Whyland Road, a logging road, descends to Twelve Mile Road at a driveway and old railroad grade up Spring Brook, crossing the stream several times. Some short bushwhacking is necessary before following a gas maintenance road back to Spring Brook Road.

Miles	Description
0	From intersection of Twelve Mile, Spring Brook, and Big Spring Roads, follow Big Spring Road NE and E past gas line crossing, past driveway (left) and gas line road (on left you may see orange blazes for STS here, but stay on road).
0.8	Pass green hunting camp on Big Spring Road, joining orange-blazed STS. In 0.1 mi. The STS will turn right, leaving Big Spring Road - watch blazes at turn. After ascending the STS will turn left onto the Hartman Trail, a former North Bend & Kettle Creek Railroad cut-and-fill grade.
1.4	STS leaves Hartman Trail (old railroad grade), following path to top of cut, then turning left (SE) onto Rattlesnake Trail, which rises at a moderate to steep rate.
2.95	Atop the ridge, STS crosses Wildcat Trail (South Link Trail).
3.75	STS turns right (SW) onto Fork Hill Road (Forestry gate limits road traffic).
3.9	Turn right off road, leaving STS and following logging road (Whyland Road) down Wildcat Hollow.
5.6	Whyland Road meets Twelve Mile Road at Forestry gate. Turn left and follow Twelve Mile Road S.
5.85	Near bottom of Wildcat Hollow turn right onto driveway, crossing footbridge and picking up grade just past the outhouse along right side of Spring Brook. In about 0.5 mi. the grade will begin to cross back-and-forth along stream.

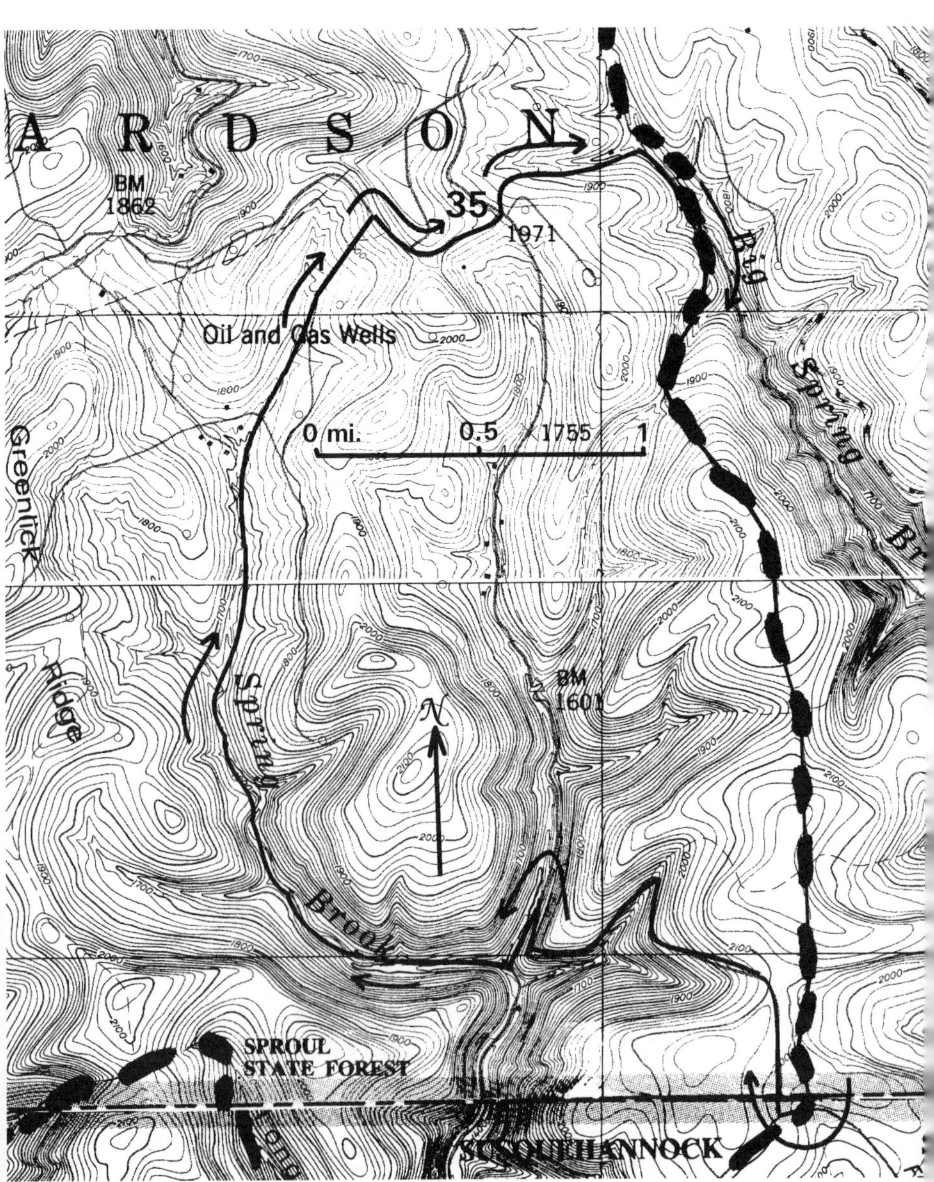
A R D S O N
BM 1862
35
1971
Oil and Gas Wells
0 mi. 0.5 1755 1
Greenlick Ridge
Spring Brook
Big Spring Br
BM 1601
SPROUL STATE FOREST
SUSQUEHANNOCK

6.75 Hollow enters on left (a small grade ascends this hollow) - continue along the main branch of Spring Brook.

7.05 After old grade crosses back-and-forth again, a hollow will enter on the right - bend left along the main branch through open area. Trail becomes an easily-followed grade along the right side of Spring Brook.

7.45 After crossing to left then back to right side of stream, the grade passes Poplar Hollow on the left (there is a grassy grade up Poplar Hollow) and enters white pines.

7.75 After exiting pines the grade will cross to the left, passing pond on left and a spring/seep on right. The grade will begin crossing back-and-forth along Spring Brook again.

8.05 About 200 yds. before a red hunting camp on the left turn right, following an old trail that leaves the grade and crosses open area and past a brown hunting camp.

8.2 Cross gas line and descend to Spring Brook, rejoining grade which will cross a road used to service gas wells. The grade will continue switching sides along Spring Brook, passing marshy areas.

8.6 At Y in stream, take the left branch. Just ahead the stream splits again and the old grade you have been following will disappear. Rise along the right side and join gas service road, continuing uphill.

9.1 Turn right on Spring Brook Road and return to intersection In about 1/2 mile.

36 WELCH RIDGE

FEATURES: forest types
DISTANCE: 5.9 miles
TIME: 3.5 hours
ELEVATION: 1600 - 2140
TERRAIN: moderate/steep grades; some bushwhacking
BLAZES: none
PARKING: Rt. 44 at Klondike Trail between Twelve Mile and Francis Branch Roads
COMMENTS: Not too hard to follow with map reading/ bushwhacking skills.

The vast majority of hiking in the Susquehannock State Forest is in a northern hardwood forest - the Tiadaghton State Forest to the southeast is mostly mixed oak. This particular hike is through a transition area, so it passes through both northern hardwoods with little under story and mixed oaks with a mountain laurel under story. In addition there are wetlands (streams, wet meadows) and a pine/ hemlock ravine.

This area, called the "Black Forest", was known for its high quality white pine, prized for masts on 19th century wooden ships. A "Number One" spar was straight, free of large knots, at least 92 feet long, and more than 18 inches in diameter at the top end.

The spars were dragged in winter to a landing and were tied together in a raft, which was steered downriver by a rudder attached to the end of a large pole operated by a pilot, a steersman, and a crew of oarsmen. On some of the rafts, called "shanty rafts", were cabins that housed the men as they floated downriver.

There are two very large pines along this hike which might have served as a spar on a ship. Of course, back in those days spar pines were more plentiful, but these will give you some idea of the magnificence of the pine of this bygone era.

TRAIL DESCRIPTION:

This route follows the Klondike Trail down and up two hollows (fairly steep) to the Welch Ridge Trail, a woods road and a skid trail that, with a short bushwack, returns you to Klondike Ridge and an old grade and driveway that will bring you back to Route 44.

Miles	Description
0	From route 44 follow Klondike Trail (sign) NE. The trail will quickly begin descending along a moderate grade, passing from an oak to a northern hardwood forest.
0.4	After crossing to left side of hollow, Klondike Trail will cross bottom of Francis Branch. Keep a sharp eye for the trail as it rises through the hemlocks on the other side. As it rises the forest will change from pine/hemlock ravine to an oak type, then to an aspen-birch type.
0.7	Continue straight ahead at old trail (Klondike Ridge Trail) intersection.
0.9	After crossing top of ridge the trail will begin to descend more steeply as it bends left through oak and then through northern hardwoods.
1.3	After crossing bottom of hollow Klondike Trail rises steeply.
1.6	The Klondike Trail deadends at an old woods road (Welch Ridge Trail). Turn right, following Welch Ridge Trail SE through oak forest.
2.0	The old woods road ends but Welch Ridge Trail continues for a few more paces before making a sharp right turn. The turn is difficult to see, so begin looking for it on your right just after the woods road ends. The route follows a skid trail down into a hollow past a couple of very large pines (3.5 ft. diameter, rising 40 - 50 ft. before branching) that allow you to imagine just how large the pine used for spar masts must have been like when they were cut more than 125 years ago.

2.25	At bottom of hollow continue following a path along the right side as you head upstream.
2.6	Pass intersection of Klondike Trail (m.p. 1.3 above). Just beyond this intersection cross to the left side of the stream and turn left up a side hollow. There is no real grade up this hollow, so just follow drainage as it rises through pine-hemlock to the left and northern hardwoods to the right.
3.2	At the top of the hollow you will intersect an old woods road. Turn left onto it - it will soon make a sharp right turn, taking you past the Klondike Ridge Trail (easy to miss), then paralleling the Francis Branch and passing leased camps.
3.85	Grade joins driveway from leased camps on left and rises to route 44.
5.3	Turn left on route 44 back to Klondike Trail sign in 0.6 miles.

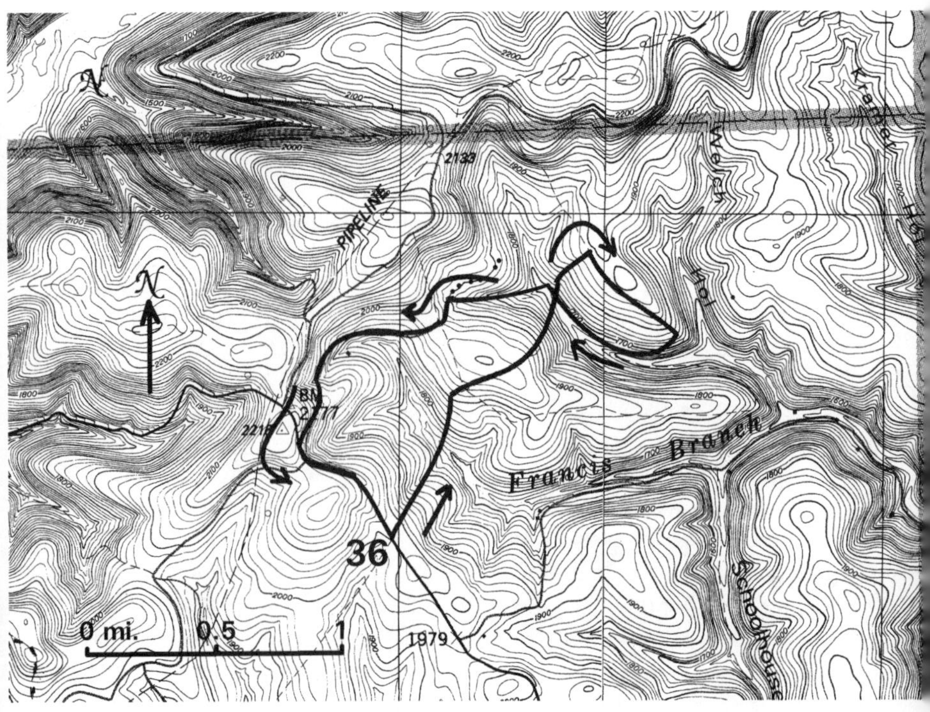

37 LEFT BRANCH - YOUNG WOMAN'S CREEK

FEATURES: forest/stream environments
DISTANCE: 11.6 miles
TIME: 6.5 hours
ELEVATION: 1260 - 2160
TERRAIN: moderate/steep grades; some bushwhacking & stream crossings
BLAZES: orange (STS), red (Donut Hole), and some salmon (Ingram Hollow); otherwise none
PARKING: Greenlick Road near Big Greenlick Trail/bridge crossing and Ingram Trail
COMMENTS: Good map reading/bushwhacking skills will be helpful. Crossing Young Woman's Creek and Greenlick Run will be difficult in higher water.

The southern portion of the STS lies over the Leidy Gas Field, a long gas reservoir that stretches NE-SW in a thin band near the top of the plateau south of Kettle Creek. In 1934 gas was discovered in the 35 - 40 ft. thick Oriskany Sandstone formation 7500 ft. below the surface. In 1951 the largest producing gas well east of the Mississippi (150 million cu. ft. per day) was discovered here. The gas reservoir has been pumped dry, but today Consolidated Gas's Greenlick gas pumping station is part of the natural gas distribution network: gas pumped from wells in the south is stored in the old gas field as it is pumped to upstate New York. The gas field gives important clues about the early environment in this area (see Geology Chapter for details).

In fast-flowing, cold streams plants and animals must be anchored to avoid being flushed downstream. Diatoms and algae, attached to rocks by slimy secretions and special cells, make them slippery to the touch, and snails and aquatic insects glue themselves to rocks and eat the algae or detritus which has washed into the stream. Life in the stream is affected by the rate of water flow, water temperature, level of oxygen, nutrient levels, and the physical characteristics of the stream bed. Almost all nutrients which determine the biological carrying capacity of fast-flowing streams come not from algae within the stream but from materials from the surrounding forest which decompose into detritus. Forest management is an important factor in the quality of water and types of life found in streams such as Young Woman's Creek.

TRAIL DESCRIPTION:

From Greenlick Road, this route follows an old railroad grade up Greenlick Run to the orange-blazed STS, which rises along Greenlick Run and Italian Hollow before following a series of maintenance roads and a gas line to the Scoville Branch and the Porter Branch. Follow the red-blazed Donut Hole Trail Young Woman's Creek to Merriam Hollow, then follow an old grade, crossing the stream to ascend Tagerman Hollow. On top of the ridge, turn sharp left and follow salmon blazes for the Ingram Hollow Trail. The blazes disappear as you bushwack your way down the rocky drainage to Greenlick Road.

Miles	Description
0	From Greenlick Road at Greenlick Run crossing start on the N side of Greenlick Run and follow old railroad grade along left (W) side of Greenlick Run. (There is a sign for the Big Greenlick Trail on the S side of the bridge, but it quickly crosses to the left - save yourself a wet crossing). The grade is easy to follow, though it makes several back channel crossings along the way.
0.65	Here the old grade begins the first of several significant crossings of Greenlick Run before joining the orange-blazed STS in 0.2 mi.
1.75	STS turns left up Italian Hollow along moderate uphill grade.
2.2	STS crosses two gas well maintenance roads and begins to descend, bending left down hollow.
2.6	STS turns right onto gas line. Just ahead the STS will

follow a gas well maintenance road to Greenlick Road, turning right briefly before exiting road left along steep jeep trail. The jeep trail will travel over the top of the hill.

3.1 STS intersects gas maintenance road, following it straight ahead and crossing gas line.

3.5 STS continues straight ahead at gas maintenance road Y intersection.

3.9 STS turns left, paralleling gas line, crossing Osborne Branch.

4.6 After crossing Scoville Branch, STS exits gas line left, paralleling Scoville Branch SE past confluence with Osborne Branch. Blazes are infrequent along this section.

5.5 STS crosses gas line.

7.0 At Left Branch of Young Woman's Creek, STS turns right across log bridge to ascend Porter Branch. Here exit the STS, following the Donut Hole Trail (red blazes) across stream and along old railroad grade. The Donut Hole Trail will cross back quickly to the right side of stream.

7.2 Manning Hollow Trail exits right off Donut Hole Trail.

7.9 Donut Hole Trail turns sharp right to ascend Merriam Hollow. Here continue along the Left Branch, crossing to the left side when convenient.

8.0 Turn left up Tagerman Hollow, following a trail up the right side. In about 1/3 mile the trail will split - there cross to the left side of the hollow and continue easy ascent.

8.7 After entering mountain laurel the trail will reach a bench, bending to the right.

9.1 On top of the ridge you will begin to descend. As you do, turn sharp left on Ingram Hollow Trail (salmon blazes), heading NE and descending. The blazes will help guide you as the trail bends left toward the main hollow drainage.

10.1 The salmon blazes disappear - bushwhack down drainage. In 0.5 mi. the route will become very rough, so watch your footing along the rocks and stream bed. The trail will be found again along right side of Ingram Hollow.

11.1 Leave Ingram Hollow Trail as you approach gray hunting camp, crossing Greenlick Run on wooden footbridge.

11.2 Turn left on Greenlick Road, arriving back at the bottom of the Big Greenlick Trail in 0.4 miles.

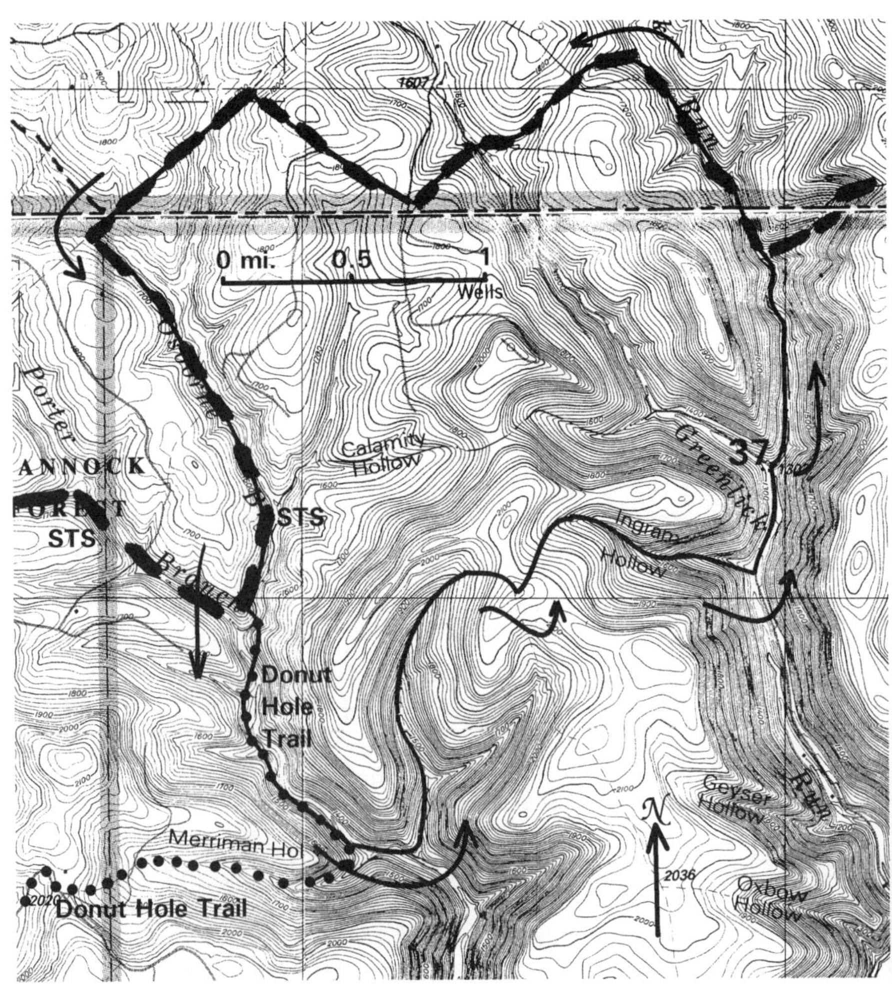

38 LIEB RUN - SCOVILLE BRANCH

FEATURES: forest types
DISTANCE: 10.6 miles
TIME: 6 hours
ELEVATION: 1060 - 1880
TERRAIN: moderate grades; some bushwhacking
BLAZES: orange (STS), otherwise none
PARKING: Cross Fork Forest Foreman's Headquarters near fire station
COMMENTS: Easily followed

At one time the American Chestnut was a common tree in Pennsylvania forests. In fact, the oak-hickory forest of today, from Pennsylvania to New England, was called the oak-chestnut forest. Its wood resisted rotting, and its bark, rich in tannin, was a main source for the tanning industry. A fungus, arriving in a shipment of infected logs in New York City in 1904, has almost wiped out this species. Very rarely do saplings grow more than four inches in diameter before they are killed by this blight, but this hike passes several that are twice as large, including a nine-inch specimen believed to be the largest in the Susquehannock State Forest.

This hike originates in the village of Cross Fork. In 1894 the Lackawanna Lumber Company built two mills there, and the Buffalo & Susquehanna Railroad was extended to transport the lumber to market. Within a year the village supported a population of 1,500, including six hotels (each with a saloon). The mills burned twice - in 1899 and in 1903 - and were finally closed in 1908. The Pennsylvania Stave Company operated a stave mill here from 1899 to 1912. The B & S line was then torn up. By 1917 the population had dwindled to 61.

TRAIL DESCRIPTION:

This route follows the STS from Cross Fork about a mile up Lieb Run, then bushwhacks across Lieb Run, ascending to Shephard

Road on logging road. A gas well maintenance road off Shephard Road joins to the orange-blazed STS, which descends the Scoville Branch and ascends the Porter Branch to Green Timber Hollow and Shephard Road before descending Lieb Run back to Cross Fork.

Miles	Description
0	From Forest Foreman Headquarters in village of Cross Fork, head SW along STS (orange blazes), paralleling edge of field and entering larch before turning sharp left and crossing field and road. On other side of road the STS will rise steeply, then follow woods road left, bending around mountain. This relocated (1994) section of trail will rejoin the old STS just above Kinney's Cabins. The STS then continues ascending along Kettle Creek and Lieb Run.
1.1	As slope to the left flattens and STS begins to bend sharp right into a small hollow, exit STS to left, descending to cross Lieb Run. After crossing Lieb Run, ascend steep slope to old woods road and turn right, ascending Lieb Run along it. There is no trail to follow between the STS and this woods road, so improvise this short bushwack.
2.45	Old woods road crosses gas line.
2.7	Turn left on Shephard Road.
2.95	Turn right on gas well service road, passing gas well.
3.35	Y in road - go left, crossing gas line shortly and continuing along service road on left side of the Scoville Branch.
3.7	Turn right at gas line onto STS, which descends to cross Scoville Branch. On opposite side, STS turns left and descends along right side of Scoville Branch past Osborne Branch confluence. Blazes are infrequent here.
4.6	STS crosses gas line.
5.6	STS turns right (NW) on hewn log bridge, ascending Porter Branch.

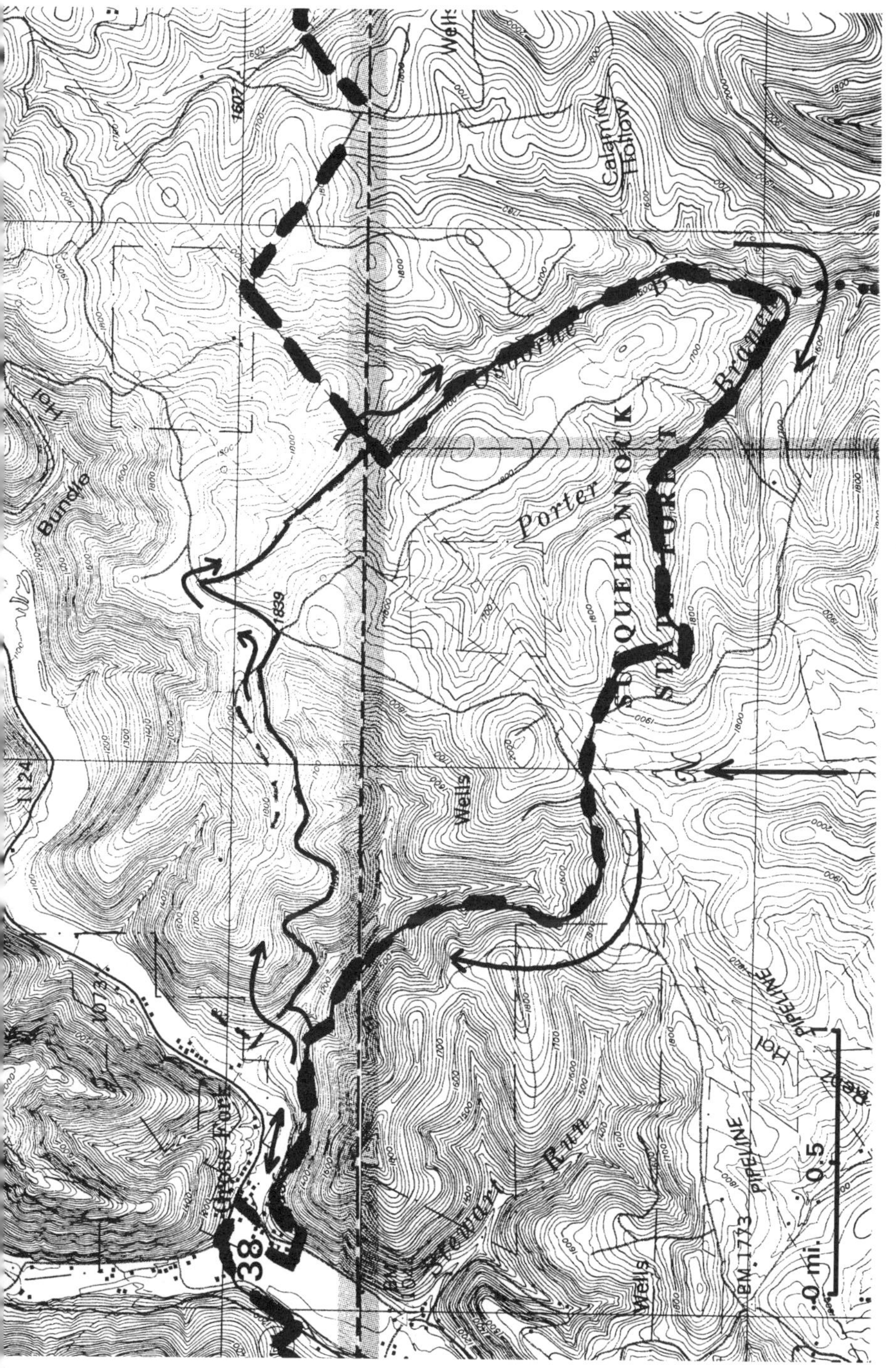

6.1 STS crosses Pine Stump Hollow and gas line.

6.5 STS turns left (W) up Green Timber Hollow.

6.9 STS turns right at grassy old railroad grade, passing 9 inch diameter American Chestnut on left at intersection. This chestnut tree may be the largest in the Susquehannock State Forest.

7.7 STS turns right at Culver Woods Road, following it past two gas line rights-of-way and crossing Shephard Road. After crossing a gas line maintenance road, STS becomes a well-defined trail that descends Lieb Run.

8.4 STS crosses old jeep trail and Right Branch of Lieb Run.

9.5 STS crosses small hollow where you exited earlier on your way up Lieb Run (m.p. 1.1 below). Continue by retracing your route from here along the STS back to the village of Cross Fork.

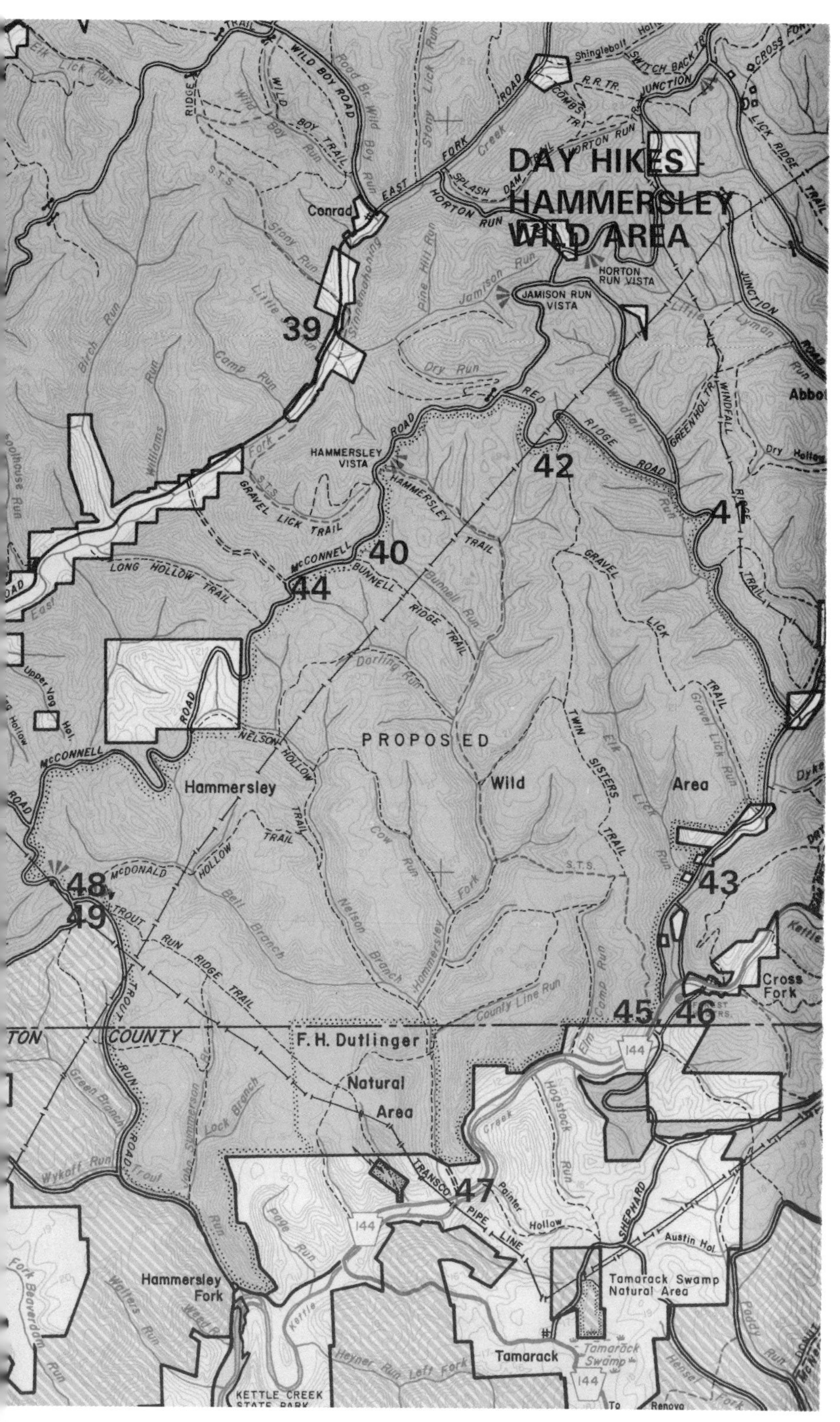
DAY HIKES -
HAMMERSLEY
WILD AREA
39
40
41
42
43
44
45, 46
47
48,
49
Conrad
HORTON RUN VISTA
JAMISON RUN VISTA
HAMMERSLEY VISTA
PROPOSED
Hammersley
Wild
Area
F. H. Dutlinger
Natural
Area
Tamarack Swamp
Natural Area
Hammersley
Fork
Tamarack
Cross
Fork
Abbot
KETTLE CREEK
STATE PARK
To
Renovo
EAST FORK ROAD
WILD BOY ROAD
WILD BOY TRAIL
RED RIDGE ROAD
McCONNELL ROAD
HAMMERSLEY TRAIL
BUNNELL RIDGE TRAIL
GRAVEL LICK TRAIL
LONG HOLLOW TRAIL
NELSON HOLLOW TRAIL
TWIN SISTERS TRAIL
McDONALD HOLLOW TRAIL
TROUT RUN RIDGE TRAIL
TROUT RUN ROAD
TRANSCO PIPE LINE
SHEPHARD
JUNCTION
WINDFALL
GREENHOL TR.
SPLASH DAM
HORTON RUN
COMBS TR
R.R. TR.
SWITCH BACK TR.
LICK RIDGE TRAIL
S.T.S.
144
COUNTY

39 BLACK MARK HOLLOW

FEATURES: forest/stream environments, old railroad grade
DISTANCE: 11.7 miles
TIME: 6.5 hours
ELEVATION: 1380 - 2080
TERRAIN: moderate old grades; some bushwhacking
BLAZES: orange (STS), otherwise none
PARKING: H.B. Williams residence on East Fork Road near Jamison Run
COMMENTS: Not hard to follow with average bushwhacking skills

When the Goodyears completed logging hemlock in this area in 1910 the Emporium Lumber Company began logging the hardwoods in the Hammersley.

The Goodyear logging railroad in the Hammersley was connected to the B & S mainline along the East Fork of Sinnemahoning Creek via a rail line up Road Hollow and down Long Hollow to the B & S. This fairly steep route meant that the logging trains had to be split into four-car lengths to get them over the mountain. Instead of using the Goodyear route and having to split and reassemble trains, Emporium constructed a new route from the Hammersley up Black Mark Hollow and then down Dry Run to the B & S mainline at the bottom of Jamison Run. Switchbacks in Dry Run and at the top of Black Mark Hollow (to what is now Red Ridge Road) allowed the trains to get over the mountain without having to be disassembled.

This hike follows most of the Emporium Lumber Company's rail route from Jamison Run to Black Mark Junction in the Hammersley. Emporium used this route for three years, until 1913 when the company completed its hardwood logging operations in the Hammersley. The hike also follows the STS along a portion of a Goodyear spur track in the upper Hammersley and the B & S main line along the East Fork of Sinnemahoning Creek.

TRAIL DESCRIPTION:

This route follows the STS from East Fork Road to Jamison Run, and a driveway, easy bushwhack, and a logging road ascend Jamison Run and Dry Hollow to McConnell Road. An easy bushwhack down Black Mark Hollow gets you to the STS. The orange-blazed STS (via upper Hammersley Fork, Gravel Lick Run, and the former B & S mainline) leads back to Jamison Run.

Miles	Description
0	From East Fork Road at bottom of Jamison Hollow (H.B. Williams residence), follow STS across E Fork - Sinnemahoning Creek along road. After crossing creek leave STS, bearing left along driveway up Jamison Hollow.
0.55	After passing the beige stucco camp with the yellow brick chimney, rise right to a trail at the base of the mountain, crossing a small hollow entering on the right, across open area, and into hemlocks. After entering the hemlocks look for signs of an old trail ascending on right.
0.75	Trail will rise and bear left on a cut grade, following it uphill.
1.05	Turn right on logging road up Dry Hollow. The logging road will switch back right, then left, rising to McConnell Road.
3.55	Cross McConnell Road, dropping down hollow (Black Mark Hollow) to right of Red Ridge Road intersection. The slope becomes more gentle as you descend, and you may have to detour around blowdowns. Although there are intermittent trails and old railroad grades down Black Mark Hollow, don't expect too much - generally, follow the right side or bottom of the hollow (though the bottom may be wet in places). In about 0.4 mi. the two upper branches of Black Mark Hollow will meet (old switchback grade off to the left rises to Red Ridge Road) and in another 0.4 mi. you will cross a gas line.
5.5	After crossing a small branch of the Hammersley Fork, scramble up the bank to the STS (orange blazes), which you follow to the right, ascending Hammersley Fork.

6.0 STS crosses gas line.

7.15 STS turns right, crossing Hammersley Fork, continuing to rise along right side of Hammersley Fork before bending left and rising steeply to McConnell Road.

7.45 After crossing McConnell Road STS follows Gravel Lick Trail, descending along moderate/steep grade. Trail will cross Treachery Run Trail (grassy road), Duffy's Campsite, and the Green Hollow Trail. After crossing the State Forest boundary STS turns right to skirt the edge of private land.

9.9 STS turns right, following old B&S grade.

11.5 STS enters mowed area at bottom of Jamison Run, turning left, crossing East Fork - Sinnemahoning Creek to East Fork Road in 0.2 mi.

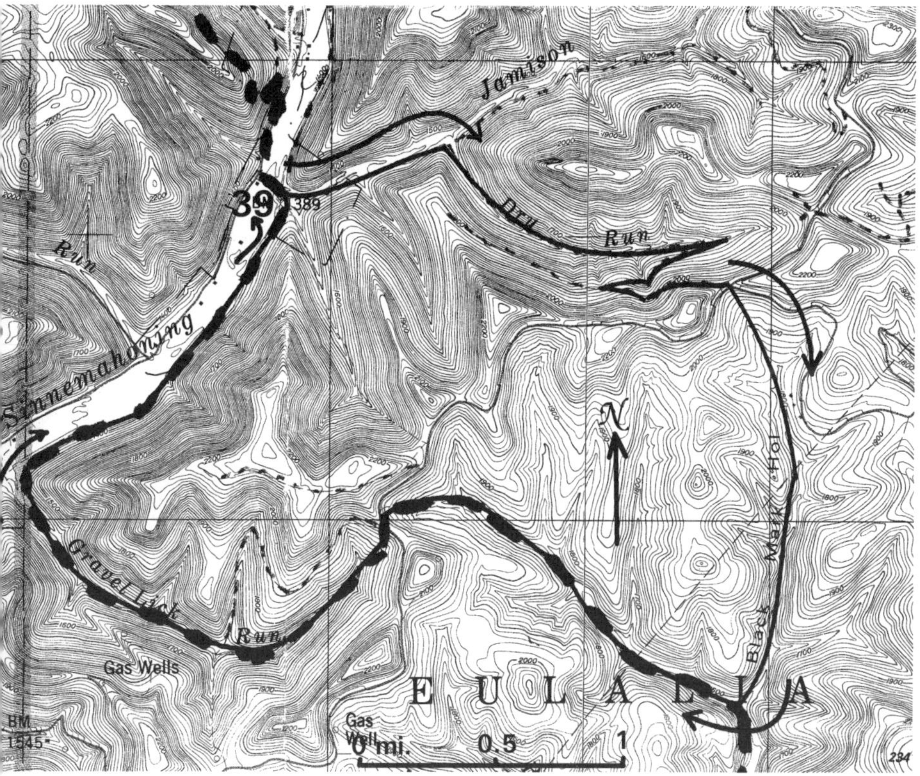

40 BUNNELL RUN

FEATURES: forest/stream environments
DISTANCE: 4.1 miles
TIME: 2 hours
ELEVATION: 1360 - 2040
TERRAIN: moderate/steep old grades; some bushwhacking
BLAZES: orange (STS), otherwise none
PARKING: McConnell Road at Bunnell Ridge Trail
COMMENTS: Easily followed

The proposed Hammersley Wild Area consists of 30,253 acres, primarily within the Hammersley Fork watershed. Although it is managed as a Wild Area, its designation is not official because the gas, oil, and mineral rights are under private ownership. Consequently, the Bureau of Forestry cannot ensure protection of the area until it owns the mineral rights, when it will then request that the designation become official.

The Hammersley Fork was logged for hemlock by the Goodyear Lumber Company between 1906 and 1910. To get their logs to market, the Goodyears operated the most extensive standard gauge logging railroad operation in the history of Pennsylvania lumbering, and many of these grades can still be found in the Hammersley. The Emporium Lumber Company then logged the area for hardwoods from 1910 to 1913. The Commonwealth bought most of the land (25,950 acres) in the proposed wild area from the Emporium Lumber Company in 1929.

Designation as a "Wild Area" means that the Bureau of Forestry limits logging to salvage operations and manages the area to preserve and protect its remote, scenic, and primitive qualities. Vehicles are prohibited in Wild Areas.

TRAIL DESCRIPTION:

This route follows the Bunnell Ridge Trail from McConnell Road to Hammersley Fork and returns along Bunnell Run.

Miles	Description
0	From McConnell Road at Bunnell Ridge Trail (sign), follow woods road across the top of Bunnell Ridge.
0.72	Trail crosses gas line and becomes a narrow old woods road. Trail becomes faint trail here (some surveyor's tape is usually here to help). Within 0.25 mi, as the trail begins to descend, it will become more evident (and become steep).
1.9	Y in trail - descend left then turn left on STS (orange blazes)
2.0	Turn left at intersection of Bunnell Run, following old railroad grade (several stream crossings).
3.1	Cross gas line.
3.45	Y in hollow - bear left.
3.85	An old grade exits left - follow it up to McConnell Road or follow drainage to road, about 0.25 mi. above.

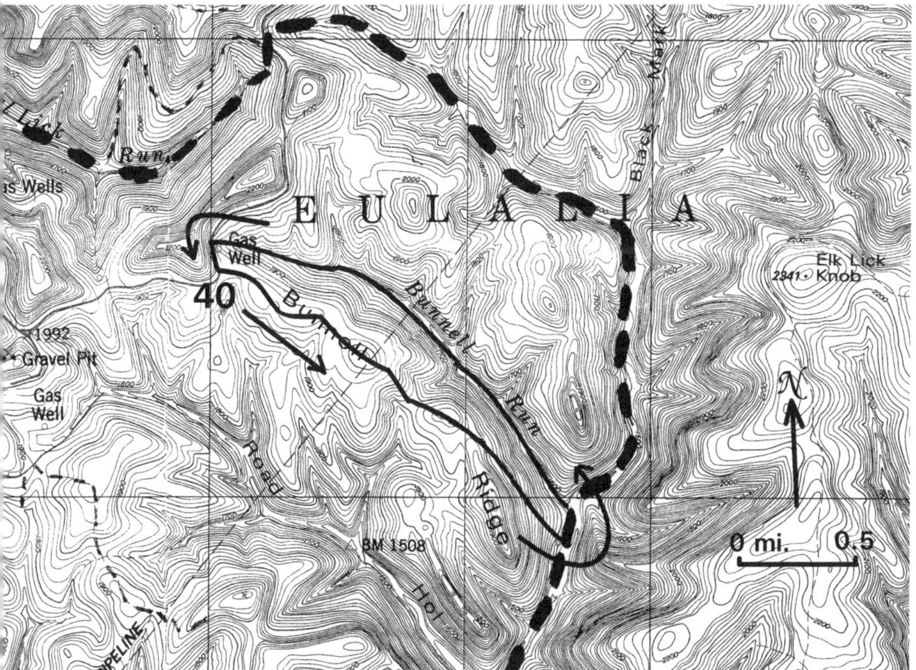

41 BLACKSMITH HOLLOW & LOST SILVERMINE

FEATURES: views, "lost silver mine"
DISTANCE: 8.5 miles
TIME: 5 hours
ELEVATION: 1400 - 2230
TERRAIN: moderate old grades; some bushwhacking
BLAZES: orange or salmon blazes on Twin Sisters Trail, otherwise none
PARKING: Windfall Road at Mud Lick Hollow Trail
COMMENTS: Not hard to follow with average bushwhacking skills. Blacksmith Hollow is rough and rocky.

Almost every county in Pennsylvania has a legend about a lost silver mine, even though silver is not indigenous to the state. Etienne Brulé, a French explorer who came to North America in 1608, explored the Pennsylvania area in 1614 - 1618, including the Susquehanna watershed. According to legend, he learned that Native Americans in the area had a secret source of silver, and he spent a good portion of his time searching for it. He discovered it on the narrow ridge between Knickerbocker and Mud Lick Hollows, above the Twin Sisters area. After digging the silver ore he brought it to his camp near the bottom of Twin Sisters Hollow, where he constructed a furnace, and there he smelted the ore into pure silver. One of his men was killed by Indians, who cut off his head - when the moon is full in October his ghost can be seen at midnight walking along the Hammersley near Twin Sisters, carrying his head under his arm.

This story, while interesting, does not explain why Brulé felt compelled to bring the ore such a distance to refine it. No silver has ever been found near the "silver mine", though some limestone has.

Robert R. Lyman, Sr., in *Amazing Indeed: Strange Events in the Black Forest* (Leader Publishing Co., Coudersport, PA, 1973), suggests that the mine was used by Native American Mound

Builders for smelting iron. Their presence in the region dates back 900 years, and they knew how to smelt iron from bog iron ore. He suggests that they mined the pit for limestone, combined it with charcoal and bog iron ore, and then removed the slag from the molten iron. Their smelting furnace at the bottom of Twin Sisters Hollow, close to the bog iron ore (heavier than limestone), was dismantled by the CCC in the 1930s for its stone.

And the ghost of the headless Frenchman? Marsh gas?

TRAIL DESCRIPTION:

This route enters the Hammersley Wild Area via the Mudlick Hollow Trail (logging road) from Windfall Road. After crossing Windfall Run the Lick Hollow Trail (former logging road) leads to the top of Blacksmith Hollow, and a bushwhack down Blacksmith Hollow and up Elk Lick Run brings you to the orange/salmon blazed Twin Sisters Trail at a vista. After following the Twin Sisters Trail to the top of Mud Lick Run, an easy bushwhack across the narrow neck between Mud Lick and Knickerbocker Hollows provides the opportunity to see the "lost silver mine". Mud Lick Hollow (a bushwhack and logging road) returns you to Windfall Run.

Miles	Description
0	From Windfall Road near bottom of Robin Hollow, follow Mud Lick Hollow Trail (sign) down to Windfall Run.
0.35	After crossing Windfall Run logging road splits - turn left, following logging road downstream along Windfall Run.
0.7	Bear right at logging road intersection at bottom of Lick Hollow, following logging road up Lick Hollow.
1.6	Bear right at intersecting logging road, continuing ascent.
2.5	Logging road bends sharp right.
2.8	Turn left where terrain on left levels at top of Blacksmith Hollow. There is no real trail here, so you will have to bushwhack your way along the bottom of the Blacksmith Hollow drainage to Elk Lick Run.

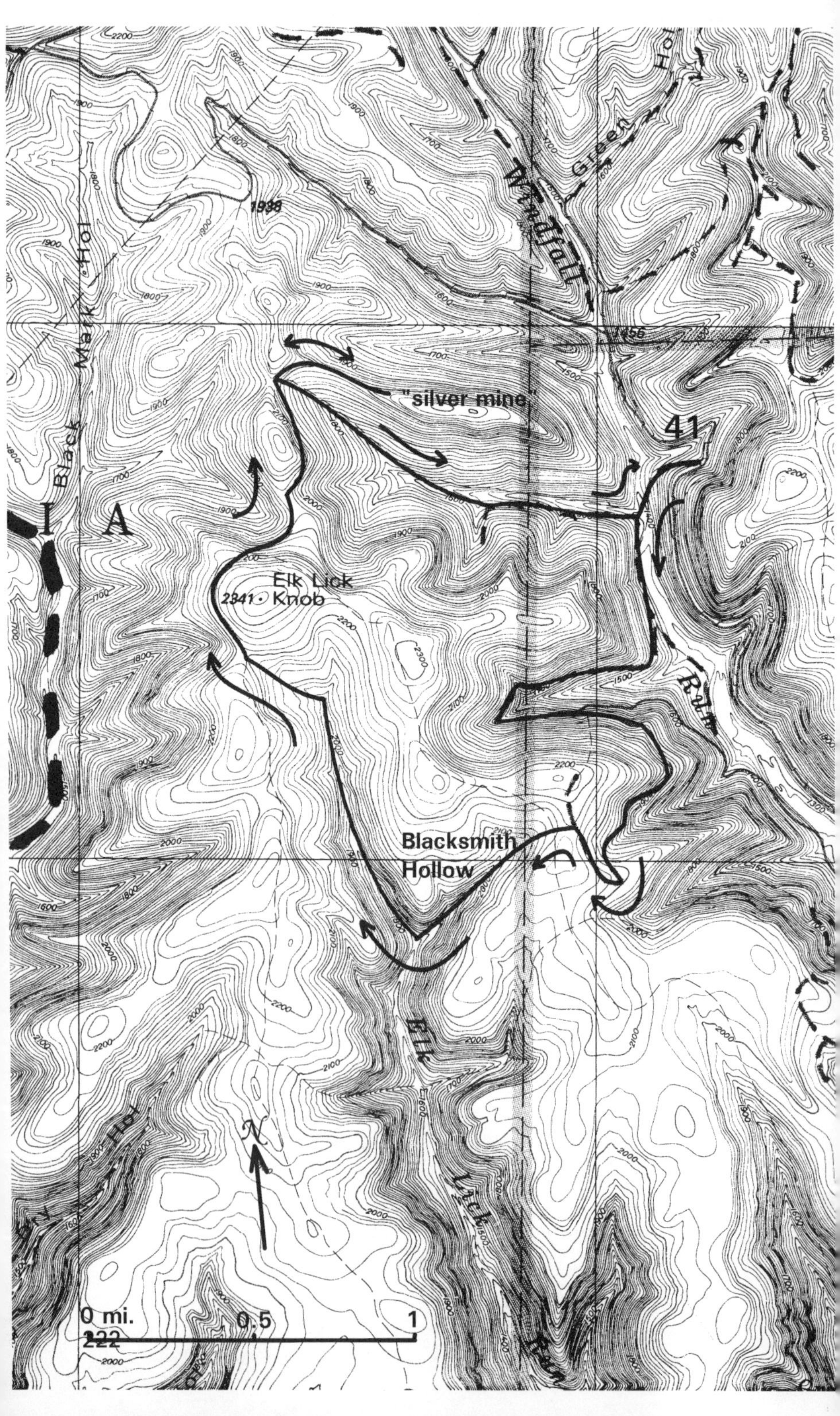
"silver mine"
41
Elk Lick
2341 · Knob
Blacksmith
Hollow
Black Mark Hol
Windfall
Green
Run
Elk
Lick
I A
1938
1456
0 mi.
0.5
1

3.7 Turn right and bushwhack your way up Elk Lick Run (no trail, several blowdowns, particularly along left side).

4.8 Bear left where hollow branches, ascending left side of this branch through open forest.

5.2 Turn right on Twin Sisters Trail (salmon or blaze orange blazes) in bottom of saddle. Trail will pass through old burn area with expansive vista of Hammersley and west plateau.

5.6 Pass Gravel Lick Trail (tree with yellow band; yellow blazes to right). Continue on Twin Sisters Trail.

6.3 Top of Mud Lick Hollow (orange "M" at the top of Mud Lick Hollow and "T" at Twin Sisters Trail). Turn diagonally right along trail (two salmon blazes to guide you) toward narrow ridge between Mud Lick and Knickerbocker Hollows.

6.4 As you approach the narrow ridge between the two hollows you pass several 6' x 4' x 3' deep pits at base of hemlocks. Continue along ridge another 0.25 mi. to a 10' x 10' x 10' pit - the "silver mine". Retrace steps to Mud Lick Hollow.

7.0 Turn left and bushwhack your way down Mud Lick Hollow.

7.75 After crossing a hollow on the right rise right to old logging road that descends Mud Lick Hollow along the right side.

8.1 Intersection of Lick Run and Mud Lick Run Trails (logging roads) at bottom of Windfall Run. Cross Windfall Run and return to Windfall Road in 0.35 mi.

42 TWIN SISTERS

FEATURES: views, "lost silver mine", Hammersley Fork
DISTANCE: 12.9 miles
TIME: 7 hours
ELEVATION: 1320 - 2280
TERRAIN: moderate old grades; some bushwhacking and rough areas
BLAZES: orange or salmon (Twin Sisters Trail), orange (STS), otherwise none
PARKING: Red Ridge Road at Twin Sisters Trail
COMMENTS: Good bushwhacking skills required. Dry Hollow is rough and rocky. Several stream crossings required.

Twin Sisters Hollow is said to have been named for two large pine trees near the bottom but could be just as easily been named for its symmetrical, appearance: it splits into two branches, each of which is topped by a knob.

In May 1964 a forest fire burned 275 acres here, creating one of the most expansive trail vistas in the Susquehannock State Forest. From it you can easily see a large portion of the Hammersley Wild Area from the top of Hammersley Fork to Trout Run Ridge. It is also easy to see the extensive changes that fire can produce in a forest - after over 30 years this burn is still substantially ferns and grass, with few trees.

After original logging, forest fires were common here. Only in a few areas, however, did the frequency and intensity of fire make it possible for only aspens, gray birch, and fire cherry to grow.

About 1500 forest fires, involving 10,000 acres, are reported annually in Pennsylvania. Only 1% of them are due to natural causes, so fire is not managed as an important element of the natural forest ecosystem. Some controlled burning may be used as a forest management tool, but all other fires are fought. At first towers were manned by personnel whose job it was to spot fires. The towers are no longer in use, and most have been dismantled. Most fire spotting and fighting is now done by air.

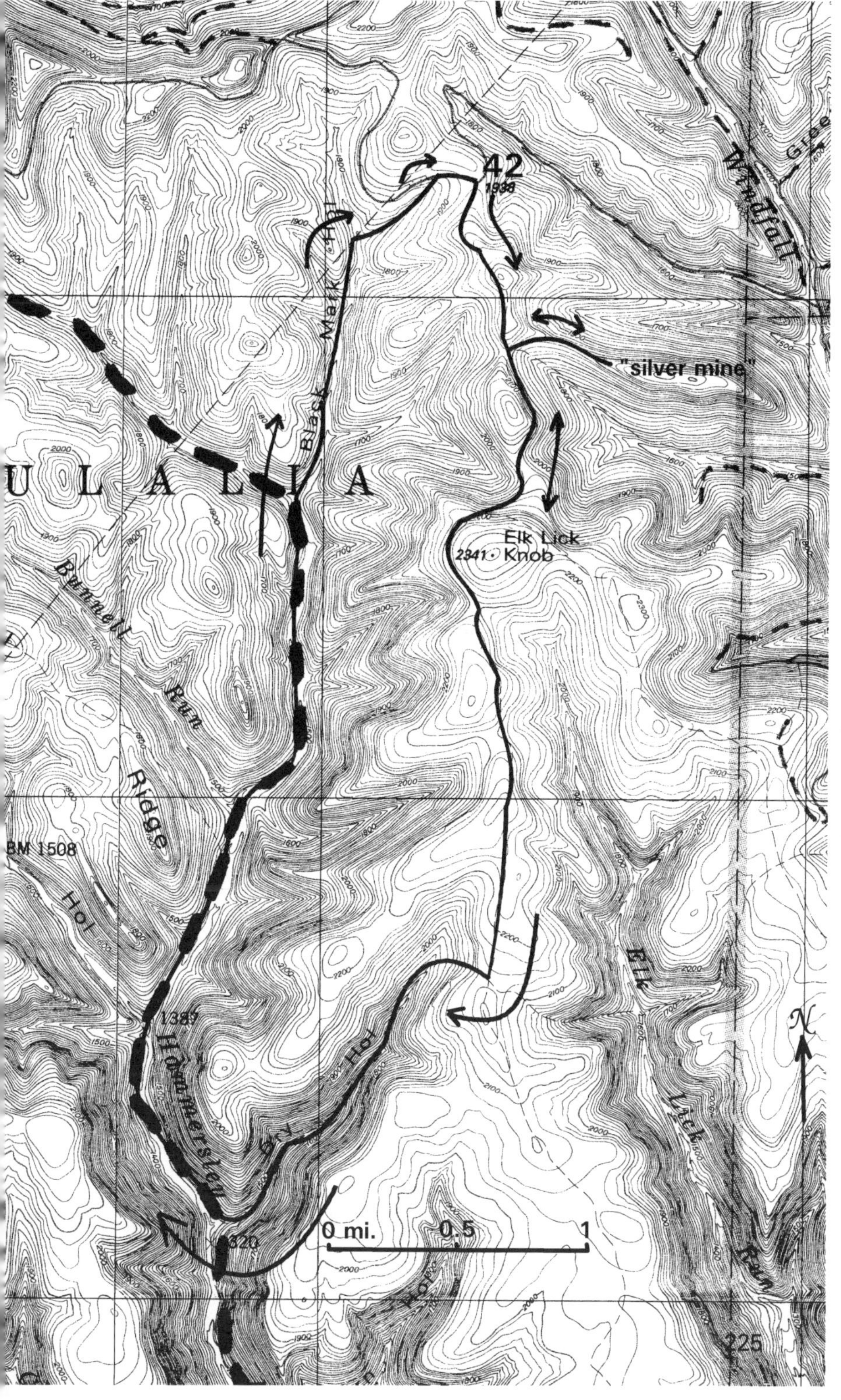

42
"silver mine"
Elk Lick Knob
2341
Black Mark Hol
Windfall
U L A L I A
Bunnell Run
Ridge
BM 1508
Hol
1389
Hammersten Hol
1320
0 mi.
0.5
1
Elk Lick Run
N

TRAIL DESCRIPTION:

This route follows the Twin Sisters Trail from Red Ridge Road to the top of Dry Hollow (with a side trip from the top of Mud Lick Hollow to the "silver mine"). After bushwhacking down Dry Hollow, the orange-blazed STS will bring you to Black Mark Hollow, where a bushwhack up the hollow and along a gas line will return you to Red Ridge Road.

0 From Red Ridge Road, follow Twin Sisters Trail S along a well-worn grade marked with orange blazes.

0.75 At top of Mud Lick Hollow (orange "M") turn left and follow trail toward the narrow ridge between Mud Lick and Knickerbocker Hollows (there are two salmon-colored blazes to guide you if you need them). As you approach the ridge you will pass several 6 ft x 4 ft x 3 ft deep holes on your left at the base of the hemlocks. Continue following ridge.

1.1 Stop at the 10 ft x 10 ft x 10 ft deep pit - this is the lost silver mine. Retrace steps to Twin Sisters Trail.

1.45 Turn left at Twin Sisters Trail, following it south.

3.15 Pass Gravel Lick Trail (yellow blazes off to left; intersection marked with double yellow-banded tree on right). Continue along Twin Sisters Trail

3.45 Expansive vista W across Twin Sisters Hollow in burn area. Continue to follow the florescent blazes of the Twin Sisters Trail across ridge and into woods.

4.55 At a Y there are orange blazes that go off to the left, but you continue straight (right branch) following florescent blazes. The blazes disappear within 0.5 miles, but the trail is easy to follow across the top of the ridge.

5.25 Turn right, bushwhacking down Dry Hollow drainage (Dry Hollow marked by rock column with orange paint on top, beech tree marked "Dry Hollow Trail", and tree with 3-slit blaze). Watch footing over rocks and stream bed.

8.05 Turn right (N) from Dry Hollow onto orange-blazed STS.

8.6 STS turns left, descending steeply and crossing Hammersley Fork over wet crossing. Blazes follow old railroad grade and there are several wet crossings involved.

11.1 STS bends left at Black Mark Hollow. Leave the STS, bushwhacking your way up Black Mark Hollow. (I followed a series of trails above left side of the hollow.)

12.3 At gas line, turn right and cross Black Mark Hollow, bushwhacking up the hollow that parallels the gas line.

12.74 Turn right on Big Springs Road and return to beginning of Twin Sisters Trail in 0.15 miles.

43 ELK LICK RUN/GRAVEL LICK RUN

FEATURES: views, stream/forest environments
DISTANCE: 10.5 miles
TIME: 6 hours
ELEVATION: 1100 - 2230
TERRAIN: moderate old grades; some bushwhacking and stream crossings
BLAZES: orange or salmon (Twin Sisters Trail), yellow (Gravel Lick Trail), otherwise none
PARKING: Cross Fork Road at Elk Lick Run Trail
COMMENTS: Good bushwhacking skills a plus. Stream crossings and rough in spots.

Game animals frequent seeps and springs, where they may eat soil and lick rocks for trace minerals and salt. Early pioneers called these "licks", and they were good places to hunt.

In the Susquehannock State Forest are two Elk Lick Runs and three Gavel Lick Runs, which can cause some geographical confusion. There are also a Mud Lick Run and a Stoney Lick Run.

The name "Sinnemahoning" is a corruption of a Native American word for "Stony Lick". Philip Tome, an early pioneer hunter, called the Sinnemahoning "the greatest elk country known" (*Pioneer Life or Thirty Years a Hunter*, originally printed in 1854). The last elk killed in Potter County was in Wharton Township in 1856. It weighed 1200 lbs. and had six-foot antlers.

TRAIL DESCRIPTION:

This route follows a path and logging road up Elk Lick Run, bushwhacking its way along the upper drainage to the Twin Sisters Trail. After passing an expansive vista the Twin Sisters Trail passes the yellow-blazed Gravel Lick Trail, which returns you (with an occasional easy bushwhack) to Cross Fork Road.

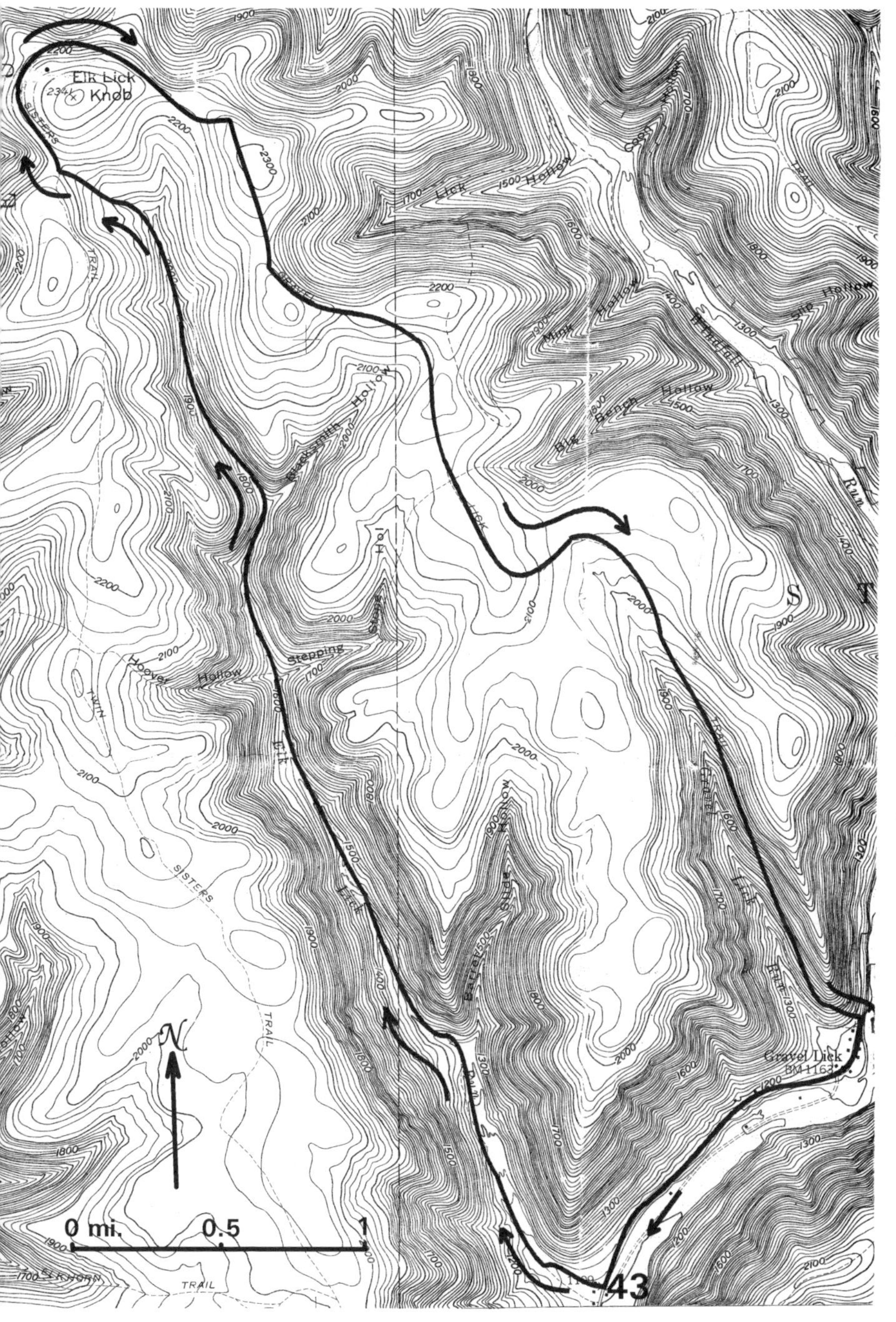
Elk Lick Knob
2341
Lick Hollow
Coon Hollow
Slip Hollow
Mint Hollow
Big Bench Hollow
Blacksmith Hollow
Stepping Stone Hollow
Hoover Hollow
Elk Lick
Slide Hollow
Gravel Lick Run
Gravel Lick
BM 1163
SISTERS TRAIL
TWIN SISTERS
ELK HORN TRAIL
N
0 mi.
0.5
1
43

Miles	Description
0	Follow right side of Elk Lick Run (sign at first bridge - yellow steel N of Cross Fork on Cross Fork Rd.) past the footbridge.
0.15	At State Forest boundary cross to left side of Elk Lick Run and follow old logging road along the left side.
0.7	Logging road splits (right ends at dam on stream).
0.95	Hollow enters on right, and logging road becomes more like a path, descending to cross to right side of stream. You will pick up an old grade now along the right side of the stream - this old grade may deteriorate occasionally.
1.6	Off to left is a large, moss-covered rock landslide. The path degrades here and you end up following the bottom of the hollow, as grade will become intermittent.
2.3	Stepping Stone Hollow enters on right (surveyors' tape and old grade), then Hoover Hollow enters on the left.
2.9	Blacksmith Hollow enters on right - continue bushwhacking up the left (main) branch of Elk Lick Run.
4.0	Bear left where Elk Lick Run drainage branches, following the left side of this branch through open forest.
4.4	Turn right on Twin Sisters Trail (salmon or blaze orange blazes) in bottom of saddle. Twin Sisters will pass expansive vista in old burned area.
4.8	Turn right onto Gravel Lick Trail (yellow blazes off to right; intersection marked by tree with yellow band), following it around knob. The yellow blazes will become older and difficult to see, but the path is fairly easy to follow.
5.25	Detour around mountain laurel, rejoining the yellow-blazed Gravel Lick Trail shortly on the other side. The trail will then quickly bend left to the left side of the knob and rise, swinging back to the right at the top of the knob.

6.0 Newer yellow paint blazes disappear, but there are still some old yellow blazes.

6.3 With the lack of blazes the trail becomes difficult to follow in flat area - keep to right side and you should be able to find the old trail as it crosses the top of Blacksmith Hollow.

6.65 After crossing Blacksmith Hollow trail rises to the top of small knoll where yellow blazes go off left, but you continue straight ahead.

6.8 Top of Big Bench Trail (triple yellow stripe; "Big Bench Trail" carved in beech tree; Big Bench Trail is marked with yellow blazes). Continue straight along the Gravel Lick Trail.

7.0 Trail passes a tree with a yellow "GL" and an arrow, indicating that the trail turns left here. The trail is difficult to see here, but the blazes will help you across flat area.

7.4 Trail begins to descend gently as some orange blazes mix with the yellow blazes. The trail will begin to drop more noticeably shortly along the left side of the hollow and will become better marked by yellow blazes.

8.8 Bear left at Y near bottom of Gravel Lick Hollow (right side descends to private land), and round point. Rhododendron and mountain laurel will appear. As you round the point you will see the white blazes of the State Forest boundary. Follow the State Forest boundary to Cross Fork Road.

9.2 Turn right on Cross Fork Road, returning to the bottom of Elk Lick Run in 1.3 miles.

44 MURDOCKS (ROAD HOLLOW)

FEATURES: Hammersley Fork; forest/stream environments, old logging railroads
DISTANCE: 12.85 miles (Alternate Route: 10.35 miles)
TIME: 7 hours (Alternate Route: 6 hours)
ELEVATION: 1110 - 1990
TERRAIN: easy/moderate grades; some bushwhacking; stream crossings
BLAZES: orange (STS), otherwise none
PARKING: McConnell Road at top of Road Hollow and road intersection 0.4 mi. W of Green Hollow Trail sign
COMMENTS: Good map reading/bushwhacking skills will be very helpful after leaving the STS for your return. The alternate route up Cow Run, while shorter, is more rugged and steeper. Crossing Hammersley Fork and its tributaries can be either challenging or very wet, but there are usually enough downed trees and debris dams to allow a dry crossing if care is exercised.

At the bottom of Road Hollow the Goodyear Lumber Company constructed a freight yard. Here their trains of eight log cars each were split into four-car consists to be pushed up the 7% grade along Road Hollow and Darling Run. At the top of Darling Run the trains were then reassembled for the trip down the other side of the ridge, along Long Hollow, to the B & S main line along Sinnemahoning Creek. The railroad made four trips a day up Road Hollow and down Long Hollow, each time moving about 3,200 - 3,500 board feet of timber across the divide.

The Emporium Lumber Company, who logged the hardwoods in the Hammersley between 1910 and 1913 after the Goodyears finished here, used a route up Black Mark Hollow and then down Jamison Hollow to eliminate the need to split the train and then reassemble it to get it to the main line.

TRAIL DESCRIPTION:

This route follows the Road Hollow Trail and the STS to Elkhorn Run. From Elkhorn Run old grades are followed down the Hammersley to the Bell Branch and Nelson Branch. The trail up the Nelson Branch becomes an easy bushwhack near, then up, Shang Hollow. At the top of Shang Hollow the gas line, woods roads, and a logging road will return you to Road Hollow. There is an alternative route from Elkhorn Run, bushwhacking along the Hammersley and up Cow Run, then down into upper Shang Hollow.

Miles	Description
0	Follow faint grade down Road Hollow from McConnell Road. By 0.1 mi., the faint grade will become more distinct as you descend along the right side of the hollow.
0.4	Hollow enters on right - the old grade along this side hollow is part of the return route. After crossing this side hollow follow the skid trail above right side of Road Hollow.
0.6	Take the left branch (fairly level) of Y in skid trail. Green Hollow enters on left.
1.25	Gas line crosses Road Hollow. Darling Run enters just ahead on the right.
1.4	Old trail goes off left at Y - stay on main trail (right branch).
1.75	Carpet Cart Hollow enters on right (sign).
2.55	Turn right on STS (orange blazes) at bottom of Road Hollow. The former freight yard of Murdocks was located nearby. STS generally follows an old railroad grade along Hammersley Fork, which it crosses several times before crossing in about 1/3 mi. and ascending to a path above the left side of Hammersley Fork.
3.45	STS crosses bottom of Dry Hollow and passes "The Pool" along old railroad grade down Hammersley Fork before rising along footpath on the left side of Hammersley Fork.

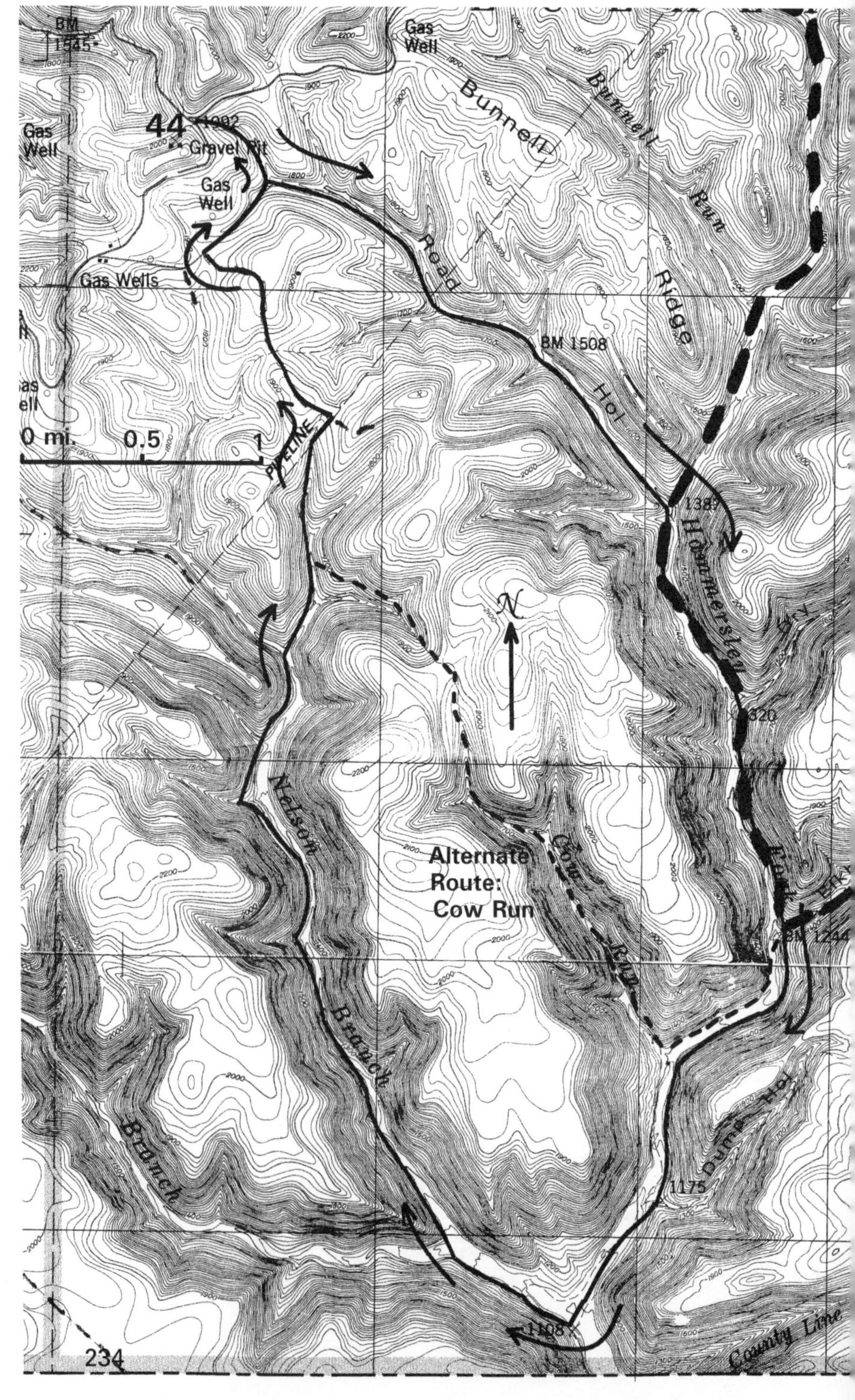

BM 1545
Gas Well
44
Gravel Pit
Gas Well
Gas Wells
Bunnell
Bunnell Run
Road
Ridge
BM 1508
Hol
1389
Hommersley
1320
PIPELINE
0 mi. 0.5 1
N
Nelson
Branch
Alternate Route: Cow Run
Cow Run
Branch
Dume Hol
1175
1108
County Line

4.5 Leave STS at bottom of Elkhorn Run, paralleling Hammersley Fork along old railroad grade.

4.65 Leave old railroad grade (which descends to Hammersley Fork), following skid trail straight ahead (left branch of Y) above left side of Hammersley Fork.

[ALTERNATE ROUTE - COW HOLLOW: Follow grade to Hammersley Fork and cross to W side of Hammersley.
5.25 Turn right at bottom of Cow Run and follow trail (sign) along the right side of the hollow.
5.8 Trail disappears and route becomes a rough bushwhack along drainage.
6.15 Take left fork in stream - becomes rough.
6.55 Bear right at next hollow, following grade on right side.
7.1 Bushwhack left, crossing saddle in plateau and bushwhacking down opposite side along left.
7.8 Turn right at Shang Hollow (m.p. 10.3 below)]

5.85 Skid trail crosses Dump Hollow. After passing Dump Hollow sign, descend to the bottom of Hammersley Fork and follow well-defined jeep trail, which fords Hammersley Fork and stream channels several times before making final major crossing of Hammersley Fork about 0.5 miles S of Dump Hollow. These crossings are wet, but the Hammersley Fork usually provides debris dams and downed trees which may provide dry crossings - exercise care when crossing.

6.5 Turn right at intersection of jeep trail on west side of Hammersley at base of mountain just below Bell Branch.

6.9 Bend left up Bell Branch. The grade now becomes a trail.

7.15 Exit right along skid trail and cross Bell Branch at Nelson Branch. Ascend point on W side of Nelson Branch to trail at base of exposed rock about 20 ft. above Nelson Branch. Follow trail along left (W) side of Nelson Branch.

8.6 Trail crosses a hollow - on other side McDonald Trail exits steeply left but you continue paralleling Nelson Branch.

9.1 In this vicinity the skid trail you have been following becomes more difficult to discern, so keep a sharp eye for it as you continue to parallel the Nelson Branch.

9.25 Skid trail splits at hollow - cross hollow along old stone bridge and continue paralleling the Nelson Branch about 20 ft. above Nelson Branch. The trail will become an easily followed old grade shortly.

9.55 The old grade bends left and becomes a logging road up side hollow. Here cross this side hollow and continue paralleling the Nelson Branch - no trail to follow for the next 1/3 mile, where trail resumes 30 ft. above Nelson Branch.

10.0 Skid trail descends to Shang Hollow. Here cross the Nelson Branch and turn right up Shang Hollow, following trail along left side of hollow.

10.3 Bear left at split in hollow and follow trail along right side of the left branch (right branch rises to top of Cow Run).

10.6 Hollow splits - continue on skid trail along right side of left branch (right branch rises to top of Carpet Cart Hollow). Trail will cross to the left side shortly where a hollow enters left, then you encounter a number of blowdowns, making your route an open forest bushwack along the left side.

10.95 Turn right and follow gas line to avoid blowdowns in hollow.

11.1 Turn left on old woods road where gas line crests.

12.05 Turn right, following logging road downhill.

12.45 Turn left at intersection of Road Hollow, ascending Road Hollow to McConnell Road in 0.4 miles.

45 ELKHORN RUN

FEATURES: forest/stream environments
DISTANCE: 10.2 miles
TIME: 5.5 hours
ELEVATION: 1080 - 2065
TERRAIN: moderate/steep grades; some bushwhacking
BLAZES: orange (STS), some hot pink/surveyors tape (Dump Hollow), otherwise none
PARKING: Rt. 144 just S of Cross Fork Rd.
COMMENTS: Easily followed but some map reading/bushwhacking skills required

Until 1867 elk lived in north central Pennsylvania. They were hunted to extinction. The PA Game Commission reintroduced elk from Yellowstone National Park in this region (including Potter County), from 1913 to 1926. 177 elk were released - their descendants today live in Elk and Cameron Counties.

The word "elk" is of German origin. Native Americans called them "wapiti", or "white deer", though they were much larger than today's white-tailed deer. The elk is no longer a Potter County resident and plays no role in forest management in the Susquehannock State Forest, but the white-tailed deer is and does.

The deer, with a territory of about 1.5 sq. miles, is a browser, and browse and cover are readily available along the forest edge. In the forest the deer brows up to about six feet above the forest floor, so high deer population adversely affects natural forest regeneration by quickly eliminating the next generation of forest trees. The deer also eliminate certain species of plants, decreasing the forest's biodiversity. Clear-cuts are now fenced to keep deer away from new growth until it has gotten a head start.

Elkhorn Run probably derives its name from its topographical similarity to the large branching antlers typical of elk.

TRAIL DESCRIPTION:

This route follows the STS from Rt. 144 over the plateau and down to the mouth of Elkhorn Run. There it follows a trail above the east side of Hammersley Fork to Dump Hollow. A trail up Dump Hollow and a bushwhack at the top of Elm Camp Hollow return you to the STS, which you follow back to Rt. 144.

Miles	Description
0	From Route 144 at STS just S of Cross Fork Road, follow STS N, ascending left side of ravine briefly before switchbacking S to the Twin Sisters Trail (sign). STS then climbs along a moderate slope to the top of the plateau.
1.1	Vista of plateau. STS bends left and levels shortly.
1.35	STS turns right and meanders through mountain laurel.
2.0	STS turns left (W) and leaves Twin Sisters Trail
2.7	After crossing wet areas, STS begins moderate to steep descent down Elkhorn Run.
3.8	STS turns right to cross Elkhorn Run. Here leave the STS and follow old grade that bends left (S) shortly.
3.95	Leave old grade (old grade descends right to Hammersley) and follow skid trail above left (E) side of Hammersley Fork.
5.2	Skid trail crosses Dump Hollow. Here turn left, ascending along right side of Dump Hollow. At the first hollow on the right bear left, following the grade up the main branch of Dump Hollow along a moderately steep path.
6.2	Trail bends right and flattens. Hot pink blazes guide you along the trail. The trail will cross to the left side of the drainage and pass a hemlock swamp on the right.
6.45	Trail enters large, flat, open area, passing a 15 ft. tall, fire-damaged stump. Trail is marked with surveyors' tape here.

6.75 Intersection of County Line Hollow and Dump Hollow Trails (sign). Continue descent along grade to Elm Camp Hollow.

7.2 Bear left at intersection of Elm Camp Hollow, following drainage uphill then picking up old grade along left side. The grade becomes difficult to follow near the top - bushwhack your way along the drainage and you will eventually cross the orange-blazed STS.

7.9 Turn right onto STS and return to Route 144 in 2.3 miles.

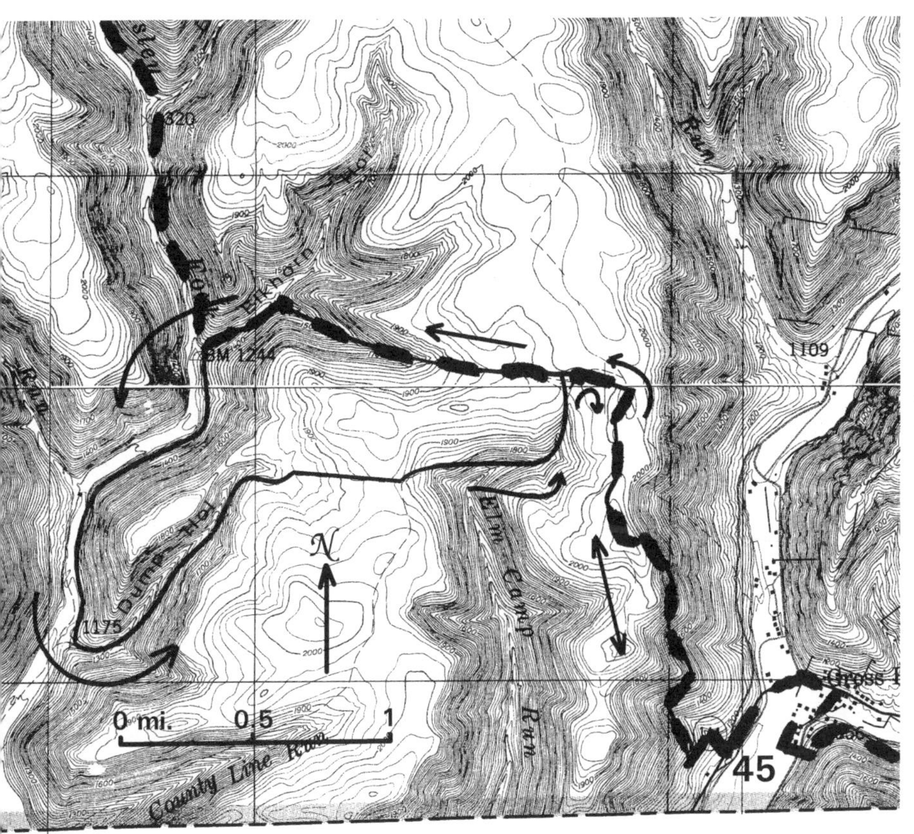

46 COUNTY LINE - DUMP HOLLOW

FEATURES: forest types
DISTANCE: 11.3 miles
TIME: 6 hours
ELEVATION: 1080 - 2065
TERRAIN: moderate/steep grades; some bushwhacking
BLAZES: orange (STS), some florescent orange (County Line), surveyors' tape (County Line/Dump Hollow), and hot pink (Dump Hollow), otherwise none
PARKING: Rt. 144 just S of Cross Fork Rd.
COMMENTS: Easily followed, but some map reading/bushwhacking skills required

Disturbance (logging, fire, windthrow, farming) changes the local environment and habitat. The first species to appear in a disturbed area are the tough pioneer plants, and these are eventually replaced by others until the regional pattern of vegetation is re-established. There are numerous pioneer plants, including grasses, ferns, goldenrod, ragweed, mosses, red maple, aspens and birches. They grow, die, and enrich the soil for the next plant species.

Along the Dump Hollow Trail you will pass areas of white birch, an open field with ground pine and clubmoss, aspen, and a large stump that has been charred from forest fire. The pioneer plants here are re-colonizing areas that have been disturbed by fire. Over time it will begin to look like the rest of the surrounding forest - either northern hardwoods or mixed oak.

TRAIL DESCRIPTION:

This route follows the STS from Rt. 144 S of Cross Fork to the top of Elkhorn Run. From there you bushwhack your way down the Elm Camp Run drainage to the County Line Hollow Trail (sign), which is a bushwhack at the top. At the bottom of the County Line Trail, bushwack along the Hammersley Fork to Dump Hollow, which returns to Elm Camp Hollow, and retrace the STS to Rt. 144.

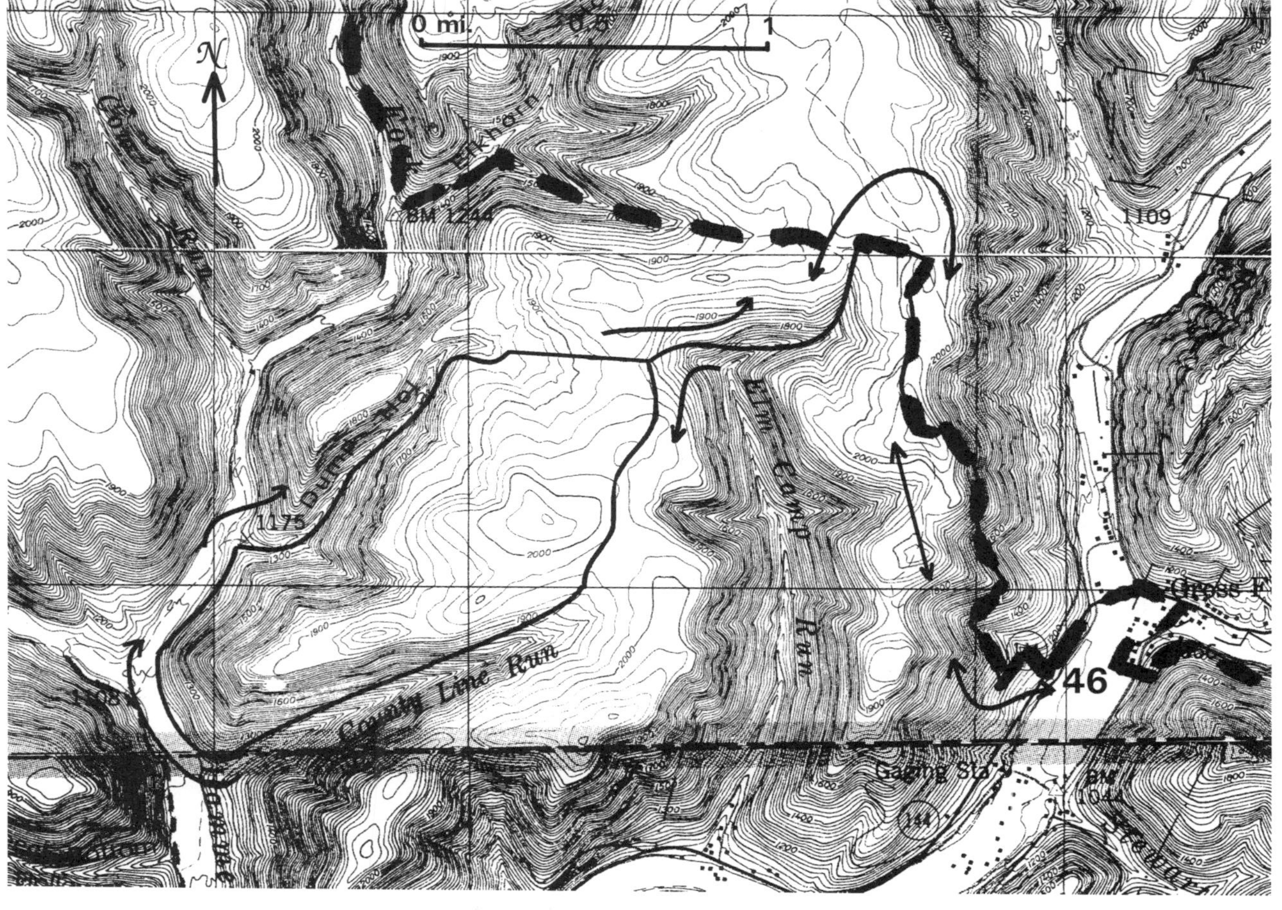
0 mi.
0.5
1
N
Elkhorn
Fork
BM 1244
1109
Dump Fork
1175
Elm Camp
Run
County Line Run
46
1108
Gaging Sta.
144
Cross F

Miles	Description
0	From Route 144 at STS just S of Cross Fork Road, follow STS N, ascending left side of ravine briefly before switchbacking S to the Twin Sisters Trail (sign). STS then climbs along a moderate slope to the top of the plateau.
1.1	Vista of plateau. STS bends left and levels shortly.
2.0	STS turns left (W) and leaves Twin Sisters Trail
2.3	Where STS begins to rise, leave STS and follow drainage to the left downhill (easy bushwack) down Elm Camp Run.
3.0	Bear right at Y onto grade marked with "County Line Hollow Trail/Dump Hollow Trail" sign, following grade uphill.
3.2	Bear left at Y in trail, following more used branch, then bear right at next Y in 0.15 mi.
3.45	Intersection of Dump Hollow and County Line Trails (sign). Turn left along County Line Trail, following well-defined trail marked with florescent blazes and surveyors' tape. Within a quarter mile, as you cross the top of the plateau, the trail will become more difficult to follow through the mountain laurel - the pink blazes, orange surveyor's tape, and an occasional faint blue blaze will help you through.
4.15	Trail begins to descend County Line Hollow and becomes a well-defined path along the right side of the drainage.
4.45	As the mountain laurel becomes thick the hot pink blazes and surveyors' tape disappears - look ahead for the trail opening in the trees or for scuff marks over the blowdowns. This section of thick mountain laurel is brief - you will exit it along a dug grade along the right side of the hollow.
5.5	Trail crosses to the left side of County Line Hollow. Just ahead, bushwhack right and follow the right side of Hammersley Fork (N) near the base of the mountain (several stream crossings will be required).

5.9 Across from the confluence of the Bell Branch with the Hammersley you ascend the mountainside on your right about 40 ft. to an old trail. The old trail will follow a rolling route above the Hammersley. [If you miss the skid road you can pick up a jeep trail along the bottom of the Hammersley. The jeep trail will make several wet crossings before you bend right and ascend to Dump Hollow along an old skid trail. Dump Hollow will be marked with a sign.]

6.3 Bear right to ascend the right side of Dump Hollow. A sign marks the hollow just downstream to the left near the Hammersley. At the first hollow on the right bear left, following the grade up the main branch of Dump Hollow along a moderately steep path.

7.3 Trail bends right and flattens. Hot pink blazes guide you along the trail. The trail will cross to the left side of the drainage and pass a hemlock swamp on the right.

7.55 Trail enters large, flat, open area, passing a 15 ft. tall, fire-damaged stump. Trail here is marked with surveyors' tape.

7.85 Intersection of County Line Hollow and Dump Hollow Trails (sign). Retrace route to Route 144 in 3.45 miles.

47 BEECH BOTTOM HEMLOCKS

FEATURES: virgin hemlock stand
DISTANCE: 5.3 miles
TIME: 3 hours
ELEVATION: 975 - 1920
TERRAIN: moderate/steep uphill
BLAZES: none
PARKING: Old Rt. 144 at Hammersley Fork bridge
COMMENTS: Easily followed; heart-pounding climb along Beech Bottom Hollow

The Eastern Hemlock, Pennsylvania's State Tree, can grow in thick stands and prefers cool, moist areas. In dense stands the air and soil below, being shaded, remain cool. Hemlock seedlings are well-adapted to this type of environment and survive under the low light for many years (full sunlight actually slows growth!). They grow slowly, however, and may only be six-feet high after half a century. As the forest becomes more open, their growth will then speed up. Lacking a strong tap root, they are susceptible to being uprooted by wind and are sensitive to drought. The oldest hemlock recorded was 988 years old, and the tallest was 160 ft.

Hemlock bark is rich in tannin, and it was a primary source of tannic acid, used to tan hides in the late 1800s. 75 - 85% of the Potter County forest at that time was hemlock.

Pine was the first timber of choice, but by the end of the 19th century the price of hemlock had increased fourfold, to $10 per thousand board feet (plus the bark for tanneries). Wages had remained fairly constant, so big profits were possible for large hemlock operations, and the largest was the Goodyear Lumber Company. The Goodyears cut 27% of the 600 million board feet of lumber cut in Potter County in 1897, and its percentage increased as others exhausted their timber supplies. From 1903 to 1907 the three Goodyear mills in Potter County cut 200 - 250 million board feet of lumber per year, more than three times that of the second largest producer, the Lackawanna Lumber Company.

Because the hemlock bark was saved and would peel only from May to August, most hemlock was cut in summer. The Goodyear's lumber camps employed several hundred men, were used less than two years, and cut all the marketable hemlock they found. In contrast, pine operations were much smaller, used the same camp for several years, and cut only selected trees.

The Beech Bottom Hemlocks, which are old-growth hemlocks of 32 - 40 inches diameter, are believed to have been left uncut because of uncertain ownership boundaries. The largest hemlock is over 43 inches diameter and 112 feet tall.

Today all hemlocks in Pennsylvania are threatened by the wooly hemlock adelgid, an aphid species that arrived in the Pacific Northwest from Asia in the 1920s and first showed up in southeastern Pennsylvania in the late 1960s. Like the chestnut blight, there is no natural defense that the hemlock has against this new pest, nor is there much that can be done at this time to prevent its spread (it is currently moving northward from southern Pennsylvania). The insect sucks sap, retarding growth, discoloring needles, and creating premature needle loss and twig dieback. Defoliation and tree death occurs within several years.

TRAIL DESCRIPTION:

This route, identical to the route that Tom Thwaites outlines in *50 Hikes in Central Pennsylvania* (Backcountry Publications, 3rd edition, 1995), follows a gravel road from old Route 144 up Hammersley Fork to Beech Bottom Hollow, where a steep trail brings you to the hemlock stand. Retrace your route back to the start.

Miles	Description
0	From old bridge over Hammersley Fork, just off Route 144, follow gravel road NW.
0.7	After crossing State Forest boundary, gravel road will cross to W side of Hammersley Fork. Cross Hammersley Fork over footbridge just ahead and then continue following gravel road up Hammersley Fork along W side.
1.6	Turn left near Beech Bottom trail sign just before crossing Beech Bottom Run. Trail will ascend along the left (S) side

of Beech Bottom Run along moderate/steep grade that passes several springs and wet areas near the top.

2.65 Trail register in virgin hemlock area. Retrace route back to vehicle.

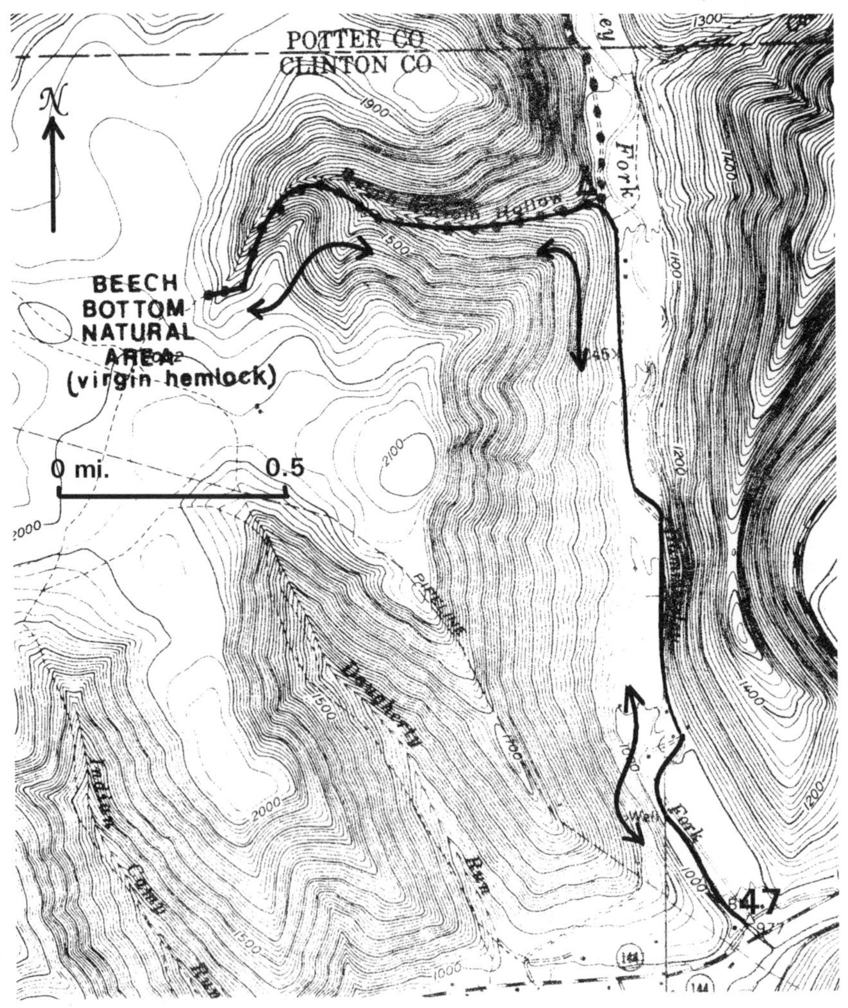

48 TROUT RUN

FEATURES: virgin hemlock stand, forest/stream environments
DISTANCE: 11.25 miles
TIME: 6.5 hours
ELEVATION: 1140 - 2160
TERRAIN: easy/moderate grades; rocky bushwhacking, stream crossings
BLAZES: none
PARKING: Trout Run Road at Trout Run Ridge Trail
COMMENTS: Easily followed

The Forrest H. Dutlinger Natural Area contains 1,521 acres, of which 158-acres is old growth hemlock. In addition to the hemlock are some old-growth white pine, red oak, beech, sugar maple, and gum. Along Beech Bottom Hollow are second growth northern hardwoods. Aspen-birch are pioneer species in areas that have been burned.

In the early 1950s a salvage timber operation was conducted after a large timber blowdown. Now that it has been designated a Natural Area, however, no further cutting is permitted.

Forrest Dutlinger was the first professional forester assigned to the Sproul State Forest. He also was District Forester for the Rothrock State Forest. In 1958, after 50 years of service, having served in the PA Department of Forests and Waters longer than any other person, he retired. The Natural Area is named in his honor.

TRAIL DESCRIPTION:

This route follows the Trout Run Ridge Trail from Trout Run Road to the top of Beech Bottom Hollow. After a side trip to the old growth hemlock it continues along Trout Run Ridge Trail to the gas line and descends the Lock Branch Trail to the John Summerson Branch of Trout Run, which you follow back to Trout Run Ridge Trail near Trout Run Road.

Miles	Description
0	From Trout Run Road, head E on Trout Run Ridge Trail (grassy logging road).
0.5	Trail crosses gas line, rising over knoll. Grassy road will cross several drainages, large sandstone boulders.
2.4	Y in road at wet area. Bear right, then left at next Y to avoid severe drainage problem in hemlocks. You will rejoin the main grassy road (Trout Run Ridge Trail) on the other side of the hemlocks.
3.2	Trail crossroads - right is Indian Camp Run Trail, left is to the Beech Bottom Hemlocks and is marked with a "BB" and an arrow painted on a tree. Turn left and follow trail (surveyors' tape will guide you over the flat, wet upper section). In 0.25 mi. The trail will become easier to follow as it begins to drop down the Beech Bottom drainage. The Beech Bottom Hemlocks trail register is 0.35 mi. from this crossroads. Retrace your steps to the crossroads and turn left (E) continuing along the Trout Run Ridge trail.
4.2	In grassy clearing with a lone hemlock and a cement obelisk marker, turn right and follow grassy grade to the gas line.
4.3	Cross gas line and enter woods, heading SE on Lock Branch Trail (grassy road marked by orange arrow and "LB" painted on a tree across gas line).
5.25	Trail descends more noticeably, crossing small drainage.
5.45	Trail exits hemlocks and bends left around point, becoming a logging road. After passing a view across the Lock Branch and toward the Summerson Branch of Trout Run, trail descends more steeply.
5.8	After passing a rocky sandstone outcrop on the left (road cut along logging road), the logging road will bend sharp right, descending hollow.

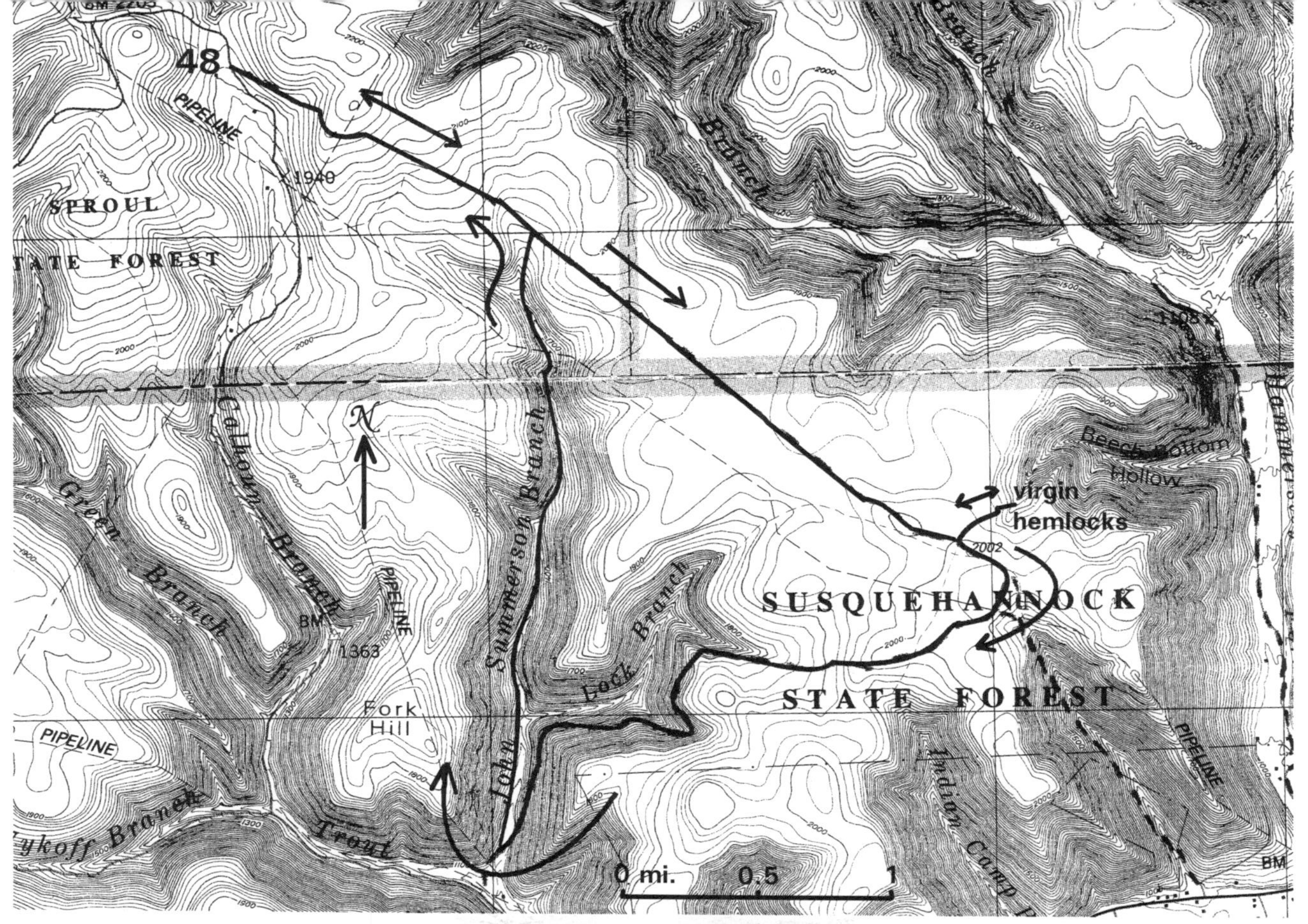

48
PIPELINE
1940
SPROUL
STATE FOREST
Branch
Calhoun Branch
Summerson Branch
Green Branch
PIPELINE
BM
1363
Fork
Hill
PIPELINE
Lock Branch
John
Trout
Beech Bottom
Hollow
virgin
hemlocks
2002
SUSQUEHANNOCK
STATE FOREST
Indian Camp
PIPELINE
BM
0 mi.
0.5
1

6.4 Trail bends left at confluence of Lock and John Summerson Branches. View across Trout Run.

6.9 Bottom of logging road - ford stream here or descend 0.15 miles to hunting camp and cross on small footbridge. On other side follow old grade upstream along left side of Summerson Branch.

7.8 In lower water cross to right side of Trout Run and follow skid trail along right side of stream. In higher water continue along the left side.

8.5 Confluence of Lock and John Summerson Branches of Trout Run. Shortly you will pick up a skid trail rising from stream at a fairly easy to moderate grade about 15 ft. above stream (if you are on the right side of the stream, cross here to the left side).

9.1 Cross to right side of stream and follow skid trail.

9.4 Trail crosses gas line.

9.75 At Y in stream, follow right branch along skid trail. As you rise and terrain flattens trail will disappear - bushwhack up drainage.

10.0 Turn left onto Trout Run Ridge Trail and retrace steps, returning to Trout Run Road in about 1.25 miles.

49 BELL BRANCH

FEATURES: virgin hemlock, forest types, ghost town
DISTANCE: 9.6 miles
TIME: 5.5 hours
ELEVATION: 1060 - 2160
TERRAIN: a few steep grades, rocky at top of Beech Bottom Hollow
BLAZES: none
PARKING: Trout Run Road at Trout Run Ridge Trail
COMMENTS: Easily followed

The village of Hammersley was located at a Goodyear Lumber Company railroad junction at the Hammersley Fork, the Bell Branch, and the Nelson Branch. Along the Hammersley on the south side of the village were about 60 homes. The center of town was located at the mouth of the Bell Branch and Nelson Hollow and contained a store, a boarding house, a saloon, and a school. On the north side of town was the engine terminal and railroad yard. Several times a day the train would take 8-car loads of hemlock from Hammersley Village to Murdocks, at Road Hollow, where the train would be split in half for the steep journey up Road Hollow and down the other side of the ridge to the B & S Railroad main line.

This hike follows part of what was once Main Street of the village of Hammersley Fork, from Beech Bottom Hollow to the Nelson Branch. Like most Pennsylvania ghost towns, not much is left of Hammersley Village - most has either been salvaged or burned, rotted away, carried away in floods, or covered by debris. It is sometimes difficult to imagine that the grades and paths over which you walk today were once bustling with people going about their daily business much as you do today. How much did they think about the future: what would happen to their lives, to their homes and village, and to the local economy after they completed razing the forest? How would they be remembered?

Times change. The landscape changes. The players change. We have a lot in common with the folks who once lived here.

TRAIL DESCRIPTION:

This route follows the Trout Run Ridge Trail from Trout Run Road to the top of Beech Bottom Hollow, then down Beech Bottom Hollow then up the Bell Branch and the McDonald Hollow Trail back to Trout Run Road.

Miles	Description
0	From Trout Run Road, head E on Trout Run Ridge Trail (grassy logging road).
0.5	Trail crosses gas line, rising over knoll. Grassy road will cross several drainages, large sandstone boulders.
2.4	Y in road at wet area. Bear right, then left at next Y to avoid severe drainage problem in hemlocks. You will rejoin the main grassy road (Trout Run Ridge Trail) on the other side of the hemlocks.
3.2	Trail crossroads - right is Indian Camp Run Trail, left is to the Beech Bottom Hemlocks and is marked with a "BB" and an arrow painted on a tree. Turn left and follow trail (surveyors' tape will guide you over the flat, wet upper section). In 0.25 mi. the trail will become easier to follow as it begins to drop down the Beech Bottom drainage.
3.55	Trail register at virgin hemlocks. Continue descent along Beech Bottom Trail (skid trail).
4.6	At bottom of Beech Bottom Trail, turn left onto jeep trail, crossing Beech Bottom Hollow and following grade N around base of mountain.
5.3	Bend left up Bell Branch. The grade becomes a trail.
5.55	A skid trail exits right and descends to cross Bell Branch at bottom of Nelson Branch - continue ascending Bell Branch along left (S) side. Along the route you will pass a field of moss-covered sandstone boulders and several small hollows.

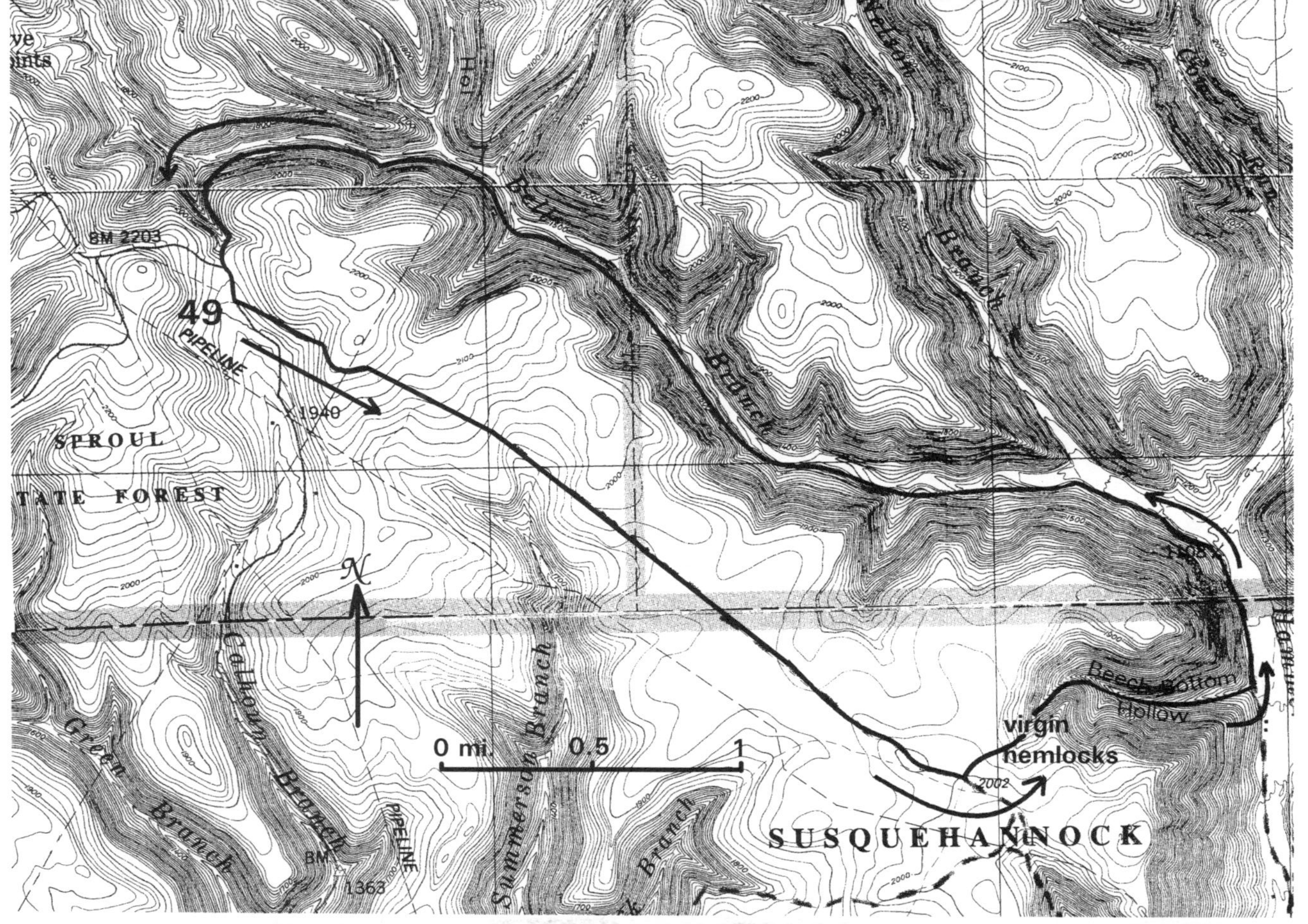
SPROUL
TATE FOREST
SUSQUEHANNOCK
49
PIPELINE
PIPELINE
BM 2203
BM
1363
1940
2002
1108
Bell
Branch
Branch
Summerson Branch
Calhoun Branch
Green Branch
Beech Bottom
Hollow
virgin
hemlocks
0 mi.
0.5
1

8.25 A skid trail exits right and descends to cross Bell Branch to hollow on opposite side - this is the McDonald Trail, which now shares the grade you have been ascending.

8.35 Trail crosses gas line.

9.1 Exit left on McDonald Hollow Trail (more worn branch) at Y. The intersection is also marked by a 1 ft. high column of stones along right side of McDonald Hollow Trail just after this intersection. The McDonald Hollow Trail now rises more steeply to McConnell Road.

9.45 Turn left on McConnell Road, returning to Trout Run Ridge Trail in about 0.25 miles.

Explore Pennsylvania's Northcentral Highlands

Pennsylvania's Northcentral Highlands Region holds almost half of all the State Forest Lands in Penn's Woods. Here it is possible to leave civilization behind and travel over hundreds of miles of hiking trails that contain expansive scenery, quiet forests, clean streams, and unsurpassed environmental quality and variety. Logging operations from the late nineteenth/early twentieth century have left the region with a vast network of former logging railroad grades, skid trails, woods roads, foot trails, and fire trails that provide one of the most extensive systems of hiking trails you will find anywhere.

If you look at topographic and State Forest Public Use Maps of the region you will see endless possible hiking and backpacking trips. But these maps are not updated frequently and show trails that no longer exist, while failing to show trails that have been relocated and trails that have been created by the Bureau of Forestry. What trails are suitable for hiking, and are they worth following?

Explore Pennsylvania's Northcentral Highlands is a series intended to explore these regional trails and present the hiker with a wide variety of the best opportunities for hiking and backpacking that Pennsylvania's Northcentral Highlands can offer. These routes are easy to follow, even with only basic skills in reading a topographic map and using a compass, and each hikes contains a topo map that has been updated to show present field conditions.

Short Hikes in God's Country, covering the Susquehannock State Forest in Potter County, is the second volume of this series being published by Pine Creek Press. Volume 1, ***Short Hikes in Pennsylvania's Grand Canyon***, covering the Tioga State Forest in Tioga County, was published in 1992. Volume 3, ***Short Hikes in Pennsylvania's Black Forest***, covering the Tiadaghton State Forest, will be released in the near future.

OTHER PINE CREEK PRESS PUBLICATIONS:

Pine Creek Press publishes books, maps, and guides about Pine Creek, the Grand Canyon of Pennsylvania, and the Northcentral Pennsylvania region. A partial list of books available from the publisher follows. A current list of publications and prices can be obtained from Pine Creek Press.

Regional Trailguides:
Guide to the West Rim Trail, by Chuck Dillon, 1989: Interpretive trailguide for the 30-mile West Rim Trail. Includes waterproof, annotated trail map.
Guide to the Susquehannock Trail System, by Chuck Dillon, 1991: Interpretive trailguide for the 85-mile Susquehannock Trail. Includes set of annotated waterproof trail maps.
Short Hikes in Pennsylvania's Grand Canyon, by Chuck Dillon, 1992: Volume 1 of the Explore Pennsylvania's Northcentral Highlands Series, covering 57 day hikes and short backpacking trips in the Tioga State Forest.

Other Books:
Pennsylvania's Grand Canyon - A Natural & Human History, by Chuck Dillon, Photography by Curt Weinhold, 1991: Tells the story of the natural and social history of the Canyon area and man's impact on the natural environment, profusely illustrated with color and black-and-white photographs.

Maps:
Pine Creek Waterproof River Map Set: Canoeing map for Pine Creek: Galeton to Waterville, including diagrams and logistical information.
Black Forest Hiking & Ski Trails Waterproof Map: Waterproof map for Black Forest Trail, Golden Eagle Trail, and surrounding x-country ski trails.
Denton Hill Ski & Mountain Bike Map: X-country ski and mountain bike trails in Denton Hill area.

Other Publications:
Outdoor Adventure Guide for Pennsylvania's Grand Canyon: Annual free publication of Pine Creek Outfitters, Inc. Describes outdoor opportunities in the Canyon area and associated articles useful for planning low-impact outdoor activities in the Canyon Area.